To Antoinette
All best wishes

THE KILDERRY FILES

ALSO BY MAURICE MANNING

HISTORY

The Blueshirts

James Dillon, A Biography

Irish Political Parties

The Houses of the Oireachtas (ed)

NOVEL

Betrayal

THE

KILDERRY

FILES

MAURICE MANNING

CURRACH
PRESS

First published in 2017
by Currach Press
23 Merrion Square North,
Dublin 2, Co. Dublin
www.columba.ie

ISBN: 978-1-78218-888-9

Set in Linux Libertine 12/15
Cover and book design by Alba Esteban | Columba Press
Vatican picture by Akim Fimin
Printed by xxxxxx

For Nick

AUTHOR'S NOTE

This is a work of fiction. There is no diocese of Kilderry or Bishop Concannon. Nor is there an Archbishop Valetti or a Joe Bradley. The events described in the contemporary or recent past in the novel are entirely fictitious and the characters described are not based on any living person.

However, in the sections dealing with events in the Second World War, the author has introduced several of the major and minor players of the time. These include Eamon de Valera, Archbishop Paschal Robinson, Colonel Dan Bryan, Bishop Michael Fogarty, Professor James Hogan and others, who are listed in the glossary at the end of the book.

The author has used his own detailed knowledge of the period and of the characters involved to imagine how they would have reacted in the unfolding drama.

He has taken one liberty with the truth. Colonel Dan Bryan was a teetotaller. He is allowed an occasional tipple in the book. The author felt he deserved it.

PROLOGUE

For Gonzalo Sánchez Pena this was the best day of his week – and the best week he had enjoyed since coming to Dublin in 1938. Not alone was he riding his beloved mare on a clear blue July Sunday morning through a wild and deserted Wicklow countryside, a ride which had tested his considerable riding skills to the full, but soon he would be sitting down to a hearty Wicklow breakfast in Hunter's Hotel. And by the end of the week he would be a rich man in a position to give up his dreary job in the Spanish embassy, go back to Spain and make himself even richer under General Franco's new regime.

He turned a corner on the winding track that led to Mrs Beechor's stables, from where he had set out earlier. Suddenly, he found his path blocked by a large black car. He had never seen a car in this area before. Three men stood in front of it. He recognised one of them – the one with the gun.

It was his last memory of Ireland.

1

....

February 7 1997

The old Bishop of Kilderry was dead. Nobody was particularly surprised. Most people who thought about it – and not very many did – believed that he had died many years ago. Even The Irish Times *merely recorded the demise of this elderly divine at the bottom of its front-page news digest, above the winning lottery numbers and below reports of yet another outbreak of squabbles in the Labour Party. The* Irish Times *did, however, have a lengthy obituary on page five and carried a watery tribute to the late bishop from the cardinal in Armagh.*

The truth was that most people, including some of the younger priests in his diocese of Kilderry, had long forgotten the existence of a bishop who had retired 13 years ago and who had not been seen or heard of in public since then. But the older priests of Kilderry had not forgotten. To have met the bishop and, more pointedly, to have served under him was to remember him. And not always warmly or kindly either, even though there were a few who referred to his private acts of kindness, his concern for priests who had fallen from grace and who needed a helping and discreet hand. Such protestations were usually brushed aside with the assertion that the old boy was merely sweeping inconvenient or embarrassing problems under the episcopal carpet, determined to ensure that no whiff of scandal or irregularity would ever taint his diocese or tarnish his handling of its affairs.

One way or another, Bishop Thomas Patrick Concannon had

been a force to be reckoned with. For 47 years he had ruled the see of Kilderry with an iron discipline. Knowledge, as he was fond of saying, was power and there was little that happened in his diocese that did not find its way to him sooner or later – usually sooner. And what was true of the diocese in general was true of his priests in particular. His intelligence network was so extensive and pervasive that any priest who harboured a guilty secret or entertained an unworthy aspiration knew that, as far as Thomas Patrick Concannon was concerned, they had better watch out.

Fear was indeed a great deterrent and the diocese of Kilderry had the most disciplined, but also the most fearful and least happy, priests in the entire country. This was something in which the bishop took genuine pride. Happiness was for the next world. Duty, discipline and obedience were the worldly means to that heavenly end.

Not that Concannon had always been that way. Back in 1937 he had come to Kilderry as a stranger. He was then 33 years old, Professor of Dogmatic Theology at the Irish College in Rome, already an acknowledged scholar, at least in that narrow field of his choice, and was marked out as a 'coming man' – although those who knew about such matters predicted that his future was more likely to be in Rome than back in Ireland. And that, too, would have been Concannon's own view.

He had taken to Rome and Rome to him. He liked the high-mindedness, the ritual, the certainty, the order and the power. He never questioned for a second the worldliness, the cynicism or indeed the venality of some of the princes of the Church with whom he came in to regular contact. It was enough for him to be part of it and to know too that his own qualities of deviousness and strategic obsequiousness, his strong intellect and capacity for hard work, his attention to detail, his doctrinal rigidity and total loyalty to the papacy would serve him well and ensure that he would remain at the centre of the spiritual universe, rather than find himself back in charge of some dreary Irish seminary or breaking bread with men he regarded as the second-rate provincials of Maynooth.

If Thomas Concannon had thought about himself and his career – and he frequently did, for he was not a man who normally or easily thought of others – that broadly is how he would have wished his career to go. The first Irishman to hold high office in the Curia. Even, perhaps, a red hat.

But it was not to be. God's providence, as Concannon was known to say, sometimes moved in mysterious ways. And so, one bright early morning in 1937, Concannon received a summons to present himself without delay at the office of the Cardinal Secretary of State, his Eminence Eugenio Pacelli.

Concannon had never met Cardinal Pacelli but, of course, he knew much about him. After the Pope – and some would say before the Pope – Pacelli was the most powerful man in the Church. His power was based not just on his diplomatic skills, but on his detailed, minute knowledge of what was happening in every distant part of the Roman Church and, most especially, if what was happening was displeasing to Rome.

When finally seated in Pacelli's study – and Concannon would always remember the grandeur and the intimidation of the great man's study – the Cardinal Secretary of State had wasted no time on preliminaries.

'We have followed your progress here with interest – and indeed a certain satisfaction. You have shown diligence, academic rigour and doctrinal purity. Your loyalty to the Holy See and your robust defence of its policies are appreciated and have been noted.'

Had Concannon been a curious man, he might have wondered by what means the cardinal was so well acquainted with the contents of his lectures and, more ominously, with the arguments and contro-

versies of the Common Room. Instead, he just took it for granted that the cardinal would know such things.

The cardinal continued. 'I did not summon you here to discuss your personal attributes, worthy though they may be. No, I asked you here for a purpose.'

As Pacelli expanded on his 'purpose', Concannon's heart sank.

Pacelli did not mince his words. 'The problem I wish you to resolve is the diocese of Kilderry. The old bishop died two months ago but, even before he died, I had reason to believe there was considerable laxity and irregularity in the running of the diocese. Discipline is non-existent and the finances are weak – scandalously so. Some monies destined for the Holy See are not accounted for. The senior canons are squabbling over the succession and unable to agree among themselves on anything. They have now come down in favour of the weakest of their number and are seeking to persuade the Irish bishops to support their choice.'

The cardinal here paused and pushed a file towards Concannon.

'These are the despatches from the papal nuncio, Monsignor Robinson. They make pitiable reading. Matters are grievously out of hand.'

Concannon was still puzzled as to what his own role might be, though gratified beyond measure that he was being taken in to the confidence of this powerful cardinal. After all, he was not even a priest of Kilderry.

'And so I have decided, and his Holiness has agreed, that you, Dr Concannon, will be the next Bishop of Kilderry. You will have two principal functions – to restore order and discipline to the diocese and to provide leadership to the bishops of Ireland; a disappointing lot I have to say. Yes, a great disappointment. They are more concerned with their own power and privilege than with the wishes of the Holy See.'

It was clear to Concannon that the Secretary of State had no *great regard for Holy Ireland, the self-styled land of Saints and Scholars and, for the first time, a small sense of resentment stirred in Concannon's heart. He quickly suppressed it. He was too anxious to show Pacelli that, whatever his designs might be, he would find in Concannon a willing instrument.*

'And when, Eminence, will this happen?' asked Concannon.

'It already has,' replied the imperious Secretary of State. 'At this very moment the papal nuncio is informing their lordships assembled in Maynooth of your appointment, and making no secret that you are my personal choice to do a particular job. They will not like it, but a little humility is good for them and I am sure it will all work out to the good.'

Even Concannon, so absorbed in the news he had just received, could see that the Secretary of State was enjoying the reaction his announcement would have on the assembled bishops of Ireland at their meeting in Maynooth. Had Concannon bothered to think about it – which he didn't – he might have suspected that the welcome for him from his fellow bishops would not be a warm one.

Over the following days, as Concannon reflected on what had just happened, three thoughts were uppermost in his mind.

The Pope, Pius XI, was ailing and if rumours were to be believed this hitherto despotic figure was consumed with worry, even guilt, about how closely he had intertwined the fortunes of the Vatican and the Italian Church with those of Mussolini's fascist state. His obsession with the day-to-day details of Church affairs was no more.

Into this vacuum Pacelli had stepped and in many ways he was now the effective ruler of the Church. Even if he did not become the next pope he would continue to be a figure of great power.

And now Pacelli had chosen him, Thomas Patrick Concannon, to be his instrument in reshaping and leading the Irish Church.

Concannon knew that the quality Pacelli most valued was total and unqualified loyalty to him and to the Holy See.

As he busied himself preparing to leave Rome, Concannon determined he would not be found wanting.

And so Thomas Concannon, Doctor of Divinity, came back to Ireland to be received with icy politeness by his brother bishops and with fear, trepidation and suppressed hostility by the priests of his diocese who would now be in his charge.

None of this, of course, ever became public. Things like that didn't in those days. As far as the public (including the newspapers and politicians) were concerned, Ireland had been singularly honoured. Had not the Holy Father himself personally chosen this man? The public welcome in Kilderry was long, loud and enthusiastic.

Concannon wasted no time in carrying out his instructions. Within two years he had re-ordered the affairs of Kilderry along the strictest Roman lines. He asserted his authority among his fellow bishops, helped not only in part by his natural strength of personality, but also by the contents of files that Pacelli had given him and whose existence he made no attempt to conceal. His position was also helped by the carefully nurtured impression, which he successfully developed, that he alone among the Irish bishops had a direct line to the Pope.

2

....

In early March 1997, four weeks to the day after the death of Concannon, Peter O'Donnell got a phone call from his uncle. It was a Monday morning and in Trinity College, as in most universities, the week started with no great sense of hurry. O'Donnell was bracing himself for the day with a careful reading of the weekend's sporting results. It hadn't been a great weekend. All his teams had lost – Galway once again in hurling, Trinity in rugby and Glasgow Celtic had been beaten for the third week in a row.

O'Donnell took his sport seriously and was not best pleased by a phone call before 10 o'clock on a Monday morning. He had been back in Trinity almost a year after he had given up the job, first as government press secretary and later as special adviser to the Taoiseach. He had greatly enjoyed these jobs and learned a great deal about the world of politics but, ultimately, had decided to go back to academe.

Well, if the truth be told, he decided on this because, after one indiscretion too many, his special relationship with the Taoiseach's wife Louise Mulcahy was in danger of becoming public. And if the full truth be told, for each of them, but for him especially, the affair had begun to lose its excitement. With the loss of intensity, the dangers and betrayals loomed larger until, eventually, each in their own way decided to call a halt. As a result, O'Donnell had decided to put some distance between himself and temptation and was now back teaching economics – or doing so at least part of the time.

O'Donnell's departure from government had been altogether friendly. His relationship with the Taoiseach's wife was now one of relaxed, but increasingly remote friendship. The Taoiseach, still oblivious to his wife's affair, regarded him as a valued friend and indeed, at this very moment, was urging him to run for the Dáil in the next election. And he was still friendly with most, if not all, of the Cabinet, something that helped him considerably in his consultancy work – 'opening doors' he called it.

Back in Trinity his governmental experience stood him in good stead. The Provost had recruited him to his fundraising committee, the students looked upon him as somebody from the real world rather than just another academic and, to his great surprise, some of the biggest companies in the country were engaging him to do 'consultancy'. He was surprised by this last development but, never a man to ignore a real chance, he was now dispensing advice on 'the corporate-governmental interface' and getting well paid for it. For the first time in his life he actually had some money.

And so to the phone call. It was on his direct line and it was from his only uncle, Most Reverend Monsignor James J Nestor, Parish Priest of Brannocksbridge and Vicar General of the diocese of Kilderry, but known affectionately to O'Donnell for as long as he could remember as Uncle Jimmy.

'I'm surprised to find you in the office so early. I suppose you have the sports section open before you.'

'Right in one Uncle Jimmy. What's wrong with Galway? It can't be the trainer again?'

Clearly, however, Monsignor Nestor had weightier matters to discuss and he came to the point without much further delay. 'You probably saw the old bishop died four weeks ago?'

O'Donnell had in fact noted the death of Dr Concannon. His Uncle Jimmy had been Concannon's private secretary for almost 20 years and, as such, he had featured large in the table time discussions in O'Donnell's home when he was growing up. So he had noted the death of Dr Concannon, though like most people he had assumed him long dead and felt little more than curious indifference when he read the news.

'To tell the truth I thought the crusty old cod was dead years ago. After all, the old boy had to be well over 90. You're hardly phoning me on a Monday morning to tell me this.'

'No.'

For the first time, O'Donnell could sense an unaccustomed tension in his uncle's voice. 'No. That's not why I'm calling you – well not fully.'

'Why then?'

'It's difficult to talk about on the phone, but well, the present bishop asked me to put Dr Concannon's papers in order, to act as his executor, that sort of thing and, well, not to give teeth to it, there are some major, or appear to be some major, problems.'

'But surely Uncle Jimmy,' said O'Donnell, 'any relations the old bishop had with the diocese would have been sorted out when he retired as bishop. When was that?'

'That was 13 years ago, 1984 you may remember, and yes they should. But not all were and that's the problem facing us now.'

'But why phone me? Surely this is a matter for Mother Church to sort out in her own silky way,' said O'Donnell.

'Well, that's why I am phoning you. Mother Church, as you call her, can't sort it out on her own. Only two people know what's involved, the bishop and myself, and to tell the truth we're out of our depth. We need to talk to someone with outside experience and since you are an economist, whatever that means, and since you've worked for the government at top level, the bishop and myself thought you might be able to help us.'

'I doubt it,' O'Donnell replied, but he was intrigued and was not going to turn down a request for help from his only and much-loved uncle. He was too fond of the old boy to do that and he remembered the regular supply of fivers and tenners that had come his way during his hungry days in school and university.

'Look, at this point you're the best hope we've got,' continued Monsignor Nestor. 'Would you do me a favour. Could you come down and talk to the bishop and myself? As soon as possible, I wouldn't ask you if it wasn't so urgent.'

Peter O'Donnell did not have a heavy day in store. He would be finished his lectures by lunchtime. And so he promised his uncle that he would dine with the bishop and himself in the bishop's palace that very evening. It was less than 70 miles away.

3

....

The bishop's palace in Kilderry might once have been palatial – indeed it had been in the time of Bishop Concannon, who lived there in solitary and awesome splendour. It was said he had one of the finest cellars in the country, better even than that of the Pontifical University of Maynooth, and that his table was always of the highest quality.

So it was said, though few could speak with first-hand experience. The bishop was slow to extend invitations to those he regarded as social inferiors and that, of course, included all the priests and most of the faithful of his diocese. To a great extent, the quality of the bishop's wine and table were matters of conjecture, but there was no doubting the sense of power and unchallengeable certainty the building and its occupants exuded – as it was meant to. Thomas Concannon did little other than by design and, as a result, the bishop's palace, which he had largely built, was designed to send a message to layman and cleric alike that this was the real centre of power in Kilderry, if not further afield.

Now, however, more than a decade after the retirement of Bishop Concannon, there was little of the old sense of power and awe about the building. As O'Donnell approached, it struck him that this was just another big house, well past its prime and largely divided into unsuitable offices for a variety of diocesan services – a marriage tribunal, welfare services and the like – with just a small portion of the old house serving as the private quarters of the new bishop.

As O'Donnell swept up the drive it was obvious how ill-kempt the gardens were – tended, but not cared for. One part of the garden had become a car park and the snob in him noted that most of the cars were of what he would call the social worker variety, ageing Renault 4s, Nissan Micras and rusting Fiestas. He noticed, too, the portacabins to the right of the house with signs telling him that, if he so wished, this was where he would find the education secretariat for the diocese.

It was 5.30 pm when he arrived and many of those who worked there were heading for their cars. Some of the young men he took to be priests, not that any of them wore the traditional Roman collar, but all had that shapeless uniform of baggy, unpressed trousers, V-necked lambs' wool sweaters and anoraks, while the nuns – at least that was his assumption – were dressed in the washed-out greys and browns that had replaced the traditional elegance of bygone days.

As O'Donnell walked up the steps he noted that the house could use a coat or two of paint. And as his uncle led him in, he could see for himself the effect of years of wear and tear on the once elegant fittings that were never intended to serve as offices.

O'Donnell's uncle greeted him warmly. He was a tall, white-haired man, well into his sixties. He had an air of scholarly calm about him and a smile that gave his otherwise aesthetic appearance an easy warmth and approachability. And unlike the anorak-clad curates, his dress was meticulous – a well-cut dark grey suit and, of course, an emphatic roman collar.

Monsignor Nestor was a priest of the old school – well versed in theology, philosophy and Latin. His sermons were serious in content and elegant in construction. No guitars were ever heard in his church nor had it ever reverberated to the strains of 'Michael Row the Boat Ashore'. He regretted the

passing of Latin usage and the loss of so much of the traditional liturgy, and had done his best in his own church to temper
some of the crassness of the new vernacular. But, for all of that,
he was also a practical man. He might not like change but he
accepted it and his sense of history gave him a realisation of
the inevitability of change, even for his beloved Church. He
was also a discreet man, trusted by his fellow priests and, most
of all, by his bishop.

'We will be dining with the bishop shortly,' he told O'Donnell, 'but let me first of all thank you for coming down at such
short notice. I know how busy you academics can be.'

This last was said with a twinkle, but a serious note soon
returned.

'What you will be told this evening is known only to the
bishop and myself and I want it to stay that way. We need absolute confidence.'

'That's okay by me,' said O'Donnell easily 'though after
some of the things I have been privy to these last few years, I
doubt if anything in the diocese of Kilderry can really shock or
surprise me.'

'Well it shocked us and both the bishop and myself are totally out of our depth. At this stage, you are the best hope we
have.'

'Tell me then,' said O'Donnell.

'No, that will wait for dinner. I want his lordship to give you
his full version and there is no point in repetition. You haven't
met him before? Well let me tell you a little about him.'

He poured O'Donnell a precise glass of dry sherry – a drink
O'Donnell hated – and another for himself. Then, when both
were seated, he filled in what he called 'the background'.

Bishop John Mullins was, according to Monsignor Nestor, a
good man. A bit nervy, a bit scattered and fussy at times, and

very opinionated, radical even, but a good man nonetheless. He had been appointed 13 years ago when the old bishop retired. The Monsignor then told O'Donnell something he did not know.

The old bishop, he said, had not retired voluntarily. He had in fact been pushed out. Times had changed, he had not. By the 1970s, he had few friends among the bishops, he was resolutely opposed to changes emanating from the new regime in Rome and his autocratic style was being challenged by a new generation of priests, some of whom had openly questioned his authority, one even attacking him by name on a television programme. The bishop had been outraged but the old sanctions did not work anymore and he found himself reduced at times to impotent rage.

'It was not a pleasant time,' said Monsignor Nestor, who was the bishop's diocesan secretary at the time. 'But worst of all, from Concannon's point of view, all his old Roman friends were gone too. The age of Pius XII was well and truly over. At last his enemies could get at him – and this they did with a vengeance.

'You have no idea how vicious clerical politics can be,' Nestor told his nephew. 'Bitchier and nastier than anything you encounter in real politics.

'In any event, when Concannon reached his 80th birthday in 1983, he was obliged to submit his retirement once again to the Vatican. He thought it would be no more than a formality and that someone of his standing would be a bishop for life. But Concannon could not have been more wrong. The Vatican accepted his resignation with unseemly haste, though he managed to hang on through various delaying tactics for quite some months.'

Nestor had been present when the papal nuncio had phoned Concannon to tell him that he would not be renewed.

'Talk about being resigned to the Divine will,' laughed Nestor. 'I never saw a man take news so badly. For weeks he refused to believe it. He did all he could to have the decision reversed – he even went so far as asking the Taoiseach to intervene. There was no way Garret FitzGerald fell for that one. Finally he had to accept the inevitable – but he did drag it out.'

Nestor went on to tell how Concannon had then tried to influence the choice of his successor. He was shameless about it, lobbying the nuncio, his fellow bishops, anybody in Rome who would listen to him in favour of his own nephew, a very resistible and second-rate academic, an undistinguished professor in a Dublin seminary.

'He was not even from the diocese,' said Nestor with his first show of indignation, an indication to O'Donnell that in clerical politics, as well as elsewhere, outsiders are rarely welcome.

In any event, he failed. John Mullins, neither a scholar nor a smooth man, with a reputation as a social activist, was plucked out of his remote parish and became the new Bishop of Kilderry.

Concannon was appalled. He regarded it as a personal affront that so plain a man as Mullins should be deemed worthy to succeed him. He did everything he could to be disagreeable, but eventually Mullins was installed, first in the cathedral and later in the palace, but with no co-operation and even less grace from Concannon.

'He's been a good bishop,' said Nestor again. 'He humanised the place, the reign of terror was no more and well, to tell the truth, he's a little too liberal and informal and outspoken for my liking, but then you know me.'

Peter O'Donnell was interested in what his uncle was telling him. All politics intrigued him and he was prepared to be as interested in clerical politics as any other form. Not for nothing was Trollope one of his favourite authors. But he still had to get the point of his uncle's narrative.

'One of the biggest problems we had – and I remained on as diocesan secretary for a further two years before moving to Brannocksbridge – was that the new bishop got no co-operation at all from his predecessor. In fairness, the administration of the diocese was efficient and orderly and the finances were healthy. There were no difficulties there, or so we thought.

'We did discover that the bishop had brought several boxes of files with him, files which in my view belonged to the diocesan archives and it was my job to get them back. I raised the matter with Dr Concannon and I confess I raised it only once. He told me in his iciest tones that all relevant files were in their proper place and asked whether I was accusing him of misappropriating diocesan property. He insisted that the only documents he had taken were his own personal property.'

Nestor paused, but made no effort to offer his nephew what he would regard as a real drink. He didn't even offer to refill his empty sherry glass. Instead he continued.

'That was that, at least for the time being. There was nothing we could do, but neither the bishop nor myself were happy. Time passed. The old bishop was now in retirement and the memory of him had faded. But in truth, both the new bishop and myself continued to be uneasy about the missing files, though we never confided this to anybody else. I continued to visit Concannon from time to time, as indeed did many of the older priests – some I think just to be sure he really was retired and out of their lives.

'But on my last visit, and by then he had moved from his retirement house to a nursing home, just a week before he had that last stroke, he was different. He knew he was soon to die, his concentration was poor and he had all the signs of great vulnerability. Then, he did something totally out of character. He held my hand, gripped it and whispered to me, asking my forgiveness for having misled me all those years ago about the files.

'"I had my reasons," he almost croaked at me "but they were unworthy. I have asked the Almighty to forgive me and now I ask you to do likewise."

'I noticed he didn't mention the bishop, his successor, but I immediately told him there was nothing to forgive. He asked my blessing and shortly afterwards he lapsed in to sleep. Two days later he had that last stroke and a week later he was dead.'

The Monsignor paused and looked at his watch.

'Come,' he said. 'It's the dining hour and his lordship will complete the story.'

4

....

If the bishop's palace at Kilderry had a reputation for the quality of its food and wine under the old bishop, it had none such now. That was certainly the view of Peter O'Donnell, a man who took his food very seriously indeed, as he sat down in the bishop's small dining room to a meal of bacon, egg, sausage, thick slices of fresh white bread and a large pot of tea. Not a glass of wine in sight, grumbled O'Donnell to himself – even Commons at Trinity would be better than this.

Nor was Bishop Mullins a prepossessing figure. He was short and overweight. His tousled grey hair could do with a comb and maybe even a wash, his shoes were scuffed, his suit was in need of a pressing and the large brown spectacles completed the look of a perpetually harassed and underpaid clerk. Nor were there any hidden social graces. Where the Monsignor was smooth, Mullins was plain and blunt. O'Donnell found it hard to believe that this scruffy and seemingly undistinguished man was the successor to the imperious Concannon and he saw at once why the old bishop would have taken his appointment as such a personal affront.

'You're very welcome. Thanks for coming down. Your uncle speaks highly of you and he generally knows what he's talking about.'

Mullins tucked in to his rasher and egg and, without clearing his mouth, continued to talk. 'Has the Monsignor told you all? It's a right bloody mess and I don't know what way to turn.'

'No, my lord, I haven't told him all,' said Nestor. 'I provided the background and brought Peter up to the bishop's final illness. I thought you'd better take the story from there.'

Mullins took a few minutes to clear his plate, poured himself a fresh cup of tea, added three spoons of sugar, stirred the tea noisily, spilling some in to his saucer and then told the rest of the story.

He recounted how the old bishop had refused to hand over all the files, indeed denied their existence, and there was nothing he could do about it. And as far as he or Nestor could see – and Nestor knew the business of the diocese better than anybody else – the finances were in order and were seemingly on a sound footing. Certainly, there was no sign of any missing money.

There was, however, one nagging doubt; one small puzzle. The bishop had one sister. She was a widow with four children and had been in poor circumstances. Yet all her children, including the nephew Concannon wanted to succeed him, had all got the most expensive education available – the three boys had gone to Clongowes and the girl to some posh convent in Dublin – and then all went to university. One of the boys became a solicitor and was able to buy a practice after his first year qualified; the other boy was set up in business, and well set up at that; while the girl qualified as a doctor.

It was clear to Mullins, and indeed to anybody who thought about it, that the only source of this patronage could be the bishop – but that in itself didn't worry Mullins too much. He didn't approve but said that, in those days, the distinction between diocesan money and the bishop's money was often vague. It was quite common for bishops, and even parish priests, to help out their families and, given the secrecy that surrounded all Church matters, nobody would know anyway and, if they asked questions, they would be very quickly sent about their business.

'No,' said Mullins, 'if that was all it was, then we would simply deal with it in the usual way. Sweep it under the carpet and keep our mouths shut. You'd be surprised how often that happens in this Church of ours – even to the present day.'

O'Donnell could see his uncle was less than comfortable with the openness and frankness of the bishop, but Mullins continued with his story.

There were two problems, the first was there was no record in the diocesan accounts of any monies being dispensed to the bishop's family. And yet significant sums had been disbursed. And secondly, the disbursement had continued until very recently. One of the bishop's nephews, the solicitor – 'a loud-mouthed braggart' was how Mullins described him – had made no secret of his uncle's largesse and this boasting had long since found its way back to Mullins. The question then was where the money was coming from.

'It's clear,' said Mullins, 'that the old boy had control over what you fellows would call a slush fund. And a big one. But where does it come from and where was it?'

Mullins continued with the story. Even with the unanswered questions, it was still no big deal. As far as he was concerned it was unsatisfactory, it was an irritation, but it was only one of the many secrets his predecessor would bring with him to the grave.

'And we fellows,' he said, 'are good at keeping secrets. We could teach you politicians a lesson or two on that.'

Suddenly, he was serious again. 'Your uncle has told you about the old boy's last-minute confession. He never asked my blessing or forgiveness, the old bugger. Too proud to the very end.'

Monsignor Nestor had told the bishop of his predecessor's confession and about the existence of the files. And Mullins, being a blunt and practical man, as soon as the bishop was removed to the nursing home, had sent Nestor to the bishop's house – a diocesan house – to remove all his papers and bring them back to the diocesan archive. If there was personal stuff it could be sorted out afterwards.

Mullins admitted that his principal concern was to clamp down on any potential scandal. He didn't know what might be in the papers or where they might end up. He suspected some of the material could be embarrassing and he had enough problems of his own without some sort of financial scandal from the past emerging to haunt him.

'You know how it is these days, the media would just love a story like that. It would be Casey all over again, but this time without the sex.'

'And so you organised a cover-up,' teased O'Donnell.

'Bloody right I did,' snapped Mullins. 'And just in time too.'

Mullins went on to recount that, on the day after the reading of the will, the retirement house of Concannon, had been broken into. Nothing was taken, but the place had been searched from top to bottom. It was clear to Mullins that his instincts had been right and that he'd only just been in time.

The bishop now had O'Donnell's full attention.

'And the files – what was in them? Did they help you?'

'Yes and no,' said the bishop, and O'Donnell could sense how troubled he was.

'Yes, there was a slush fund. It had been used to fund the family. By God those leeches sucked him – or rather the diocese – dry. As near a million over the years as makes no difference and almost up to the year he died. But, there is probably fuck-all we can do about it and more's the pity.'

O'Donnell could again sense his uncle's unease at the bluntness of the bishop's language.

'But we can deal with that. The family are angry, they suspect we have fooled them but they are in no position to go public. The real problem is the other part of what we have found.'

Mullins paused and poured another cup of tea. 'The truth is we're sitting on a bloody goldmine – a goldmine that could prove to be a far greater and deeper scandal than those thieving nephews and nieces ever would be, and I haven't the faintest idea how to handle it. All I do know is one false step and we are all in deep shit.'

Again, the Monsignor winced.

'How much are we talking about?' asked O'Donnell.

'Millions, at the very least. I'll tell you – enough to kill for.'

There was silence. The bishop was clearly a worried man.

'Could I see the file?' O'Donnell suggested tentatively.

'That's why I thought you were here,' barked Mullins. 'Your uncle tells me you can be totally trusted. Is he right?'

O'Donnell could have stopped at that point. But he was curious and Trinity had no comparable excitements to offer.

'Yes,' he said. 'You have my word.'

'Good. Then you'd better stay the night and read the files. The Monsignor can fill you in and we can talk at breakfast.'

O'Donnell made a brief phone call to a colleague in Trinity asking him to take his morning lecture and then returned with his uncle to the study to see the files for himself – and he still hadn't been offered a drink. That, at least, would not have happened in the old bishop's time.

5

....

The bishop's study, into which Monsignor Nestor now led O'Donnell, was the only room in the palace that had not changed in any significant way since the time of Concannon. It was a large, darkish room with heavy furniture and a magnificent Victorian desk with a green-shaded lamp. It was a room designed to intimidate and to impress, and O'Donnell could visualise errant parish priests and nervous curates summoned to report here. He could also picture how the office could be used to impress and persuade those when the bishop so wished.

Monsignor Nestor chuckled.

'Many is the time I came in here quaking in my shoes to face Dr Concannon. Mind you, once he got used to me, or rather me to him, he was not bad to work for. He could be considerate and even kind, but he rarely dropped his guard or relaxed in to any sort of informality. I think this room still intimidates Dr Mullins. He never used it as his own office – he has a much smaller room off the front hall. For some strange reason he has never changed the study.'

Nestor moved behind the bishop's desk and pressed a button on the wall. Slowly the oak panel slid back to reveal the door of a large walk-in safe built into the wall. Nestor produced a key. The lock turned easily and he invited O'Donnell into the safe, which was six feet high, at least 10-feet wide and as deep again.

'Rome does strange things to people,' said Nestor. 'The old bishop had a thing about secrecy and security. This is where he kept the files originally and this is where we are now keeping them. Here they are – or at least here are the ones you will need.'

With that, he produced five large cardboard boxes of a type used for storing documents in the early years of the century.

'Let me explain each of the boxes before I let you at it. By the way, even though there are five boxes, only three may be of relevance to you. I have spent the last four weeks reading through them and I am confident only three are relevant to our enquiries. I have put markers on those particular files that I think will be needed by you.'

'Why may I not see all five boxes?' asked O'Donnell, immediately suspicious that even his good uncle was covering up some juicy morsel or perhaps was conscious that they 'might give rise to scandal'.

He was right.

'Look, there is no need for you to see their contents. They are concerned with purely ecclesiastical matters.'

'But what's in them?' persisted O'Donnell, his curiosity whetted by his uncle's reluctance and obvious embarrassment. He was not going to let go that easily.

'Well...,' a little hesitation, 'I can't let you see the contents but I will tell you what each box contains. Sit down.'

Then the Monsignor explained. The first box contained file cards, indexed and neatly ordered. Files on every priest who had ever served in the diocese. Files on bishops in other dioceses. Files on heads of religious orders, on professors in Maynooth and in the other seminaries. Files on university presidents, journalists, senior civil servants and even some politicians. There were even files on ecclesiastics in Rome.

'About a thousand cards in all, over a period of 46 years,' said the Monsignor, 'including one on myself.'

'But why?' asked O'Donnell. 'Why and what sort of information did he have on these files?'

The why was easy enough, explained the Monsignor. Concannon-believed quite simply that information was power and he set out to have as much information as he could on anybody with whom he might have to do business. It wasn't that he would use his knowledge publicly or openly. In many cases the people that he was dealing with knew that he had information about them and, even if he didn't have it, the illusion was there. In most cases the information was never used but it gave him an insight into the motivation behind much of what was happening in the country. The Monsignor paused, lost for a second in memory.

'You know I can still see him sitting there.' Nestor pointed to the empty chair. 'The thin dry smile, the light of the lamp reflecting on his gold-rimmed spectacles, the affected Roman mannerisms. And he would say to me, quietly, almost as if talking to himself, "you know, people can be so foolish. If you look in the right places there are no real secrets and you know it's important to know something about everybody, and especially to know something bad about everybody."

'He would say this,' continued the Monsignor, 'as if it did not apply to him, as if he was above any of those frailties which gave rise to secrets.'

O'Donnell was puzzled, as well he might be. 'But where did he get his information? Kilderry is not exactly the centre of the universe.'

'It's easy enough if you know how to go about it and the bishop was an expert,' said the Monsignor almost sadly. 'It was extraordinary how many priests would pass on information and gossip about their colleagues – friends even. Why would they do this you may ask. In part to ingratiate themselves and in part because gossiping is a particular clerical vice – gossiping and bad-mouthing, especially their fellow priests.'

Nestor had seen his own file and the things about himself that had been relayed – though in his case they amounted to no more than the report that he broke canon law from time to time by attending horse race meetings and the theatre, which at that stage were forbidden. What shocked him was the source of these stories – two men still alive whom he regarded as close and good friends.

Concannon's system was simple enough. If a priest had a drink problem, if he was too friendly with a particular woman, if he went to race meetings, if he were suspected of even mildly unorthodox views, then the bishop would know – and what information fellow priests didn't supply, the busybodies would provide. The bishop, concluded Nestor, was a genius at accumulating information, a talent he had brought with him from Rome.

That, however, said Nestor, was only part of the story. 'He applied the same tactics on the wider society. He was particularly good at getting information on his fellow bishops, usually playing one off against the other. He cultivated key people: university professors, professors in Maynooth, especially those who had hopes of getting a diocese of their own, the editor of the *Irish Independent* which was then, as you may not know given what it is today, a strongly Catholic and conservative newspaper, the Secretary of one or two government departments – Local Government and External Affairs were two he was particularly friendly with – and of course he was the first and only bishop to be a member of a Dublin Club, the Stephen's Green Hibernian Club in his case.

'He was in the way of getting a great deal of information but, more important, he knew how to collate it and cross-reference it until he had his own rich mosaic of what was going on in the country and in his own diocese.'

The Monsignor stopped and pointed to the box. 'And here it all is. And here it all stays.'

The historian in O'Donnell was outraged.

'But, my God, just think of it – one of the most valuable historic archives of the century is in that box. You can't just file it away and leave it there.'

'Oh yes we can,' smiled the Monsignor, 'and we will.'

'But you won't destroy it?' asked O'Donnell almost plaintively.

'Well, that's up to the bishop but, as you know, I'm a bit of a scholar myself and it's not in my nature to destroy evidence. No, the files will be preserved but they will not surface in the lifetime of any of the people mentioned in them and, I suspect, for many years after that too.'

O'Donnell was still marvelling at what he had just heard and almost forgot to enquire about the nature of the other off-limits box. His uncle seemed not to have any inclination to enlighten him.

'Oh, that's just ecclesiastical correspondence between the bishop and others in the Church, mainly people in Rome, some other bishops and the nuncio. Formal and routine stuff. Not really relevant.'

O'Donnell was about to say that he would rather be the judge of what was 'relevant' but decided to let the matter rest – at least for the moment.

His uncle was already opening the first box.

'This one deals with all the financial transactions relevant to the bishop's family. The transactions start in 1940 and continue up until a year ago. The bishop was meticulous in everything he did and, thankfully for us, so too are the records here.'

'Two questions,' said O'Donnell. 'The first is the source of this money, since you say there is no record of it in the diocesan records. It had to come from somewhere. Where?'

'The source will be fully explained in this box here. What's your second question?'

'Surely the bishop left a will. Was there anything in that? Any clue as to where the money came from or anything of that sort?'

'A good question – and relevant,' said the Monsignor drily. 'Yes there was a will and the bishop didn't die penniless. The diocese owned the house he lived in and the diocese supplied all his living expenses and medical needs, so he was virtually self-sufficient.'

'But that's not all,' persisted O'Donnell.

'No. The drawing up of the will is curious – strange even. The original will was drawn up 20 years ago by Mr Archie Bowe, the solicitor to the diocese and a man of great integrity. But a year before the bishop died, he did something very strange. Without telling Archie Bowe, he had another solicitor – a Mr Cooney from Cloghan – draw up a new will. Bowe only got a copy after the bishop's death and, as you might imagine, he was furious.

'I asked Bowe how different the new will was from the old one. He claimed client confidentiality – he is a stickler – but did say it was very, very different. So all we have to go on is what was in the new will – a donation of £20,000 to the papal nuncio, the same to the Irish College in Rome and to a group called *Mysterium Fidei*, a few small bequests, £2,000 to his driver and half that to a carer, and a few other donations. The whole estate came to about £70,000 – significant, but only a fraction of what might have been there.'

Nestor was trying to recount events precisely.

'I was present on behalf of the diocese when the will was read in Archie Bowe's office. The nephews and nieces were there too. Not particularly nice people I have to say, but when they discovered there was less money than they expected, and none of it for them, you could have cut the tension with a knife.

They couldn't wait to get out to have their own private discussion. But first they pressed Bowe hard, almost accusing him of hiding something from them or even of misappropriating the money. They even looked at me with suspicion. They simply could not believe their ears. They still can't, but everything was above board – as it always would be with Bowe.

'So you're saying the will is relatively modest, with no mention of the money you and the bishop are sitting on. I don't understand.'

'That's precisely why you are here. To help us find out and to protect our interest. You will shortly see for yourself what we are talking about.'

There was a long silence. Finally O'Donnell broke it. 'The break-in at the bishop's house – surely that had to be the family. As far as they were concerned, the money had to be somewhere.'

'We have no evidence, but that is my own suspicion. It took place the day after the reading of the will. Given that there was nothing for them in the will and they found no files in the house, their suspicion that they had been bested would have been confirmed. We can expect trouble and nasty trouble from that quarter, but do you know I almost welcome it.'

O'Donnell tried to digest the full impact of what he had heard, but his uncle was already pulling out the remaining two boxes.

'Look, I have to get back to my parish, but I'll show you your room and then you can come back here to the study and work as late as you like. You can get some refreshments in the kitchen if you need them. One thing I can promise you, you won't be bored with what I leave here for you to study.'

O'Donnell, knowing that the best that awaited him in the kitchen was a glass of milk and an almost certainly stale sandwich, would have been happier with the promise of a pint.

But the Monsignor was right in one thing. He was not going to be bored.

6

....

Before Nestor left, O'Donnell asked him if the bishop had kept a diary.

'The answer to that is yes and no. Bishop Concannon was meticulous about noting all his appointments and meetings, and all are recorded here. But did he keep a personal diary? No, not on a regular or daily basis. But, he did write up detailed accounts of meetings he had if he thought them important.'

'Like what?'

'The bishop liked precision. He liked to see a problem or a situation laid out on paper. That gave him an opportunity to study all the angles and, of course, he liked to be able to keep the record straight as far as his own memory of events was concerned. For example, before a meeting of bishops in Maynooth, he would examine in writing the issues likely to come up and rehearse the arguments he would make. Then after the meeting, he would write a short account of what happened.'

Nestor explained that these personal notes and recollections were written on loose leaf pages and inserted in to binders, with each binder dealing with six or seven years. Concannon called these volumes his 'journal' and O'Donnell felt this would be the best place to start.

His first impression was that entries were made on an occasional rather than regular basis. There was much about his early days as a bishop, his preparations for the hostile meetings he expected in Maynooth, and especially on how to handle the cardinal, and he recorded his victories and occasional setbacks. What struck O'Donnell most was the bishop's self-confidence, but also how strategic he was in picking his issues.

What also struck O'Donnell were the gaps in the entries. These gaps explained why the bishop had chosen to keep these records in loose leaf binders. They could be removed without leaving any evidence. And there were gaps, O'Donnell noted, most especially in 1940 and 1945.

Having finished his survey of the journals, he had no hesitation in deciding this would be his starting point. A number of entries he thought might be especially interesting.

The first one which caught his attention was dated April 12 1939.

> Attended dinner hosted by papal nuncio at his residence. Fine house, but clearly in need of repair and no sign of any renewal in sight. Spoke with nuncio privately. He was a somewhat strange appointment. I had heard vaguely of him in Rome but never met him there. A Franciscan and said to be a good scholar but he might have expected a better appointment than Dublin given that he had been a senior Vatican diplomat at the Treaty of Versailles. He seems to have good judgement and I suspect he has good sources including politics. He is said to have a cordial relationship with de Valera and to have cultivated a few clerical spies of his own. He had obviously had good reports of me from Rome and spoke only to me about some of the bishops of whom he was critical. He finds some of them openly loyal to Rome but privately resistant and resentful both of the nuncio and of directives from Rome. He tells me my own appointment is still greatly resented

but Rome is happy with me. He is worried about state of health of the Archbishop of Dublin and suggested my name might be in contention should there be an early vacancy. I told him I would doubt it. The talk in Maynooth is either of Professor Boylan, who at least is a decent scholar, and Monsignor Ryan of Belfast.

In any event, it was a good table from a friar with a vow of poverty. The nuncio knows how to do things in proper style. Clearly a man with experience of the world, and it shows.

At table I was close to James Dillon, Professor Michael Tierney, Professor Alfred O'Rahilly and PJ Ruttledge. I have heard Ruttledge is out of favour with de Valera and may shortly leave the ministry, but if this be so, you can be sure de Valera will do it smoothly. Some difference over the IRA seems to be at the root of the problem. Talk was gloomy and pessimistic on the inevitability of war and the failure of statesmanship to avert it. The League of Nations is a joke and the so-called democracies are floundering around. The professors were loud in their lamentations on the failure of the democratic systems to rise above the lowest common denominator and professed to see signs of encroaching communism all round. Professor James Hogan of Cork, an excitable man who, I am told, was once a spy and is now a medieval historian, was particularly critical of the French Government 'which had alienated the true France, and would fall like a rotten apple at the first gust of wind. The Germans would do to France what they had just done to the Czechs'. I spoke at some length about the excesses of Nazi rule and especially of the attacks on the Church. Nor was I particularly happy about Italy either. I argued that the future for the

Church and civilisation lay in the models of government emerging in the Iberian Peninsula – especially that of Dr Salazar but I was also hopeful of what would happen under General Franco.

Only James Dillon of those present was disagreeable, He was so certain and so dogmatic as he prated on about the sanctity of representative government, of the need for the civilized world – and by this he meant, believe it or not, England, France and the USA – to stand firm against fascism. Bombastic stuff and I have no doubt that behind that polished façade lies a deep strain of anti-clericalism. I feel he did not approve of me and perhaps that is just as well for I formed a strong distaste for his bombastic certainty.

After the meal, when we were in the drawing room for coffee and brandy, I was approached by a man who had been sitting down the table from me, who had only briefly joined in our conversation but who was listening intently as I spoke. His name, which I had not caught earlier, was Henry Alsop, a name I had not heard of before. A tall, gaunt man, yellowish, almost dyspeptic in complexion and with a quiet ocular intensity. He told me he had listened very carefully to my words, that I had spoken with great spirit and great sense, that alone among the company I had a real grasp of current world realities.

I was pleased, but somewhat surprised when he said he would like very much to talk to me alone and at some length and as a matter of some urgency. I was agreeable, but vague, since I know nothing of this man and he may be a crank. I think not and in truth he interests me, when I learn a little more I will see what I will do.'

The next 'relevant' entry was for two months later – June 1939.

The nuncio dined here last evening and stayed overnight. Told me again Rome was well pleased with my efforts at restoring order and discipline in the diocese and would like to see me take a stronger role within the Hierarchy. Assured him I would make every effort but that, as a bishop, I was at a disadvantage being outranked by the archbishops. He understood, but sadly there is no likely vacancy, at least for some time, but he was not hostile to the idea, and informed me that both Cashel and Armagh were unwell and that Dublin was defying all the odds by staying alive.

He is in fact very unhappy with the lack of leadership generally within the Hierarchy. Armagh was 'genial but ineffectual', Cashel and Tuam were 'sleepy and provincial'. The nuncio is particularly concerned about Clonfert – quite out of control he said, strange economic and social theories which are none of his business and needlessly annoying the government, McEntee in particular is incensed.

I brought up the subject of Alsop. He gave me a strange look but did not ask why I had broached the question. What he told me confirms and amplifies what I have already learned. Alsop is English by birth, wealthy, a widower and childless. He is a convert, previously Church of England and with a history of over-indulgence and rakishness in his earlier years. He was a fashionable convert, influenced, it appears, by Monsignor Knox, a friend of both Belloc and Benson, but not, it appears, of Chesterton, of whose levity and lifestyle he does not approve. Since his conversion, as the papal nuncio put it, he is more Roman than the Romans. A deep thinker according to the nuncio, quietly worried about the future of the Church.

The remainder of that entry merely detailed the papal nuncio's views on various members of de Valera's Cabinet and the nuncio's fellow ambassadors then serving in Dublin. They were not, for the most part, charitable, and were particularly scathing of US envoy David Gray, whom the nuncio described as 'a quintessential WASP with an ingrained contempt for the Irish'.

The next entry that caught O'Donnell's attention was dated four weeks later – July 8 1939.

Following the papal nuncio's visit, I sought to make contact with Alsop but he was on an extended visit to the U.S. looking after some of his business interests there. I'm reliably told they are very substantial. He returned last week and immediately accepted my invitation to dine here, which he did last evening.

He is a strange brooding man, widely read and widely travelled, very much a man of the *monde entier*, given not at all to small talk, but animated, almost excited, when discussing the big matters.

Our conversation focused almost entirely on the coming war and in particular on the future of the Church and the fate of Ireland in the post-war years. He is pessimistic on both issues. He dislikes de Valera and thinks his policy will result in the worst of both worlds for Ireland and, while he told me he would be instinctively a Cosgrave supporter and personally likes Cosgrave, he feels that his party would make an even worse fist of the present situation. He is particularly hostile to Dillon who he sees as vain, unreliable, dangerous even.

His main concern, however, was the future of the Church. He sees dangers everywhere. In a changing, uncertain and dangerously unstable world, the only hope lies in a strong and certain Church, a Church with a clear message and the disciplined means to get it across. He assured me he did not mean to give offence but that the Church at the present time – and he included Ireland – was inward and complacent, ignoring the changes all round it, ignoring the revolution in mass communications and, in too many cases, fighting battles that no longer mattered.

He foresaw a great opportunity for the Church in the devastation of the post-war world, but not the Church as at present organised and led. What surprised me was that he saw Ireland as having a central part to play in such a situation. When he warmed up to this theme, he was almost violent in his emphasis (even though he never raised his voice).

I asked if he expected the current Hierarchy to lead this move. I have to admit I asked with a certain quiet malice. Certainly not, he said, for he was even more critical of them than the papal nuncio had been. No, it would be through some new departure. That was why he had been so taken by what I had to say about recent developments concerning Dr Salazar and General Franco and then, to my surprise, he told me that alone among the bishops he had met – and he also dismissed the English bishops as 'deferential doormats' – I was the only one with the vision and the personality to take the initiative the Church so badly needed.

I was surprised, but when he elaborated I discovered that his views on developments in general were not vastly different from my own and 1 assured him we could talk in total confidence. I told him at some length about what I knew of Spain and Portugal and said I would use my contacts in Rome to get as much further information as possible.

We talked late in to the night and he invited me to dine with him in his Dublin club on my next visit to that city. He told me I need have no worries about petrol rationing – he would send a car for me, but I assured him that as a bishop 1 had an adequate supply available. I look forward to that meeting.

The next entry of interest was dated August 6 1939.

Dined with Alsop in his club – the Stephen's Green Club. Dingy place. Discreet, he said, but free from any Masonic or Jewish influences. He suggested I should become a member. No other bishop was, but he persuaded me it offered greater privacy for my Dublin visits than did the other hotels favoured by visiting prelates, especially Wynn's Hotel he said, which was a hothouse of clerical gossip.

He is in fact very well informed of what is happening in Dublin circles and he told me that the better type of Catholic professional and business person is to be found in the Stephen's Green Club and, in addition, the ban on ladies ensures that there can never be any cause for scandal. He offered to propose me for membership and I accepted his offer. It may raise some eyebrows among my fellow bishops, but there is no interdiction in canon law on my applying and joining.

I brought him up to date on what I have found about the Iberian countries. He shares my high view of Dr Salazar but believes the regime of General Franco, because of its military discipline and Spanish passion, as he described it, is likely to be longer lasting and more effective. He was especially interested in the new Catholic action group, *Mysterium Fidei*, which he feels will be well-suited for post-war conditions.

I know little enough about this organisation, but Alsop, his eyes bright, told me that the only way to defeat communism and masonry is to adopt the same tactics – secrecy, discipline, ruthlessness where necessary and total loyalty to one single overriding objective – the establishment of Christ's rule on earth, Christ's rule as defined in the Magisterium and proclaimed through the One True Church.

I have to note that I was somewhat taken aback by his fervour and the absolutist nature of his outpouring.

The next journal reference to Alsop is three weeks later. It is clear from the contents of this next entry that there had been several intervening meetings, mostly in the Stephen's Green Club. of which the bishop was now a full member. As Monsignor Nestor pointed out, it was not the practice of the bishop to record all meetings in the journal, but only those he regarded as being of real significance. This meeting clearly fell in to that category. Or possibly, O'Donnell suspected the record of the other meetings had been removed.

September 27 1939

Dined last evening with Alsop in the Stephen's Green Club. He was late arriving, which for him was most unusual, but he had left a message advising me of this. While I waited, I noticed that Dillon, who regularly dines here, was the centre of some attention.

He had his 'man of destiny' look, but was in an expansive mood – booming voice and theatrical gestures. Some members, though by no means all, were complimenting him on his 'moral courage' in calling for the abandonment of Irish neutrality. He was cool with me, though exceedingly proper. I made no reference to his speech, but I am certain, and it is the view of the nuncio also and indeed of Geary of the *Independent* and Walshe of External Affairs that his political career is well and truly over. I shall not grieve if this be so.

When Alsop arrived, I was shocked by his appearance. His face was even more gaunt than before, his skin yellow and his whole being had an emaciated, careworn look. His clothes were almost hanging off him. He apologised for his late arrival and got to the point immediately. He had been to see a consultant in Fitzwilliam Square who had confirmed to him what he had known himself – that he had but a short time to live. His condition was quite simply without hope.

I expressed my concern and my regrets but he brushed them aside, almost brusquely. What time he had left he intended to use to the full and did I mind if he got to the point without preliminaries. By now his eyes were shining and there was a strange intensity in that diseased face. If I did not know him better, I would have called it the look of a fanatic – a face almost from an El Greco painting.

His proposition was sudden and staggering. He reminded me of the long discussions we had about the nature of the challenges facing the Church and the type of response these challenges required. He talked again about *Mysterium Fidei* and of the unique opportunity open to the Church in Ireland. It was ground we had covered many times before and I wondered what it was he now wanted me to do. Almost as if reading my mind, he looked me straight in the face with a burning intensity, the like of which I had never experienced before and said: 'This is what I am going to do and this is what I want of you.'

He was, he said, a wealthy man with no relatives and no dependents. He had converted virtually all of his assets into stocks and shares or banked capital. His house and its contents he would leave to a close friend. The remainder of his assets were to be transferred to me within a matter of days but on certain conditions which I was free to accept or reject. The monies involved, he repeated, were substantial, very substantial, and, as he had organised them, had a capacity to grow even more substantially.

The bulk of the funds would be in shares over which I would have sole control and were to be used at a time which, in my judgement, would be appropriate to the setting up in Ireland of an organisation such as *Mysterium Fidei* or its equivalent, which would lead the way to the winning back of Christ's Kingdom, first in Ireland and later in the world as a whole. He had total trust in me and total confidence in my judgement. I would have total discretion how best to attain our objectives at any given time.

Would I accept?

I have to say I did not hesitate. I was not fully sure on the exact detail of his plans but Christ's work and the Church's work took many shapes and, if I did not agree fully with what he was proposing, somebody who knew his thinking less well than I would almost certainly take my place. He seemed relieved when I accepted and said we would attend to the details presently.

He then told me of the second part of the bequest. As a man of affairs, he knew that the work entrusted to me would involve preparation, research, recruitment and the like, and in order to preserve the value of the main bequest until I was ready to implement his plans, he proposed to give me a capital sum in my own sole control to be used privately and at my discretion towards the achievement of the main objective.

By now he was tired but also elated, almost light-headed it seemed to me, but delighted I had accepted the challenge. He thanked me profusely and asked could I attend at his home in Lansdowne Road in three days' time where his solicitor, Charles Ruddock, would arrange the 'details'.

The next entry was a few days later.

Alsop was curiously excited when I called to his house today. Instead of behaving like a man facing death, he was more like a young man about to embark on an adventure. His solicitor, Mr Charles Ruddock, a leathery little man whom I had seen more than once in the club, clearly did not approve of what Alsop was proposing and I sensed they had been arguing before my arrival. Alsop, however – or so it seemed to me – had made it clear to Ruddock that he was here to obey instructions, not to argue.

Ruddock was cold with me, but then he was losing control over major funds. He certainly didn't like that and probably guessed I would not be using his services.

Alsop was precise and to the point. He was opening an account in the Munster & Leinster Bank in Dame St in my name; it would be in two parts. One hundred thousand pounds would be placed on deposit, with a current account of 10 thousand pounds. This money could be used at my discretion and as I thought best in order to secure the purpose dear to both our hearts. The current account should never be under 10 thousand pounds and, if I needed lump sums, the capital account was open to me at my sole discretion. I could sense Ruddock sniffing with disapproval as Alsop outlined his conditions.

Alsop then handed me a padlocked, medium-sized steel box and a key. As he did so, I could sense the fury and consternation on Ruddock's yellow face. He did not seem to have anticipated this development – nor indeed had I. Alsop told me the box contained all his stocks and shares certificates, an inventory of which would be found in the box. I could calculate their value for myself and record their appreciation value. They were to be kept safely, nobody was to know of their existence or their provenance, and they were to be kept for use at the appropriate time for the glory of Christ the King and in the way he had so often discussed with me. And with that he handed me the box. Ruddock, I could see, was beside himself with rage, but there was nothing he could do or say.

What an awesome responsibility I had thrust upon me. Awesome responsibility indeed. Christ be praised! We talked for a further half hour, but Alsop by now was tired.

As I was leaving, I remarked to him about the magnificence of the desk in his study. It was truly a fine piece of furniture but I'm not quite sure why I remarked upon it to him. He looked at me and then said: 'It will be yours. It is the least you deserve and it will be a reminder of me.' He instructed Ruddock to make sure that his instructions about the disposal of the desk were followed. Ruddock was even angrier, but again there was nothing he could do.

The remainder of this entry contained very precise details of how Concannon took control of the funds, the opening of his personal accounts in the Dame Street branch of the Munster & Leinster Bank, and of his taking control of the stocks and shares and their transfer to the secure safe he had recently installed in Kilderry.

By now it was 4.00 a.m. O'Donnell looked in to the fourth box. Inside was the metal box mentioned in the bishop's journal, aged, but very secure. It was locked, but Nestor had left the key and, on opening, O'Donnell found neat bundles of documents containing details and certificates of stocks and shares on yellowing but thick paper. The names and figures jumped off the faded pages at O'Donnell. Blue-chip investments, substantial in 1940, but today their value could be reckoned in millions of pounds and dollars. Many millions. Even O'Donnell could see that here certainly was money to kill for.

On further examination, he was surprised not to find any inventory. Presumably what was here was what had not been realised or cashed in over the years. Curious, he thought. It would be helpful, and indeed important, to know just how many of the original shares had been cashed in over the years. Maybe it would turn up elsewhere, although, given how methodical Concannon was, he doubted it.

He put the boxes back in the safe, closed and locked the huge door, and headed off to snatch a few hours' sleep. He might well be tired in the morning, but at least he would not have a hangover. His head, however, was swimming with the information he had just seen and all he had learned that evening.

7

....

At the very same time as Peter O'Donnell was reading through the files in Kilderry, Richard E Murdock was lowering his sixth gin and tonic of the evening in the corner of his golf club bar 60 miles away in the West of Ireland. Richard E, as he was known – though few people knew that the 'E' stood for Eusebius and Murdock did not make it his business to tell people – was alone, not because there were no others about, but because his morose bad manners led people to avoid him as far as possible. Murdock was a nephew of Bishop Concannon – it was actually Concannon who decided that the name Eusebius be given to Murdock and in family as in other matters, what Concannon asked for, he generally got.

This particular evening Murdock was even more morose than usual. He glowered into his gin and tonic, his sirloin and port complexion matching the crimson Clongowes tie he habitually wore, almost as if he felt a compulsive need to affirm to the world that he was indeed an old Clongownian. Recalling his days at Clongowes, and his own prominence there, was one of his staple conversational items and was one, but only one, of the reasons his fellow golf club members gave him such a wide berth.

This particular evening Murdock had much to glower about. He had discovered just a few hours earlier that his wife was having an affair or, more accurately, was engaging in sexual gymnastics with not just one but with two of the apprentices in his legal practice – her third apprentice in three years. And these, Murdock suspected, were only the ones he knew about.

For some reason, she seemed to go out of her way deliberately
to seduce these young men, and the greatest part of her pleasure
seemed to consist in letting Murdock know what she was up to.

He had discovered this latest indiscretion or 'outrage', as he
termed it, only this afternoon. The district court had ended early and he had come home sooner than expected. Normally he
would head in to the nearby hotel bar for a drink with a few
of his colleagues, but this afternoon he did not. On his arrival
home, he heard loud noises coming from the guest bedroom.
When he opened the door it was to confront his wife in bed
with not one but two of the apprentices. So frenetic was their
activity, and so intricate their positions, that it was 10 or 20
seconds before they were aware of his presence. Even then,
his wife made no great effort to extricate herself – or more
accurately to have the apprentices extricate themselves – or to
cover her nakedness.

Murdock had been incandescent with rage, but there wasn't
much he could do about it. The apprentices would be gone by
Monday, but the story would already be around the office and
no doubt would travel much further afield within hours. He
knew he was becoming a laughing stock. And that was the rub
as far as Murdock was concerned. There was simply nothing
he could do about it. It was his wife's revenge – and exquisite
revenge it was.

Murdock barked at the barman for another gin and tonic,
and his already florid complexion grew even redder as his indignation rose. Revenge.

Three years earlier, Murdock's wife, tiring of his endless
philandering, had hired a private investigator to collect what
information he could on Murdock. The harvest had been rich.
The existence of Murdock's mistress in a nearby town had been
quickly discovered and there was also a married woman living

15 miles to the other side of the town, the wife of a District Justice no less and a woman Murdock's wife cordially detested. But juiciest of all had been the discovery of Murdock's frequenting of brothels in Dublin, especially those specialising in some unusual practices.

Murdock's wife had all the information – times, places, photos of Murdock entering and leaving these establishments, photos of him kerb crawling around Percy Place and a written statement from one of the women involved.

It had cost a few pounds to pay the private detective, but she had got what she wanted and now Sally Murdock had her husband where she wanted him. Murdock knew that, being the tough Kerry woman she was, she would not hesitate to use the information and use it ruthlessly. His wife had discovered the sweetness of revenge and the joys of uncomplicated sex – and was enjoying both in roughly equal measure.

Strangely, however, it was not his wife's behaviour that was the main source of Murdock's ill temper this particular evening. It was, if anything, a matter more ominous and more serious. His legal practice was in serious trouble. His arrogance and frequent drunkenness had lost him some of his more valuable clients. His income had dropped but his lifestyle and his wife's spending had not. He was in serious financial trouble.

He knew there were rumours and it was only a matter of time before they reached the ears of the Law Society and then there would be an investigation. Of that he was certain. The Law Society had been stung too often by defaulting solicitors to ignore even the slightest rumour. And he knew too that such an investigation, when it came, would show that substantial monies had been transferred from his clients' accounts to his own accounts and, most ominously of all, that money was no longer there.

Until recently, it had not worried him unduly. He knew that, just as at every other stage in his life so far, 'the Bish' would oblige, would sort out his problems. Ever since his father died, way back in the 1940s, Richard E Murdock had always had this particular safety net. Whether it was for his fees for Clongowes, pocket money for 'extras', fees for university, money to buy out an established country practice or funds to sustain that practice, his uncle 'the Bish' had always been on hand. And even when his uncle retired, that support had continued. All he had to do was ask and his request was granted.

He knew his uncle had a fearsome reputation as a cold and unapproachable man but, as far as his sister's children were concerned, the door was always open. There was no great warmth, no easy familiarity, but there was never any stinting either.

Murdock was not a speculative man and he had come to take it all for granted, almost as if it were a fact of everyday life, as permanent and unchanging as the Town Hall that dominated the Market Square of Murdock's home town. But then, just over a year ago, the money had dried up. Requests for help went unanswered, requests to come to see the bishop were turned down – the bishop was not in a position to receive visitors, not even family, Murdock was told. In his selfish way, Murdock was not surprised that a nonagenarian was unable to see people and he made no effort to find out the reason why.

He was sustained by the belief that, as soon as the bishop passed away, and he expected that to happen soon, the real jackpot would be at his disposal. Financially, Murdock had no doubt that his uncle was sitting on a goldmine and that it was only a short matter of time before a large portion of it would be his. After all, where else would it go? And so, even as his own financial situation had worsened appreciably during the previous year, Richard E. Murdock had no real worries. Time, which even Thomas Patrick Concannon could not defy, would see him right.

As Murdock ordered his seventh gin and tonic he knew with a stomach-churning feeling that he was in serious trouble. He had known it for the past two weeks, ever since that prissy little solicitor, Archie Bowe, had read the contents of his uncle's will. Not a bob. Not a sou. A bequest – and a hefty one – to the nuncio, another to some crowd 'Mysterium' or other and to the Irish College in Rome. Then, as if to add insult to injury, he left a few thousand pounds to old Johnny Ryan, his former driver and general factotum, a few to his carer, and that was that. Nothing for the family.

Murdock, however, knew better. It was he who had organised the break-in to his uncle's house. It wasn't really a break-in – he had long ago equipped himself with a duplicate key to the bishop's house and, over the years, he had got to know the layout of the house very well. It had taken him less than half an hour to realise that boxes and files were missing and to know that his uncle's study was not as he had known it. In his frustration, he had messed some things about and made no effort to disguise the fact that the house had been searched. That, he knew now, had been a mistake, something which had aroused suspicions but, in his mind, was not a major blunder.

Murdock was not in the habit of blaming himself. No. The significant fact was that boxes were missing, and he had no doubt that the missing boxes contained the money he believed to be rightfully his. Nor had he any doubt as to who had stolen the boxes. For stolen he believed them to have been. It had to be that fat, greasy little bishop, that styleless imposter his uncle had so detested and his accomplice in this theft could be none other than that dry as dust academic, that sleeveen Nestor, who had been his uncle's secretary, but whom his uncle had, and in Murdock's view rightly, never fully trusted. These were the thieves, the bastards who had stolen what was rightfully his.

As he ruminated, his anger grew. It welled up inside him, until he could contain himself no longer. His large, meaty fist thumped down on the bar counter. Those within hearing range were astonished to hear the man, who had boasted all these years about his uncle 'the Bish', exclaim: 'That little bollocks, that greasy little fucker of an imposter. I'll murder the fucker if he doesn't give me back what is rightfully mine. Murder the fucker.'

With that he stormed out of the club, slumped into his Mercedes and fumbled for his car keys. He pointed his car in the direction of the nearby town and the comforting arms of his long-suffering mistress, who was none too pleased to see him, but could ill afford not to make him welcome.

8

....

Breakfast with the bishop next morning was little different to the meal of the previous evening. Strong tea, toast and more bacon and eggs. Bishop Mullins was a man who relished his food. Plain fare and plenty of it.

Peter O'Donnell was surprisingly rested after his few hours' sleep. Monsignor Nestor would join them later, but the bishop was not going to waste time.

'Well, what do you make of it?' he asked O'Donnell through a mouthful of fried egg.

'Where do I start?' O'Donnell replied. 'I'll need more time but, from what I've seen so far, you're probably the richest bishop east or west of Texas. You could probably start your own church on the value of those shares I saw last night – Procter & Gamble and General Electric to name but a few.'

O'Donnell could see that his attempt at light-heartedness was not appreciated. Bishop Mullins, he suspected, did not have a sense of humour, certainly not at the moment.

He had better put some order on his thoughts.

But, before he could do that, Mullins got to what he clearly saw was the heart of the matter. 'How much?' he barked. 'How bloody much are they worth?'

O'Donnell produced a note he had made at the end of his night's work.

'This is just a starting estimate and may be well short of the final figure. The shares are just as Concannon got them from this Alsop fellow. Or rather, what's left of the shares he got since we don't know how many original shares there actually were. In fact, I'm surprised there's no inventory of original shares, but it may turn up. One way or another, it's an awful lot of money.'

O'Donnell explained to Mullins what he'd learned about Alsop, though he suspected Mullins already had a fair idea.

'Anyway, some of the shares are useless – pre-war shares in German companies that no longer exist, other shares in now-defunct US and UK companies. Quite a few are in companies that were merged or taken over and these have more than held their value, but the main bulk of the shares are absolutely as blue-chip now as they were then.'

O'Donnell paused. 'I'll have them professionally checked out and verified, but,' he paused again, 'at a conservative estimate, I would say up to five million.'

'Holy fuck. That's ten times my own estimate.'

There was a silence.

'What the hell am I going to do?'

'We can talk about that shortly but, in the meantime, I will have a professional estimate done to see just how much is there.'

'Is that safe? I mean, won't word get out –that's the very last thing I want.'

'No. We have to know. I have a friend who is a stockbroker. I'll bring the matter to him as an academic exercise without telling him about you or anybody else. He's very discreet and will have fun working out the current values – and we may need his services later if we're going to cash them in. They've been lying around for too long as they are. But insofar as you can ever trust a stockbroker, I'm told I can trust Sigerson Keane. We really need to know as soon as we can just what it is we are sitting on.'

O'Donnell detected a quizzical look in Mullins' eyes at his use of 'we', but he continued, pouring himself another cup of tea, 'Anyway, putting a value on the hoard is the least of your troubles, but we can get back to it shortly.'

Mullins was now filling his pipe, sucking noisily in an attempt to get it lighting. The foul-smelling tobacco did not increase O'Donnell's enjoyment of the greasy bacon that was now congealing on his cold plate

'There's the second question you need to know about; the bishop's relationship with his sister's family. As you told me last night, he has been funding them for years – until very recently that is. From what I can see, that money, or most of it at any rate, did not come from the main bequest Alsop made – and don't pretend you haven't read the old boy's journal. It seems to have come from the working capital Alsop gave Concannon to get the whole enterprise under way. He seems to have used this as a sort of personal slush fund, which he may have topped up from time to time from the capital fund, and it's the residue of this that ended up in his will. Or he may have siphoned off some of the original shares in to that fund. He obviously cashed in some shares and spent money, maybe an awful lot of money, but we have no idea where he spent it, how he spent it or on what he spent it on.'

Mullins was clearly uncomfortable with the use of the words 'slush fund', even though he had used it himself yesterday, but he did not interrupt. Nor did he have anything to offer as to where the money might have gone.

'From what I read, it is more than clear Concannon was a greedy man. He just could not say no to the money, but I doubt he had any idea how he would use it to realise Alsop's so-called vision. This was wartime, remember. And I feel the sheer enormity of the money and the size of the task he had undertaken just paralysed him. So the money, or rather the shares, just lay there accumulating in value while he did nothing and, more importantly, had no idea as to what he might do. But I could be wrong. He may have spent large chunks of it. But we just don't know.'

O'Donnell paused for a sip of cold tea. The bishop was silent.

'So how then did he help the family?' asked O'Donnell and immediately answered his own question. 'I'm fairly sure that came from the working capital Alsop gave to cover the early expenses. It was a lot of money, a hundred thousand in 1940 which, if wisely invested, as I'm sure it was, would provide a nice annual supplement to whatever other income his lordship had. And as I said, he probably topped it up from time to time by the sale of some of these shares or maybe from the hefty dividends produced by some of the shares.' O'Donnell couldn't help adding that there were few poor bishops in those days.

Mullins gave him another sour look but O'Donnell continued. 'It would be easy enough for Concannon to pay school and university fees and help his sister's family out of this fund and, indeed, live well himself. Remember, school fees, even for Clongowes in the 1950s, were no more than a few hundred pounds a year and university fees even lower. So Concannon wouldn't have had to dip in to diocesan funds as other bishops might have, not that I suspect that would have bothered him had he deemed it necessary.'

Mullins made no attempt to deny this and O'Donnell went on. 'This was the money he disposed of before his death, the money his family expected would be theirs.'

'I can confirm that,' Mullins interjected. 'In the strictest confidence, of course. Concannon got rid of close to a hundred thousand in his last year. Remember we told you he changed his will and, strangely, old Archie Bowe was not the solicitor he used. He used another solicitor but then deposited the will with Bowe, who was furious but could do nothing about it. But by then most of the money had gone elsewhere and we have no idea where.

'But I can say he was a snob, or maybe a shit, to the end because not a penny came to the diocese, his own diocese – and we could have used it – but half of it went to some crowd called *Mysterium Fidei* and to the Irish College, and the rest to the Holy See through the papal nuncio in Dublin. A few bob too to his old driver, but that was that.

'It was a slap in the face to us but not a surprise because Bowe had tipped me off. Mind you, he hadn't bothered to prepare the family for the shock and I think he enjoyed seeing their reaction.'

'And not a word in his will about the treasure trove in your safe,' said O'Donnell.

Mullins was now mopping his brow with a not too clean handkerchief. 'What the hell am I going to do with it. I can't spend it all on the diocese. And how do I explain where I got it if I start to give it away?'

O'Donnell pushed back his plate and looked at Mullins – the wrinkled face, the shaving cuts, the thick-lensed glasses. A week ago, he had too little money for his good works. Now he had too much.

'Are you jumping ahead a little too quickly?' he asked quietly.

'How do you mean? I'd better start moving fast. I want all this sorted out before word gets around. You know how grasping and greedy people are. That's why I want everything sorted out, shipshape before word gets around. There's too much money to be good. It can only do harm if the word gets out. That's why I want shot of it – or most of it at any rate.'

O'Donnell listened in silence. When he spoke, it was quietly.

'You're missing my point.'

'What point?'

'The point is, who owns the money?'

'I do of course – not personally, but as Bishop of Kilderry. It's diocesan money surely.'

'Why "surely"?' persisted O'Donnell.

He could see the bishop was annoyed. The thought had not crossed his mind and, for all his eagerness to get rid of the money, he was not at all pleased.

'It's obvious why. It was left by the bishop. He got it as Bishop of Kilderry and I have possession of it as his legal and indeed apostolic successor,' he added a little pompously.

But even as he spoke, O'Donnell could see the doubts cloud up in Mullins' mind. He might have been reluctant to inherit the money – he knew it meant trouble – but as a farmer's son, a farmer and cattle dealer to be precise, he didn't like the idea of giving up something he had begun to think of as 'his' and for which he had many worthwhile causes. He was too stubborn a man and, until a more worthy claimant came along – and he could think of none such offhand – what he had, he would hold. And as for that bloodsucking family – the bishop had begun to feel sorry for himself.

By now they had been joined by Monsignor Nestor. O'Donnell reckoned it was time to get to the point.

'This is how I see it. Let's start with the worst-case scenario.' He could sense the tension on the other side of the table.

'Let's say the money was given to the bishop not as Bishop of Kilderry but as Thomas Patrick Concannon, a powerful Church figure, and was given for a very specific purpose. He did not execute that purpose, or may have only done part of it for whatever reason. It may have been a daft proposition in the first place; he may have tried and failed. And remember, the 1940s was a dangerous time and he may have judged the circumstances inappropriate. It may simply have been all too much for him, but one thing is clear – Alsop gave the bishop one set of funds for his personal use, though not I suspect for his sister's family, and that's past tense now anyway.

'But, and this is the point, the other money was for a very clear purpose. Do Alsop's intentions still matter? By what right can you – or anyone else – decide Alsop's original purpose is no longer valid or relevant? And how was the money spent? Did Concannon adhere to Alsop's intentions or did he go his own way? Did Alsop leave any instructions with somebody else? Did he ask some friend to monitor Concannon?

'Alsop may have been generous to the point of fanaticism, but he was a very successful businessman and was unlikely to entrust such a huge sum without some sort of safeguard that his intentions be respected. We don't know any of this. We don't know if anybody else knew the story – somebody in the Vatican perhaps. They are surely all dead, but did they leave records? What about the papal nuncio – did he suspect anything? Surely he must have known something.

'And what if Concannon broke the law in funding some group or other in wartime? Are there any records in Special Branch or in the Department of Justice? Not much escaped those boys, especially during the so-called emergency. And you know those files are no longer sacrosanct. We are only a few years off the 50-year rule. This could go as far as the Supreme Court. Maybe even to Europe.'

He paused for a drink but found only cold tea. He wouldn't have minded a gin and tonic. But even with cold tea, he was warming up to his topic.

'What's to stop some high Vatican figure coming in and saying it is best placed and best suited to carry out Alsop's work. They could make a reasonable case and wouldn't hesitate to squeeze any objections the diocese of Kilderry might have. You know better than me how rough those boys can play, especially with juicy funds at stake. It will be shut up and cough up.'

Mullins was subdued. He knew enough about ecclesiastical thuggery to know that O'Donnell was not exaggerating. But O'Donnell had not finished.

'I'd reckon this *Mysterium Fidei* might have an even stronger case. They were very small and insignificant when Alsop spotted them. Small, single-minded and very determined, or so I've read. Today they're still all of those things, but not small. Today they're a very real power, still single-minded and determined and, from what I've seen of them, not nice people.'

He paused, now quite animated. 'I know a bit about them. They had a hold of sorts over the last attorney general when I was working for the Taoiseach. She eventually shook them off but, from what I saw of them, I wouldn't like them to hear about this. If they do, they'll make the boys from the Vatican look very tame indeed.'

O'Donnell was not finished. 'There's still the family. They don't know they were paid out of a slush fund and may feel they've a legitimate claim to all their uncle's loot. They're greedy people, or at least one of them is, and we've had one break-in already. So, they'll fight hard and, if the courts say that Alsop's intentions are no longer relevant, they could be in with a chance. Or at least they'll see it that way.'

The bishop and the monsignor sat in gloomy silence. In spite of their protestations, they did not fancy losing the money. They were both very human and, in their own minds at least, they put Kilderry first.

'Fuck,' said the bishop.

'Oh dear,' said the monsignor – and this time he did not even notice the bishop's profanity.

O'Donnell waited and then very quietly said: 'It's not over yet. I've given you the worst scenarios. But we're not beaten yet. We still have a few strong cards in our hand.'

'Like what?' growled the bishop.

'Possession of the money and the shares, and the information in the bishop's journal. The money is in stocks and shares, the whole thing happened decades ago and nobody alive today has the faintest idea about any of it. Clearly, if any of the potential claimants had even a whiff about this, they would have been sniffing around by now.'

'But what if Alsop had relatives or told *Mysterium Fidei* or the nuncio about his intentions?'

'No, he had no family. Of that I am certain. As to *Mysterium Fidei*, well he was a dying man and I think he trusted Concannon to sort all that out. No contact had been made and if they felt there was something there for them, they would surely have asked questions before now. Maybe there is something about it in the documents you haven't let me see or in his diary entries. It's a loose end and I don't like it. I may have to see the other files to make sure.'

Monsignor Nestor had been silent up to now.

'I would be surprised if he had not mentioned something about his intentions to the papal nuncio. They were good friends, or so I heard. The story was that he had been chosen for the job by the nuncio, but I can't say for certain if that is true. Certainly, he was a frequent guest at Dr Robinson's table, or so his previous secretary told me. We just have no idea if Robinson left any records and, if he did, they remain just that – archival documents.'

'And as you say, they are all dead now,' continued Nestor. 'But I know how the Church works, and I would be more than surprised if there is not a note somewhere in the nuncio's files.

These fellows cover every angle. And remember, the new nuncio was left some money in the bishop's will – a fair amount at that. These bequests were unexpected and they may even be a bit curious. We must be careful.'

'All that is possible I have to admit, and I hadn't given it any thought,' said O'Donnell. 'We're in a bit of a minefield alright. But we have to assume we are the only ones who know and we have to move quickly.'

'What do you mean, move quickly?'

'Well, let's get all our facts and get the best advice we can. I need to have a better look at Concannon's journal to get as full a picture as I can. And hopefully, we may be able to put in place some sort of trust or legal structure where the money can be quietly disbursed in the interests of the Church or humanity or whatever.'

O'Donnell was not as confident as he sounded and he sensed the others were even more uneasy. He needed to give them a little reassurance.

'What all this means is that we have to keep the whole thing utterly secret for the moment. Not a word must get out and, if and when it does, it must get out the way we want it.'

O'Donnell stopped himself with a jolt. This time yesterday Concannon was but a vague and indifferent memory. What had he got himself in to? Why was he back in his old spin doctor mode, and working for an obscure bishop about whom he knew nothing and cared less?

But his interest had been engaged. He was intrigued and he knew it. He could get out now, but he knew he wouldn't.

He had a final warning as he prepared to leave.

'If word gets out about this then anything could happen and it could turn rough. We need time and we need to keep it to ourselves.'

But O'Donnell, as he drove back to Dublin, reminded himself of the first law of politics. Leaks happen when you least
expect it and they rarely come from the source you suspect.

9

....

Before leaving for Dublin, O'Donnell used the bishop's photocopier to copy all the financial documents and shares. He would have the shares professionally evaluated by Sigerson Keane without giving any indication as to their provenance. He would explore some of the ownership issues with a few of his Trinity law colleagues, again without disclosure of any of the specifics. Everything would be raised in hypothetical terms. He hoped it would stay that way – but he had his doubts.

The bishop and his uncle would carry on, business as usual, with all documents locked securely in the safe. They would meet again in a week's time.

As O'Donnell headed back to Dublin, the small sense of unease he had felt earlier became stronger. It was not just the question of what he was doing in the first place. This was none of his business he told himself. Apart from his affection for his uncle, he had no particular attachment to the Catholic Church. He was, he told himself, an agnostic and, apart from a liking of Gregorian chants, there was no loyalty owed by him to that institution. So why get involved when there were so many more pleasant things to divert him?

Why indeed? Well, he had given his word that he would help and he wouldn't let his uncle down. But he knew it was more than that. He was curious and he was not happy that he had not been given anything like the full story, uncle or no uncle.

There was more to this than he had been shown. There was much still in the bishop's archive that he had not seen and which he reckoned they had no intention of letting him see. The journal excerpts he had seen were not enough to satisfy him that he had anything like the full picture.

The academic in him warned him never to make an assessment on the basis of partial information. He had been denied access to the bishop's cards, the information he had on so many people, and not just his priests. And his uncle had been keen to point him towards particular parts of the journal. Why? Why would he not give him a free hand? Why indeed?

Maybe his uncle was unwilling to let the secrets and maybe the scandals of the diocese be exposed to the light of day after all these years. Let the dead rest in peace. But what about the living? Maybe his uncle was following the time-honoured Church practice of 'not giving scandal to the faithful' or, as O'Donnell saw it, cover it up and brazen it out.

O'Donnell was beginning to feel a sense of grievance. Was he being used? Or was he becoming slightly paranoid. Maybe he should just go ahead and check out the legal and financial aspects.

But here, too, the more he thought about it, the more he was disturbed. The money, the sheer size of the amounts involved. It was too much and the story was too neat. They only had Concannon's version of events. Was his account necessarily a truthful one?

What about Alsop, long dead and with few, if any, surviving relatives? Might they, if they existed, have a different version?

And what about Charlie Ruddock, the solicitor who had been cheated out of the administration of huge sums of money. Was he still alive? Did his firm still exist? Would it have records or even a folk memory of the events described in Concannon's journal?

And there were the questions about Mysterium Fidei and the Vatican. Surely there was something buried in their files that would resurface if any suspicions were aroused.

He also began to ponder a little about the man himself, Thomas Patrick Concannon.

The more he thought about it, the more uncertain he became of his original assessment – that Concannon had been frightened or paralysed by the enormity of it all and had simply sat on the money all these years, his only indulgence being his worthless family, his fine dining and wine cellar. But that didn't tally either. Concannon was a man of power. No, it just did not make sense that Concannon – a powerful, ruthless, and ambitious man who ruled his diocese so effectively – would simply sit on this hoard and do nothing.

But he had to admit that, in spite of his misgivings, his interest was engaged and he was curious. And he had given his word so, for the moment at any rate, he would do as he promised. But he would do it his own way and he would keep his enquiries to himself for the time being.

10

....

Archie Bowe was both old and old-fashioned. He accepted the former, recognising he had no choice in the matter, but was proud of the latter. He equated his old-fashioned views, his expensively unfashionable suits (which he still had made to the specifications of an earlier time) and his outmoded but punctiliously correct working practices with a sense of standards – standards that he saw in sad decline all round.

It would be easy to call Bowe stuffy and snobbish, and some did. It would be easy to see his style of dress and his studied speech as affectations, and in some ways they were. And it would have been easy, as his impatient nephews did, to characterise him as a man afraid to face change, unable to come to grips with the modern world.

Such things missed the main point of Archie Bowe. He was not a subtle or sophisticated man. He saw the world in simple and straightforward terms – black and white, right and wrong, good and evil. His emotions, such as they were, he kept to himself. His loyalties, few and selective – the law, the Catholic Church and the Fine Gael party – had been unshakeable and never in doubt, but, in recent years, each in turn had given him cause to doubt. But, he kept these doubts to himself and never publicly wavered.

The Bowes were a long-lived family. His grandfather, Archie Bowe senior, had been solicitor to the diocese of Kilderry from 1865 to 1919; his father, Nathaniel Bowe, had been solicitor from 1919 to 1958; and, on his death, young Archie, then in his thirties, had taken over. He was proud of this continuity of service the Bowe family had given to the diocese of Kilderry and hoped that, in turn, his nephew Nathaniel Bowe would continue the tradition.

There was little about the bishops of Kilderry that Bowe did not know. Much of what he knew had been passed on to him by his father, who in turn had learned much from his father. What he had not learned there, he had found in the files in his office – files kept under lock and key, and for Archie's eyes only. It was a fundamental principle of Archie's very being that whatever secrets the diocese might have, whatever that might be unseemly or worse, were matters meant to be kept secret. Archie prided himself in the certainty that, in the Bowe family, the diocese of Kilderry had loyal and faithful servants.

This had always been a matter of pride to Archie, but today he was worried – worried and troubled – and Archie was not the sort of man who could confide his troubles in anyone. Others confided in him. Never the reverse.

He was worried about the diocese. Something was wrong and, worse still, he was not being told what it was. His father used to say that things changed with the appointment of Thomas Patrick Concannon in 1937. Concannon had always been proper, courteous and punctilious with Nathaniel Bowe, but there was always a distance between them. Nathaniel complained, not frequently and only to Archie, that he never felt he had the same relationship with Concannon as he had had with his predecessors, Bishop Nalty, and then Bishop Flood. In spite of this reservation, the firm had continued to handle all the business of the diocese – apparently to the full satisfaction of the bishop.

Archie had put his father's reservations down to his dislike of change and perhaps also to his father's own coldness.

Archie had no such reservations when he took over in 1958 and
liked to think he had the bishop's full confidence on all matters.
He had expected a formal relationship with Concannon, who
by then was probably the strongest ecclesiastical voice in the
country and whose views on moral and ecclesiastical matters
thundered from pulpit and pastoral letter – and were always
widely reported.

Bowe found himself reflecting on the bishop he had known
in those years. Concannon was always measured and never
frivolous. He was fearless in promoting the official line and engaged very effectively in public controversy with government
ministers on health and educational matters. He had occasional
exchanges with Protestant bishops on theological issues, especially his defence of the hard line on inter-church marriages.
And he had little appetite for the new-fangled ecumenism that
was seeping out from fashionable theologians. But Bowe remembered that the bishop was never personal or bullying and
what distinguished him from his fellow bishops was his ratio-
nal and intellectual approach. But Bowe remembered too that
the bishop was never wrong, never admitted to doubt or error.
That, thought Bowe, was his great strength.

And why should he admit to error with the truth of the
Church and God's own infallibility behind him, thought
Bowe, who would have been happy to return to a time of such
certainties.

No, Bowe was an admirer of Concannon and very much in
awe of him. And in turn Concannon –though he would never
say so – had total confidence in Bowe's probity and discretion.
And it has to be said that, from Bowe's perspective, the affairs
of the diocese was profitable business.

But Bowe also had charge of the bishop's personal finances
– or so he thought, even if now he had serious doubts, indeed

certainty, that he now knew only part of the story. He may have wondered at the size of these personal finances but never questioned or doubted its provenance. Chastity may have been a requirement of the priesthood, but poverty never was – at least not in the diocese of Kilderry.

But while Bowe did what he had to do, he found the whole thing slightly distasteful. He disliked the smug mendaciousness of the bishop's nephews, the Murdocks, especially that gormless priest and the insufferable and boorish Richard E Murdock. Bowe did sometimes speculate – but only to himself – how Concannon, who came from such a modest shopkeeping background, had managed to accumulate such funds.

It was not his job to speculate, and certainly not to question such matters, but he did note that the bequests left by pious ladies only amounted to a fraction of the estate he handled. He comforted himself that the Vatican also had its financial secrets – and was Kilderry not just a small mirror image of the Vatican?

But something new and strange had happened. Bowe could feel it. There was something wrong, something he did not understand.

He had found the 'new' bishop hard to take at first – as had Concannon. He was not a bishop as Bowe would have wanted – a bit brash and vulgar, with little sense of the dignity of the office and little respect for its traditions. But, with the passage of time, he had come to respect, if not like ,Mullins. And as for Nestor, a man who epitomised for him what the priesthood should be, he had as close to a friendship as he permitted himself. Yet even Nestor he found odd and evasive of late. Something was happening and, when something was happening in the diocese of Kilderry, Bowe deemed it both his duty and his right to know.

He had in front of him a faded cutting from the *Irish Independent* of June 19 1937.

> The papal nuncio, Most Rev Dr Paschal Robinson, announced yesterday that His Holiness Pope Pius XI has appointed Most Rev Dr Thomas P Concannon DD Professor of Dogmatic Theology at the Irish College in Rome to succeed the late Dr Finbarr Flood as Bishop of Kilderry. In making his announcement, the nuncio said Dr Concannon was the personal choice of the Holy Father for this important diocese, and our correspondent in Kilderry writes that the news has been received in the diocese with great joy by both priests and people. Dr Concannon is a distinguished scholar and has been an eminent member of the faculty since his ordination in 1928.
>
> The President of the Executive Council, Mr de Valera, has sent his good wishes to the new bishop, as has the leader of Fine Gael Mr W.T. Cosgrave.
>
> Dr Concannon is expected to return to Ireland in early July and will be consecrated by Cardinal MacRory in early August.

Bowe could remember, almost as if it were yesterday, his father describing the new bishop's first public appearance in Kilderry. He could hear his father's soft voice and see his eyes twinkling and his yellowed moustache quivering as he told the story.

'Nobody knew what to expect. Nobody, not even the senior priests, had ever heard of him before. The papers made a great deal of the fact that he was the pope's personal choice and that was good enough for the people, some of whom were secretly surprised that the pope even knew where Kilderry was. But it was clear to me that some of the canons had their noses out of joint at the arrival of this "outsider" and one of them even told me that Concannon was as big a surprise to the bishops in Maynooth as he was to everyone else and that they were not one bit pleased.

'Anyway, the big day arrived. First of all there was the consecration. Very solemn and formal, the cardinal, the nuncio and all the bishops. Priests by the dozen, a long sermon, Gregorian chant to beat the band, politicians, de Valera leading most of his Cabinet in bowing and scraping to the new man.

'But then came the public bit. It transpired that the Church had asked that there be a public meeting of welcome. And so there was. John Shiel's biggest lorry placed in the middle of the Market Square and festooned in papal flags, the Ballinahowan band, an army guard of honour and of course all the speeches – Kelly the TD; Humphreys, the chairman of the county council; and then Browne, the chairman of the town commission – even though he was a Protestant. All the usual old blather.

'And then came Concannon. I can see him as clearly today as if it were yesterday. Six foot two in full episcopal attire, his mitre making him taller still. The round gold glasses, the beaky nose and those thin lips. Even the way he stood awed the people. When he spoke in that strong, cold voice of his, there was total silence. There was no small talk.

'He told them that the pope had great hopes for the diocese of Kilderry; he wanted it to be a model for all others and he intended to be an instrument of the Holy Father's will. He told them he looked forward to being their leader in all things spiritual and their guide in all things temporal. He would interpret the moral law and explain the teachings of the Church. They need not look elsewhere.

'And then, dramatically, as if to drive home his point that Kilderry had a new leader, he asked –ordered – them to their knees for his first episcopal blessing, even though the ground was wet and dirty. Even the hard chaws outside Kilderry's pubs, fellows who never darkened the door of a church, went on their knees. And then the blessing, the Holy Father in St Peter's Square couldn't have been more imperious.'

Nathaniel Bowe never forgot that day and Archie himself felt almost as if he had been there. Thomas Patrick Concannon had told the people and the priests – especially the latter – that they had a new boss and that he intended to continue as he had started.

Archie felt it was time to look in to his files, not just the recent ones but those from his father's time. He was not happy about the will he had so recently administered – but not drawn up. And, even though he believed he had been Concannon's only solicitor, he had always felt – indeed was certain – that there was a whole side to Concannon's life from which he had been excluded.

Concannon had always been formal with him and never asked his advice on anything other than diocesan legal matters. The bishop had seemed to regard him as a servant rather than a trusted confidante. There was something going on and Archie did not like not knowing.

Archie was a great believer that problems did not arrive overnight; their roots were usually embedded in the hidden past. So delve he would. It was time to make a few phone calls and pay a visit to his Dublin club.

11

....

Monsignor Nestor was a gentle man and, insofar as the word has any meaning, he was a holy man. He believed in his God and his Church, though he was finding it increasingly difficult to sustain the latter belief given what he saw as the general lowering of standards, the flaccid intellectual qualities of the bishops, the moral and physical sloppiness of so many of his clerical colleagues, and the indifference of so many of those he used to call the 'faithful'. But beneath everything, James Nestor was a man of faith.

He should have been made a bishop but he was passed over more than once, not because he was unsuitable, but because he was too suitable. And because his old classmate and academic rival, Tom Johnson, the bishop of a nearby diocese, had borne an old grudge against him and had injected a little poison and many doubts in to the system so that the word got around that he was in some way 'unsound'. And so, preference never came and he eventually found himself pastor of the unremarkable parish of Brannocksbridge.

It would be wrong to say he had borne all of this with stoic indifference. He was, like many priests, an ambitious man and the repeated rejections had hurt. For a while it had embittered him but, in recent years, as he saw those who had been preferred over him flounder ineffectually from one crisis to the next, especially their shameful handling of the new and worrying stream of sex abuse allegations – something that horrified and disgusted him – he felt the loss of office less and less.

In his distaste for bishops in general, he was prepared to make one exception – his own bishop. This in its own way was strange. Bishop Mullins had, after all, been plucked from obscurity and promoted over his head. But over the years, he had come to see it as a wise choice. Mullins was a rock of integrity: straight, direct and humane. The people liked him, they trusted him and they believed him. Mullins and Nestor were a good team and, he had to admit, he genuinely liked the man – even if he did find some of his opinions and his certainties a pain in the neck at times.

And it was this very thought that was giving Nestor his third sleepless night. He had been indiscreet, and he knew it. It had all happened so easily, so innocently really, but he had been caught off guard and he knew it was only a matter of time before a price had to be paid. But paid it would be.

How could he have been so foolish?

Certainly not drink, absolutely not. Nestor was abstemious, as his nephew's thirst would attest. No, the only explanation was that he was preoccupied and had let his guard down. He had said the wrong thing at the wrong place to the wrong person. It was as simple as that.

He had been to the funeral of an old parish priest in the southern part of the diocese. Such funerals were generally followed by a substantial lunch for all visiting clergy, an important part of clerical life – not so much for the food, which was always the same overdone roast beef and overcooked vegetables followed by sherry trifle, and not so much for the drink either, but because it was one of the increasingly rare opportunities for priests to get together in some sort of collegial way, exchange views and experience some of that solidarity which had been such a characteristic of their life in years gone by.

Nestor usually enjoyed these occasions. They reminded him of an earlier, more certain age and he had enough of that great clerical weakness for gossip to find these lunches – or dinners as they were usually called – worthwhile.

On this particular occasion, it was his bad luck to be seated beside John James Gilmartin, the parish priest of Ballinbo. JJ was a plump little man, red-faced, heavily jowled, with no neck and wobbly chins. He was the only child of an elderly merchant and his wife and, on their death, he had inherited a comfortable fortune. He had spent four years as a student in Rome and, on foot of that, considered himself a sophisticate, a cut above his rough and ready brethren and, more than that, he had the money to prove it. It showed in his dress – his suits were tailor made, not in Dublin but in Rome, his shoes handmade in Tutty's of Naas. He spoke with exaggerated precision, affected an old-world courtesy and liked it to be known that he was a personal friend of the papal nuncio and that he moved with ease at the highest levels of Dublin society.

In fact, nobody took JJ Gilmartin seriously. He was already showing himself lazy as a parish priest and it was only a matter of time before he found himself shifted to a smaller parish; he had little to say on the things that really interested his colleagues – hurling, farming, racing, stipends, school managers, alcoholic teachers, and church repairs.

He was, however, a master of gossip, but it was not the gossip which interested his fellow priests – which of their number might be hitting the bottle or getting involved with some woman, who might get what parish and more recently what Christian Brother (or even one of their own) would be next before the courts on child abuse charges. No, JJ liked to pride himself on his grasp of high gossip, on the sort of questions and issues he felt were engaging the wielders of power in the corridors of Maynooth, the embassies of Dublin or the quiet corners of the National University. For that reason, among many, few rushed to sit beside him.

As he lay sleepless, Nestor asked himself again and again how he could have been so foolish. He realised now he had only been half-listening as Gilmartin minced on and on, whispering in to Nestor's ear about cardinal this, monsignor that, ambassador something else, even the Minister for Foreign affairs got a mention. He had been lulled, preoccupied, when suddenly the question had been asked.

'I suppose our dear late bishop must have left quite a tidy pile. When can we expect the will to be published?'

'It won't be published, not if I can help it,' replied Nestor absent-mindedly, almost to himself.

'Oh, you mean he left nothing.'

'No, the opposite. He left too bloody much.'

The words were out before Nestor realised just what he had said. Gilmartin was in like a shot.

'How do you mean too much? That must be wonderful news for the diocese – that is if the diocese gets the money. I'm sure his awful relatives will have some claim.'

Nestor knew he was in trouble. He tried to backtrack.

'No, no I didn't mean too much money. What I meant was that the money was small and that there are some tricky legal complications. When things were sorted out, there was very little left and all of that went to the Church.'

With most other priests that would be that, but not with JJ Gilmartin.

'But he must have left money. He had money when few others had and, apart from his palace and those worthless relatives of his, he spent almost nothing in his later years. I would have thought he was worth close on a million.'

'If he was, he must have given it to good causes before he died,' said Nestor lamely, not happy at all at the way things were going.

'Why not publish the will then,' cackled Gilmartin. 'Surely news of such generosity would do us a lot of good at this time?'

'I told you there were legal complications and, before you ask me what they are, I cannot tell you. Now, where are you taking your spiritual retreat this year?'

It brought the conversation to an uncomfortable end, but Nestor knew it was too late. Gilmartin had smelled a rat. He almost certainly guessed that Nestor's first reply was the truth. He could hardly believe his luck that so tasty a morsel had fallen his way.

Nestor groaned. It would only be a matter of time before Gilmartin would be on the phone. The story would not lose in the telling. And before long, the rumours would start floating. Once started, they would not be easy to stop.

He would have to tell the bishop straight away. It had to be done and, if he knew the bishop, he would simply shrug it off and attach no blame to Nestor. Which is exactly what he did.

Nestor was also right about the real problem. It did not take Gilmartin long to get started. He was barely five minutes in to his sleek black Audi before his pudgy little fingers were punching out a series of numbers on his car phone – the first car phone in the diocese, he had boasted. Before he even arrived back to his parochial house in Ballinbo, questions were being asked about the 'mystery' of Bishop Concannon's 'missing' will, its 'suppression', just how much money the old boy had actually left, where the money was and who would get it.

And, as Nestor had feared, the stories did not lose in the telling.

It was only a matter of time before something would happen.

12

....

The papal nuncio, Archbishop Francis Valetti, was taking his morning coffee and smoking a Toscanello in his sunlit study. *The Irish Times* and the *Irish Catholic* lay unread at the edge of his desk. He rarely paid much attention to either paper, but the *Financial Times* was different. He often thought that, if he had not been a priest, he might have been a banker or stockbroker and often regretted that this had not been the case.

On the wall facing him was the picture of his boss. A severe looking Pope John Paul II looked down at him. He liked John Paul – not for any spiritual or personal reason but because, in his view, John Paul minded his own business. As long as his bishops and priests stayed on song on questions of doctrine and as long as there was no 'scandal', John Paul did not care too much about what his people got up to. The only golden rule was not to get caught, especially by the media. For somebody in a remote outpost like Dublin, the nuncio had pretty much a free hand.

But in spite of the sunshine and the good quality of his specially imported Italian coffee, he was not in a particularly good mood. He was worried – and with good reason.

The papal nuncio did not much like Ireland. In fact, if pushed on the subject he did not much like being a priest, but being an archbishop with no diocesan responsibility did have its compensations. The principal one was being very much his own boss in Ireland and answerable only to his distant superiors in Rome whose indifference to matters Irish was legendary, as long as everybody behaved or, more to the point, did not get caught out.

Valetti had long lost what little faith he once had, but never once had he considered resigning from the priesthood or abandoning his life as a career diplomat. It was not a matter of faith; it was a matter of practicality. Where else would he have at his disposal a large house, full-time servants (even if they were elderly nuns), a modest but certain income and the privacy to indulge his particular interests away from prying eyes or uncomfortable questions.

Prospective employers were unlikely to waste much time looking over the CV of a 54-year-old Canadian, overweight, bumptious and secretive, who had spent all his life since the age of 14 living within the sheltered confines of his Church, a man who had mastered the skills and secrets of diplomacy and clerical intrigue but had few, if any, real achievements to his credit.

More than that, Valetti was living under a cloud, ever since his last posting in Cyprus. His recall to Rome had been abrupt and there had been some speculation as to its cause. But not very much. Cyprus was a backwater and Valetti not a figure of any great significance, little more than a clerical apparatchik who merged back in to the Roman landscape while his case was investigated.

Unlike too many of his ecclesiastical colleagues, his 'weaknesses' were neither young men nor alcohol. In his case it was money and, more specifically, an apparent addiction to gambling – both on horses and the stock exchange. In the event, it was not so much his gambling but the large sums of money passing through his bank accounts that raised suspicions in Cyprus.

He always suspected he had been set up but, when challenged by the Church authorities, confessed to a gambling addiction. When pressed further, he could seemingly document a winning streak and some good investments that explained the large sums of money. The money was quietly transferred in to the Vatican's own banks – or one of them – and he, equally quietly, returned to Rome. There was no publicity, no 'scandal' and, from the Vatican's perspective, that was all that mattered. Indeed, there was even a little sneaking admiration among some of his colleagues for his financial prowess.

Insofar as there had been a cover-up, it had worked and that should have been the end of the matter. But it was not.

The Vatican investigation had not been thorough and had not intended to be. It did not ask how such large amounts of money got in to the account in the first place, nor did it question his truly awesome run of winning horses or show any curiosity about the identity of some of his closest associates on the island of Cyprus. Had the investigators done so, they might have suspected that money laundering, rather than gambling, was the main source of the cash that coursed through the Church accounts controlled by Valetti. And, had they looked further, they might have considered his associates and his own background – Canadian born but the son of Sicilian immigrants with strong family ties to Catania. Catania was where Valetti still holidayed and from where he shipped his wine, though when asked he always referred to his roots as 'Italian' rather than Sicilian.

These could have been awkward questions, especially if the activities of some of the leading members of his Catania family had been probed, but they never were. Therefore, after a year or so Valetti, who was both efficient and doctrinally orthodox, found himself in Dublin – which he hated from the beginning. It was not just the climate and the food, but the dull Irish bishops he was meant to supervise or, as he said himself, 'spy' on. But as he quickly learned, they were –with one exception – a grey lot and he soon became bored.

Once bored, he found his old habits died hard. He began to gamble again. At first on a modest scale and with a seemingly discreet bookmaker who was happy to extend him credit and who boasted to his friends that he was the only bookie who numbered a bishop – no, an archbishop among his customers. But it was not proving to be a happy experience. There was no run of good luck this time, no injection of outside capital and, of late, his losses began to mount – and with them his debts. Nor were his stock exchange 'flutters' doing any better.

His creditors were getting impatient and even a little sour. He knew if word got back to the Vatican, he would not be treated so lightly this time. He did not want to go back to his old 'friends', who had been understanding about their Cypriot losses and blamed one of their own disgruntled colleagues for shopping him. They had made clear to him on his appointment to Dublin that they still saw him as a valuable 'asset' and his services would always be welcomed.

It was not a road he wanted to go down but, as he brooded, he increasingly realised that he soon might have no option.

And in truth his options were limited. Perhaps he could borrow from some rich Irish Catholics for a fictitious charity. Or maybe set up some fund or other he could dip in to. Or maybe – and he knew he was at desperation level – there was some old and forgotten fund lying buried here at the nunciature. All he knew of his predecessors was that they had been discreet men, secretive even, but the more he thought about it, the more a long shot it appeared to be.

And so he was not in a particularly good mood when his phone rang and his private secretary told him that a Father Gilmartin insisted on speaking to him.

'Ask him what he wants and tell him I'm busy.'

'I've told him that already and he won't tell me the nature of his business, but he insists on talking to you and you alone. He says that you know him, that he was educated in Rome so you understand each other and that he has some very important and urgent news for you.'

The archbishop groaned. Yes, he knew Gilmartin, an oily and obsequious man, full of self-importance. He had cornered him at a reception in some embassy or other. Gilmartin had invited him to dinner in his club, the Stephen's Green he remembered. He declined but Gilmartin did not seem to notice the brush-off. He had no intention of ever meeting him again and absolutely no desire to go to that club. And he was quite prepared to be rude to him if necessary.

'Put him on,' he growled. 'It will be a short call.'

But once on the line, it was clear that Gilmartin would not be easily brushed off

'Excellency, what I have to say could become a major scandal. I feel it my duty to tell you and you alone.'

And tell he did. His estimate of the old bishop's hoard was now well over a million pounds and he believed there was some sort of cover-up going on. He suspected the motives of the bishop who had not been educated in Rome and he feared the money might be in danger of disappearing. And of course, he finished piously, 'there was always the danger of scandalising the faithful.'

The nuncio was now interested and became even more so when Gilmartin told him that the old bishop Concannon had been on the closest of terms with every nuncio from Pascal Robinson, the very first nuncio, until his own retirement and that there may well be some files relating to the money in the nuncio's own archives. In fact, he would be astonished if there were not.

'The secret of where the money came from and who rightfully owns it are probably buried in your very own files. This money may be lost to the Church forever if you do not act.'

For the first time, Gilmartin now had the nuncio's undivided attention.

He pressed for more details but Gilmartin insisted he could say no more over the phone but, if the nuncio could meet him for lunch in the Stephen's Green Club, he would tell him all he knew.

Valetti knew he was hooked. And he remembered a recent 'windfall' that had arrived at the nunciature – a significant bequest from some deceased bishop of whom he had never heard. He was about to pass it on to the Vatican, or at least some of it, a few thousand maybe – with his past record he had to be very correct about such matters – but maybe he better take his time until he knew more. And now Gilmartin was telling him this was just the tip of the iceberg. He immediately sensed some possibilities.

It was a long shot, but the best he had and meanwhile he would dig around in the archives. In fact, his Roman training had given him a good knowledge of archives and his natural cunning made him a good researcher. At the very least it would be a diversion, and one of the things he liked about archives was that he did not have to deal with real live people.

And if the price was lunch with Gilmartin in the Stephen's Green Club, then so be it.

13

....

Peter O'Donnell had been busy. He was certain the bishop and his uncle had not told him the full story, or at least all they knew. His natural instinct was to be wary of big institutions – there were always secrets to be shielded and that was especially true of the Catholic Church. He needed to do a bit of digging around for himself.

His first call was to his stockbroker acquaintance Sigerson Keane, or Mr Pickwick as O'Donnell liked to call him – fat, bald, and genial but with a sharp eye and predatory mind, and a lot of information about some of the richest people in the country who happened to be his clients. And some of the newly poor too, though he never blamed his own advice for some of their 'setbacks', as he tended to call them.

'So, you want to know about all those old stocks and shares,' said Keane, taking out the list O'Donnell had sent them. 'Could I ask you why?'

'Oh, just intellectual curiosity, a research project I'm working on.'

Keane did not believe him for a second. He knew O'Donnell did very little academic research these days – consultancy paid much better. There must be some money floating about and, if so, he would want to be around to get any business that might be there. But he could play a waiting game.

'Okay, so what is it you want to know?'

O'Donnell's list had included only the shares he thought still had some value. But even in its pruned state, it was a substantial list.

Keane's reaction showed an immediate quickening of interest. Almost a physical excitement.

'GE shares bought in 1908, General Motors in 1924 and most of the others bought in the 1930s. Standard Oil in 1930, then Good Year Tyres that same year, Proctor and Gamble 1933, DuPont 1936, Sears and Roebuck 1938.

'Holy hell, all of them Dow Jones 30 shares, bluest of blue-chip.'

Keane was now giving O'Donnell his full attention. 'And you want a present-day estimate of their value – what sort of numbers of shares are you talking about?'

O'Donnell had no intention of answering that question. Cards close to the chest he thought. 'Oh, no actual numbers. Just an intellectual exercise for an academic article I am doing. I'm just trying to figure out what shares bought in those years would be worth in present-day values.'

He knew Keane did not believe him. It was Keane's job to know what the very few academics who knew anything about the stock market were publishing – not that he had any respect for any of them. And he knew for sure he had never come across anything written by O'Donnell for the simple reason there was nothing to come across.

'Ah, your students must find this fascinating,' Keane goaded, knowing full well – he had taken the trouble to check the Trinity yearbook before the meeting – that O'Donnell's lecture courses were narrowly confined to national economics and there was no evidence of any research publications.

'Okay, on the basis of the scanty information you have begrudged me, I can make a few general observations.' He decided he would curb his impatience and bide his time. He took out his calculator. 'All are good investments. All on the Dow Jones 30 when purchased. The index was stable in those days.'

He paused and, to O'Donnell's surprise, took out a pouch from which he took a pinch of snuff, most of which spilled on to his desk and on to the large volume he was now consulting. He was in no hurry as O'Donnell grew increasingly apprehensive.

'Well, as I said, the market was stable in those years. Things fluctuated during the war years but, surprisingly, all the shares you have given me survived intact. Have you not chosen any shares – for this exercise of course – that did not make it through the war? Surely nobody would have only had winners? Even the most successful investors pick a loser now and then. Even Warren Buffett backs the odd loser.'

O'Donnell knew straight away he had made a mistake. Had it been a serious academic exercise, he should of course have factored in the risk element. He knew now that Keane did not believe his 'academic exercise' story. He just shrugged his shoulders. 'Yeah, I suppose to make it a bit more realistic I should have factored in a few failed entities.'

Keane had made his point and he knew that O'Donnell now realised he was fooling nobody. And the more O'Donnell dithered, the more certain Keane became that there was a story – and maybe even a profit for him somewhere in there. But he could wait. And he could make a few enquiries of his own.

'Okay, let's take 1949 as our starting year. Stability was returning and the index stood at 200. Today, 1997, it is about 10,000.'

'Which means what?' asked an increasingly nervous O'Donnell.

'It means each share has increased in value by 50 times its face value. And that will be a bottom-level sale price. Some of those you mentioned would have gone up by even more.'

He paused, a sly smile on his lips. 'Are you sure some old grand-aunt hasn't left you a few? Even a few would be huge.'

O'Donnell was now very uncomfortable. He realised, when it came to money, you can trust nobody. He knew Keane would do some nosing around and he had contacts in a great many places and probably at the highest levels of the Catholic Church. It had been a mistake. If he was a genuine researcher, with some expert knowledge in stocks and shares and economic history, he could have found all this out through his own resources.

He tried to laugh off Keane's question – 'No such luck, genuinely an academic exercise' – knowing how ridiculous it was beginning to sound. He thanked the openly sceptical and very engaged Sigerson Keane and left.

As O'Donnell walked back to Percy Place, he dropped into Smyth's of Haddington Road – his favourite Dublin pub – for a much-needed pint. He had been doing his calculations. The shares and stocks had to be worth up to eight million. At least, Eight million with no clear owner and possibly a few who thought they had a strong claim. This could turn very nasty if any suspicions were aroused. He had better get back to Kilderry and bring Mullins up to date but, meanwhile, there were a few more questions to pursue.

In particular, he needed to know a little more about the original benefactor, Henry Alsop, and the conditions under which he had entrusted Concannon with the stocks and shares. Were there terms or conditions attached? The answer to that might help clear up the ownership issue. But Alsop was dead for the past 50 years and his solicitor – his disgruntled solicitor – Charlie Ruddock was long dead also. The only possibility, and a very slim one, was that Ruddock's office still existed and there might be someone there who could help.

O'Donnell was beginning to feel he was getting out of his depth. 'Too much money,' he kept repeating to himself as he nursed his late-night pint. The pub was quiet and he liked it that way. *'Too much bloody money,'* he repeated to himself.

'And what had happened to the shares Alsop had given but were no longer there? Had they been cashed in – and where was that money?'

Concannon, at least according to his journal, had been given that money for a purpose. He was to implement Alsop's great world strategy for the Catholic Church. But what was that strategy? And what, if anything, had he done? Was there even a strategy? There was no reference to any strategy – at least not that he had seen in the journal. There was no evidence that he had spent any money, no big buildings or new churches, and no further reference to Alsop.

There was no reference to Alsop's death, which must have come soon after he gave the money. Or did he linger on and, if he did, had he enquired as to what progress if any the bishop was making? There was no record of any monies being disbursed so had Concannon just sat on the funds, seeing them grow from year to year, perhaps even paralysed into inaction at the enormity of what he had undertaken to do?

O'Donnell thought about this as Kasia put another pint in front of him. 'More woman trouble?' she asked. He liked Kasia . She was a good listener and he occasionally confided in her when she asked him about the absence of any permanent relationship in his life in spite of having a number of girlfriends. He was always open with her, telling her he liked relationships but was not a big fan of commitment. Kasia, he knew, was strictly a commitment woman and had little sympathy with his predicament, but she was a good listener.

But, this evening at least, he was in no mood for talking. And Kasia knew when to leave him alone.

So, what had happened to the money? Or maybe more precisely he needed to know why nothing seemed to have happened. He needed to get another look at the journal, this time the full journal and, maybe even more important, at the bishop's file cards. The 'blackmail' files, as he was beginning to think of them. He would need a good reason to get past his uncle and the bishop on that one.

Was there a file on Alsop? Had he told anybody about Alsop's bequest? Did the papal nuncio know anything about it? Or had Concannon, being of sound peasant stock, just decided to hold the money?

O'Donnell decided he should at least look in to Charlie Ruddock as another possible line of enquiry. Ruddock, the solicitor who handled Alsop's account, had been none too pleased – furious in fact if the bishop's journal could be believed – when Alsop ignored his advice. Although he must surely be long dead, his practice may still exist. He remembered some reference in the journal to it being in Lansdowne Road, or was that where Alsop lived? It was a long shot and, even if it was still there, would anyone remember Concannon?

His friend Tommy Newrie had by now joined him for another pint. But even Tommy could not help him. Nor was he reassuring. He sensed danger. Too much money always meant danger. He advised O'Donnell to get out of the whole thing as fast as he could. Tommy was not a man for too much risk. But O'Donnell knew he was too far in and much too curious to give up now.

Alsop, he felt, may be the key to it all. And the only way to Alsop might be through records left by Charlie Ruddock. It was unlikely, but worth a try.

14

....

For the first time since coming to Dublin, Archbishop Frank Valetti was in a good mood. Now at last he had a project that interested him and, more importantly, the prospect of easing his financial worries.

He had met the odious JJ Gilmartin. But before doing so, he had his secretary check out the will of the late Bishop Concannon. Yes, there had been a bequest to the nuncio. Not bad, £20,000, but with total discretion to the nuncio as to how it might be spent. £20,000 was a nice figure – not big enough for anyone in Rome to notice but enough to keep his creditors at bay for the moment. The money had not yet arrived but the firm of Archie Bowe & Son Solicitors assured him it would be despatched shortly as soon as all details were complete. If challenged, he would say the money would be sent to some appropriate charity, but he did not think that would arise.

He didn't like Gilmartin, nor had he expected to. Small and oily, jowls swimming over his Roman collar, his expensive light-grey suit unable to conceal an unhealthy paunch, his eyes framed in horn-rimmed spectacles.

Gilmartin had ensured their table in the Stephen's Green club was a prominent one. It was important for him to be seen entertaining the nuncio. There was bound to be some professor from Maynooth who would bring word back of his dining with the nuncio and maybe conclude that he was being considered for some bishopric or at least that he was a man of influence.

Or perhaps some diplomat present might be reminded to put him on an embassy invitation list.

Valetti knew his man. Looking across at the expensive but ill-fitting suit, the eyes darting around the room to see who might need to be impressed and listening to the affected accent that could not fully conceal his rough Kerry origins, he saw a type of man he despised and many of whose like he had met in Rome. But he also saw a man who could be very useful to him. Valetti did not often do charm. Today would be an exception.

He quickly realised Gilmartin was no insider and most of his information was second or third hand, but he did have an endless supply of gossip, mainly about people he did not personally know – judges, politicians and diplomats – but he did at least have some useful and malicious things to say about some of the bishops, which Valetti filed away for possible future use. It was tedious stuff for Valetti, who clearly had little interest in things Irish, but he indulged Gilmartin and listened as he talked about his own special qualities. He needed little prompting to tell of the clerical conspiracies that had prevented his own promotion to the rank of bishop.

Valetti showed himself an attentive listener, insisting on addressing Gilmartin as *dottore,* even though he knew Gilmartin had no more than a pass BA from Maynooth and an undistinguished *licentiate* from his days in Rome. But everybody in Rome was a *dottore.* Gilmartin beamed, hoping the nuncio would be overheard, and made no attempt to correct the record.

'*Dottore,* I am a stranger here. The brother bishops tell me little and I am told in high places that you know a great deal about what really goes on. I would not like to presume on you and I know you have your own loyalties, but I value greatly any help you could give me which would deepen my understanding of this country. And between ourselves, you know

I am beginning to feel that the best men have not always been promoted while obviously more distinguished people have been left on the sidelines.

'If I am to recommend some changes, and I may have to soon, then I need an honest and discreet adviser. Unofficially, of course, but somebody with whom I can speak my mind and not find myself tied in knots by some of those soutaned fools around me.'

His words had the desired effect on Gilmartin. Surprise, pleasure, but most of all opportunity. The opportunity to be someone who really mattered. How proud his parents would be if they could see him now – a parish priest who was not taken seriously by his peers being taken in to the confidence of the most powerful cleric in the land.

He realised to his embarrassment that his excitement had become physical. At times like this he got an involuntary erection and he squirmed a little to ensure no evidence was visible. Women never had that effect on him – men neither – but it had happened on the day of his conferring in Rome and on the day of his ordination. There had not been much reason since then for any such excitement and this sudden onset troubled him, but he was glad his napkin concealed his situation.

Valetti was unaware of his companion's discomfort and would have cared less. Being a practical man, he was no stranger to the erratic rumblings of the flesh and had his own way of dealing with them.

He had no intention of letting Gilmartin know the real purpose of the meeting. So, one more diversion. 'Tell me about the bishops. I've read all their biographies and have met most of them, but I can't say I really know them. I'm not prying, but it would help me make better judgements if I had your insights –just between the two of us of course.'

Gilmartin was happy to oblige and Valetti realised at once that it was second-hand gossip. Valetti saw straightaway that Gilmartin was not close to any of those he spoke about and had nothing of value to offer. This was what Valetti had expected, but he let his companion talk on, feigning an interest he did not have.

Finally, he got to the only topic which interested him.

'Your late bishop, who of course I never knew, left me a small bequest in his will. I already have a charity in mind for it. I'm very grateful to him for including me, especially since it seems he left such a small estate.'

'But that's just the point,' spluttered Gilmartin. 'He was a wealthy man. He indulged his useless nephews and niece for years. He lived like a prince. It's even said he had his own bankers and stockbrokers. And there were rumours, only rumours mind you, of his being given stewardship of a major fund or bequest during the last war.'

'What sort of bequest?'

'No one ever knew, but there were stories of strange comings and goings during the war. He may have thought no one noticed these things, but I'm told not all of those who worked for him liked him and word always gets out, especially in a place as small as Kilderry.'

'What sort of comings and goings?'

'Well, important people. One was head of the Department of External Affairs and later became ambassador to the Holy See. There was also a top man from Justice and some senior army people. There were even rumours of a late-night call from de Valera.'

Gilmartin had become reflective. 'None of us, certainly not someone as junior as me, ever knew him. He was remote, but he exuded power and maybe a sense of fear. I'm told he had no friends among the other bishops and was seen as a law unto himself. But he did have friends in high places, both in Dublin and in the Vatican – apparently he made no secret of that when talking to his priests. He was known personally to Pope Pius XII, apparently through another professor from his days in Rome.'

'But these meetings were all open. Why the mystery?'

'That's just the point. The meetings that started the rumours were all late at night and were not meant to be noted, but people did talk and there was all sorts of speculation. And it would have remained that way if Monsignor Nestor had not blurted out to me that the bishop had left too much money and, as we now know, no evidence of it in the will.'

'So that's it – a mystery buried in the mists of time?'

'Not quite,' said Gilmartin. 'Nestor has confirmed the existence of the money. He knows about it and so does his – my – bishop. As soon as this goes public, somebody will lay claim to it. The diocese will probably claim it, but so too will his relatives and there may be others. It is going to be a scandal, unless of course there is a second will or some hidden instructions.'

The two men sat in silence.

'You mentioned some names there of secret visits – civil servants, army, etc. Would there be a record of these visits?'

'There is probably nobody living who can tell. But, I'm sure Concannon kept a record of every meeting he ever had. He was said to have a file on every single priest in his diocese and many others too, I'm sure. I don't know if they still exist and what, if anything, they will tell us about the missing money, but surely you have your own sources. If one of the visitors was the nuncio –his name was Robinson – then surely he will have left a record in your archives.'

Gilmartin had one further piece of information to impart to an already impatient but very focussed nuncio. 'I remember from my time in Rome we had an oldish professor in the Irish College, a Dr Semple. He came from my own diocese and he sort of befriended me. He had been a contemporary of Concannon's in Rome but he very obviously disliked him, hated him I would say.'

Valetti began to fidget. Was he going to get another self-serving reminiscence.

'Semple told me more than once that Concannon was the most ambitious man he ever met. He saw Kilderry as merely a first stepping stone to where he really wanted to be – back in Rome at the very centre of things. He made sure to cultivate powerful people in the curia and other important places. He was especially close to another academic, who later became a nuncio himself. A fellow called Ramiro Marcone.

'Of all the Irish bishops, Concannon was the one with real influence and he knew who pulled what strings where. But then, sometime late in the war, or maybe just after it, his influence seemed to dry up. Semple said that sometimes happens in the Vatican, and sure you'd know that better than me. Semple never could figure out what exactly happened, but something did. After that, any chance he had of getting out of Kilderry seemed to have gone.'

Valetti was no longer listening. He had one interest only and knew what exactly he would do next. He could begin to smell the money already. But he also made a note of Semple's name. The mention of Ramiro Marcone had rung a bell. He was not sure why. Something about Croatia and the civil war there, but if it helped him know more about Concannon and his money then he would pursue it.

15

....

O'Donnell had not slept well. Maybe it was that last drink, but he knew it was more than that. There was too much he still needed to know. He had read only the early years of the journal and been given no access to the bishop's file cards. He was angry with what he regarded as a lack of openness from Bishop Mullins and his own uncle. He had begun to think they wanted a cover-up and him to be the man to provide it.

Some straight-talking was needed. It was time he got back to Kilderry.

But there was one further line he would follow before doing so – Charlie Ruddock, the solicitor who had handled Henry Alsop's affairs.

He called in to the reference library on Pearse Street on his way to Trinity and checked the Law Society's register for 1941. It was a slim volume, with fewer than a hundred solicitors' firms in Dublin and most of them small practices. Charlie Ruddock was there, a two-man, father-and-son practice – Charlie Ruddock, qualified University College Dublin 1913, and James Ruddock, University College Dublin 1940. It had an address in Upper Mount Street, five minutes away from the Taoiseach's office where O'Donnell had so recently worked.

He then looked up the current register, a much fatter volume. To his surprise the firm of Charles Ruddock still existed, though now it was Ruddock Molony Enright. Its address was still Upper Mount Street but it occupied the adjoining building as well. Obviously mergers and expansion. To his even greater surprise, among the four listed partners was a Heather Ruddock, who graduated from University College Dublin in 1972. Obviously a granddaughter of old Charlie. It was certainly worth a call. But he would make a few enquiries first.

He discovered very easily that the firm was low profile but high powered, specialising in commercial and European law. It had a reputation for discretion and high fees. And there was something vaguely familiar about the name Heather Ruddock. It was a name he had heard before but where? Oh well, it would probably come back to him.

His call was answered by a cheerful-sounding receptionist.

'You wish to speak with Ms Ruddock. And the nature of your business?... Oh, historical research. That's an unusual one for us. Not our usual line of work. Just one moment and I will see if Ms Ruddock is available. Trinity College you say?'

He expected a polite but firm brush-off but, within seconds, the receptionist was back. 'You said your name was Peter O'Donnell from Trinity College?' Another slight delay and then a throaty voice that had known too many cigarettes came on the line.

'Mr O'Donnell, what a surprise... Yes, we have met. Oh dear, I'm disappointed you don't remember, but then an important person like you must meet so any people.'

O'Donnell was not sure whether the tone was mocking or just playful. 'Well how can I help you? My receptionist says historical research but I thought you were strictly an economist with a bit of consultancy thrown in, or is it consultancy with a bit of economics thrown in?'

He was beginning to feel defensive and he still had no sense of having met Heather Ruddock. Before he could answer, she continued. 'Look, I'm sure you wouldn't ring if it was not serious. What sort of research? ... Into Charlie Ruddock, my grandfather? But he was just an ordinary solicitor, a very good one but he has been dead since 1970, two years before I started here, though he was long retired by then... Yes, I knew him well and loved him dearly. I was his only grandchild. I hope there is no scandal erupting. He was an utterly honest man.'

O'Donnell noted a defensive and slightly aggressive change in tone. He tried to be reassuring.

'No, nothing of that sort. It's about a former client of his, also a very honest person, a Henry Alsop, and a bishop who died recently, Bishop Thomas Patrick Concannon. I have been asked to do some research on Concannon.'

'New ground for you, a long way from economics and politics. But yes, my grandfather did talk to me about Alsop and Concannon. He neither liked nor trusted the bishop and, to be honest, he thought him a crook, a conniving crook he used call him. In fact, it was the only topic ever made him angry. I was too young to understand why.'

There was a silence.

'Look, I don't know if I can be of help and am not sure I would want to. I have to see a client in a few moments.' There was another pause. 'Okay, let's talk about it. How about 5 pm today? Here... And you still can't recall meeting me?'

With that she hung up. And she was right – he still could not place her.

O'Donnell then phoned his uncle. He made it very clear that he was not happy they were giving him only part of the story. He would have to see all of Concannon's papers, that he could not and would not keep going if he had only half the information. He said he would call down to Kilderry at the weekend and expected full co-operation. Otherwise he was gone and they could resolve their own problems.

He had been sharp with his uncle but told himself it was the only way. He knew full well that both his uncle and the bishop had a higher loyalty than to the truth or to him. Both would be collateral damage if the interest of the Catholic Church came first – which it undoubtedly would. He felt relieved that he had made his position clear.

He tried to read some economics journals but found he had no interest. He knew he was never going to be regarded as a serious economist, but this self-realisation did not bother him anymore. Indeed, it had not bothered him for quite some time, even though he knew his colleagues had long held this view. Maybe it was time to look for a different job but, on the other hand, what job would be as undemanding – and with so much free time to do some lucrative work on the side?

Two words struck him when he arrived at the Ruddock Molony Enright offices – discreet and understated. A small nameplate, an elegant waiting area. The receptionist who had been so friendly that morning gave him an appraising, slightly curious look.

'So you're the researcher, the historian,' and added almost conspiratorially 'you know you must be very special. Most people have to wait at least a week before Ms Ruddock will meet them.'

The moment he entered the spacious, airy office he knew exactly where he had met Heather Ruddock before. How could he have forgotten – but then he realised he had never known her surname and it was always late at night in ill-lit nightclubs.

'Know me now?' she asked as he blushed with embarrassment.

Ruddock had been a close friend and frequent companion of his old lover, the Taoiseach's wife, Louise Mulcahy. That affair was now well and truly over and he had not spoken to Louise in more than a year. But he missed her, and the affair had been one of the reasons he had left politics. He had never known Heather's surname, she had always been 'Louise's friend Heather'.

He relaxed slightly.

'I'm not very flattered that you didn't remember my name. I thought I had made more of an impression than that. When I heard it was you on the phone, I thought that maybe there was a situation vacant in your life.'

It took O'Donnell a moment to realise she was teasing him and enjoying the opportunity.

He remembered how discreet she was. She made sure Louise was never alone and then, when he arrived, she would quietly disappear. He realised now that this was a pre-arranged strategy, something he had taken for granted at the time. In a strange way, he had always seen her as part of Louise's background, never as a person in her own right.

Now as he looked at her, he saw her as a handsome woman in her mid-forties, expensively dressed, maybe a little overweight but exuding energy, her look at once sardonic and amused – and maybe even a little predatory.

She beckoned him to sit down. 'You've hardly come for lonely heart advice, so what is this research about?'

She picked up the phone and asked that some coffee be sent in.

He tried to be as honest as he could about his investigation on behalf of Bishop Mullins and his uncle without being too specific about the amounts of money involved.

'Old Bishop Concannon died recently. He had been out of action for years and most people had long forgotten he even existed. His estate is a bit of a mess. It's a significant estate with huge potential for litigation and embarrassment. My uncle is the second in command in Kilderry and he felt that, with my experience of working for the Taoiseach, I would be able to make sense of it all.'

'I doubt his lordship knows the full extent of your work for the Taoiseach. But let's leave that. Have you been of help?'

'Not really. It gets more and more complex to tell you the truth. I'm not even sure they're giving me the full story. In fact, I know they're not. The Catholic Church plays by its own rules and breaks them as it sees fit. I'm not sure I want to stay in, but I'm a bit intrigued by it all.'

'Louise always said you were not one to give up easily. In fact, she says – or said, since I rarely see her now – that you saved her husband's career. But, where do I come in to all of this? Or rather, where does my poor grandfather come in to it?'

'I'm not sure. From what I know, your grandfather knew the old bishop through a client of his, a Henry Alsop, and that he didn't like or trust the bishop. It's a long shot, but I thought there was an off-chance you might have some stuff in your archives that could be of help.'

'Archives? We don't have anything so grand. But yes, I did hear my grandfather talk of Alsop and Concannon. He generally didn't like bishops, but he hated Concannon with a passion. Whenever his name came up in the newspapers, it was enough to set him off. It was pure hatred. Surprising really since he was a very gentle and loveable man.'

She looked at her watch. 'You have my interest. I feel I owe it to my grandfather and, anyway, it makes a change from commercial litigation. I've to go to a lecture in the Law Society at 6.30 but I'll dig around and see what I can find. Our filing system is actually very good and we have all our records since my grandfather's time. He was a stickler for good record-keeping so, if there's anything there, I'll find it. Henry Alsop you say. And you can fill me in on the full story. And since I won't be charging for my time, let's meet outside office hours.

How about taking me to dinner on Thursday? Give me your number and I'll call to confirm.'

She did not ask if the arrangement suited O'Donnell. With that she was on her feet, her perfume, sharp and expensive, hanging in the air.

He looked at her again, taking in the well-cut suit, the long legs and full figure. Though she might be 10 years older than him, she was a very attractive woman. And a tough one too, he reminded himself.

'No,' he said to himself. 'Don't even think it. Out of the question. Don't mess it up.'

As he passed the receptionist's desk he could see that at least he had her attention. She looked him up and down before giving him a knowing, almost conspiratorial, smile. He was clearly not a run-of-the mill corporate client. But what did the receptionist know that he did not?

16

....

Archbishop Valetti was getting to know his predecessor and, to his surprise, he was enjoying the experience. Valetti had never heard of Paschal Robinson before he came to Ireland and he had actually been in the country a few months before he even heard the name. This in itself should have been surprising since Robinson had been the first papal nuncio in Ireland in modern times and had set up the structures and systems in which Valetti now operated. But then, there were many things about Francis Valetti that people might find surprising.

It was not that he cared much about Robinson or had any interest in Church history but, because he saw him as a possible key to the Kilderry puzzle, he might be the only way Valetti had of finding out the truth about the possible cash pile in that diocese and, more to the point, how he could get his hands on some, or all, of it.

For a start, he needed to find out all he could about Paschal Robinson. To his pleasant surprise the archives in the nunciature were housed in a light and airy room, which up to now he thought was just another storage area. Robinson's files filled four large filing cabinets – as against just one cabinet for each of his successors.

But if he expected to find the files well-ordered and professionally indexed, he was in for an unpleasant surprise. Clearly somebody had been through the files – there was no note who it might have been and he assumed one of his predecessors – and clearly, it would take some time to get them back in order. But he had no reason to believe the files were not complete.

He began by reading a few biographical notes and liked what he found. Robinson, he learned, had been born in Ireland in 1870 and had lived in Dublin in Percy Place, just a few doors up from where Peter O'Donnell now had his apartment – but this was a fact of which neither O'Donnell or Valetti would ever know or care.

Robinson had moved at an early age to the US, where he had been a successful and experienced journalist before deciding to become a Franciscan friar. He trained as a medieval historian and was clearly good at what he did, getting a Chair at the Catholic University of America in Washington. He was later appointed to the Vatican's diplomatic service and had attended the Peace Conference at Versailles in 1919. In 1929, he became the first papal nuncio appointed to the new Irish Free State.

The appointment had been big news as the political parties vied with each other to show how loyal they were to Rome. Valetti had the 1929 press cuttings in front of him and couldn't help thinking about changed times as he read one sycophantic press headline after another. One newspaper described Robinson's appointment as 'Red wine from the Royal Pope', and everywhere there was great guff about the signal honour the Pope had conferred on the new and Catholic State.

He contrasted this with his own arrival – a few grudging paragraphs in the *Irish Independent*, an ungenerous article about his predecessor in *The Irish Times* and the event totally ignored by RTÉ. Valetti did not regret or resent this change, feeling that, with his own background, the lower the profile the better.

From Valetti's perspective, the fact that Robinson had trained as a journalist and historian was a great advantage. He was clearly well organised and methodical, and this was reflected in the records he had kept. He had a sharp eye for the telling detail, especially when discussing the personalities on which he reported. His judgements were shrewd and he seemed to have a sense of humour. And there was another bonus. All Robinson's correspondence with the Vatican was in Latin – where Valetti's competence was adequate but limited – but his drafting was in English and all of these drafts had been preserved.

Valetti had some difficulty getting a grip on Robinson's lifestyle. He lived in a grand house in the Phoenix Park yet he seemed to take his Franciscan vows, especially that of poverty, seriously. While he entertained, and apparently did so in some style as the surviving menus and guest lists showed, he did so strictly as a diplomatic duty and his own lifestyle was austere – and severely so.

As he read through the files, he began to get a feel for the power and ambition of the Irish Church in those years, although he noted too the occasional tensions with the Irish State that simmered quietly but rarely surfaced. Valetti could see that it was part of Robinson's job to keep things that way.

Valetti's focus, however, was on Kilderry and it was not until 1934, Robinson's fifth year in Ireland, that he found the first reference to the diocese. Robinson had received an anonymous letter, which he felt could only have been written by a priest and almost certainly a priest of Kilderry. The letter alleged serious irregularities in the diocese – including the charge that the bishop, Dr Flood, had lost all control over his priests and, in fact, was rarely seen in public. It was claimed that the diocese was being run by a small cabal of canons who were helping themselves to diocesan funds, promoting their friends and victimising their enemies – among whose number the writer clearly saw himself.

It was also alleged that there was great 'laxity' – a telltale clerical word – in the behaviour of some priests, including the frequenting of race meetings, something forbidden by canon law, and relationships with housekeepers that could only be seen as a 'source of scandal to the laity'. The writer did not ask the nuncio to intervene – probably because, as a cleric, he knew well the nuncio had no power to intervene, but wanted him to know the facts.

A year later came the second reference to Kilderry, this time in a routine report to the Vatican Secretary of State on the general situation in the Free State. It was largely concerned with the early work on the new constitution that de Valera was already drafting and on which some of the Irish bishops had strong views.

The reference to Kilderry came at the end of the report. It was a factual, if alarming, assessment of neglect of leadership by the bishop, financial irregularities and unseemly behaviour among some clerics. Robinson reported that the bishop was old and infirm and that care should be taken to appoint without delay a successor capable of reversing these trends. The report noted that there was no obviously suitable candidate in the diocese, even though a number of priests were already making their case. The report recommended that an appointment be made soon and it should be an outsider, possibly even from the Vatican.

It would seem Robinson had been heeded – but not in any great haste. On 5 October 1936, a Bishop Ferretti had written from the Vatican to his 'Brother in Christ' Robinson, asking him to submit three names for appointment as bishop, or at least that is what Valetti saw in the Latin text that he laboriously translated.

Robinson clearly wasted no time. He replied within days that his understanding was that the local priests were divided between two candidates, each of whom was busily seeking support. Robinson named these as Canon Roughneen, the parish priest of Brannocksbridge; and the president of the local seminary, Dr Mulchrone. Robinson was insistent that neither should be appointed. He suggested instead that an Irish priest currently in the Irish College in Rome, Thomas Patrick Concannon, be the new bishop.

But that was not the first reference to Concannon in Robinson's papers. He had, it seems, been getting some advice from a colleague in Rome, a Benedictine monk Ramiro Marcone, who was a philosopher at the College of San Anselmo. Marcone had made enquiries for Robinson and recommended Concannon as a young man 'of intellect and strong character with great fidelity to the *magisterium*'.

That was enough for Robinson, and Valetti could not help wondering if Concannon ever knew of Robinson's role in his appointment. Probably not; certainly not from Robinson.

Robinson's files were not indexed and it had taken Valetti two days to get to 1937. But he was a methodical man and was happy to go at this pace. And to his surprise he was enjoying himself. Robinson told a good story and had none of the pomposity and obfuscation of so many of his colleagues in the Vatican. He had no doubt his patience would be rewarded.

He decided to finish for the day and only then did he realise he had not had a single wager or stock exchange flutter in two days.

17

....

It was a fine day but Bishop Mullins barely noticed. He knew now he had made a mistake in not telling Peter O'Donnell the full story. He knew it was a mistake, not because it was the wrong thing to do but because he had misjudged O'Donnell and his tactic had backfired. Mullins didn't usually see himself as a typical Catholic bishop but he now knew – and it was a painful realisation – that he was.

In his heart, he had wanted a cover-up, though he did not call it that. He wanted to protect his diocese, his Church and maybe even himself from what his seminary training called 'scandal'. He had hoped O'Donnell would see things the same way and would be swayed by his loyalty to his uncle. But he knew how wrong he had been. O'Donnell had been angry on the phone to Monsignor Nestor, asking some awkward questions and demanding answers – and threatening to walk away from the whole business if he did not get them.

What a fool he had been to think O'Donnell would be like one of the tame Catholic 'laymen', the accountants and others who advised on diocesan business matters. O'Donnell was tough and determined, with no sentimental attachment or loyalty to the Catholic Church and would put what he called his own 'integrity' above all else.

Mullins reflected that a bit of clerical training would have softened his cough and would have persuaded him that loyalty to the institution trumped integrity any day. Mullins at least had enough self-awareness to realise that he could not shake the seven years 'formation' Maynooth had given him. It was in his DNA, hard as he might try to follow his own instincts.

But Mullins was not going to let any self-doubts get in the way of clear thinking. He had brought O'Donnell in to help keep the whole business out of the public eye – and that was still the case. But after Nestor's indiscreet conversation with that 'odious little prick' Gilmartin, that situation would not continue for much longer. Although there was the consolation of knowing it would be no more than rumour, at least in the short term. But Mullins knew that would not last.

Mullins' main worry at the outset had been the danger posed by Concannon's grasping relatives and, in particular, by Richard E Murdock. His first objective had been to ensure that the money rightfully belonged to the diocese and that the full enormity of the sums involved would never become public.

He still had not succeeded and indeed was no closer to achieving that first objective. He knew that Gilmartin's story would travel far beyond Kilderry.

He began to look at his options.

He realised he should have been more curious about the money. Not the money in the bishop's will, but the money that had been expended by Concannon since his benefactor had given it to him in the early 1940s. From what he knew of his predecessor, he was not a man to sit on the money and do nothing. He was a man of action whose ambitions went way beyond Kilderry and who ultimately saw himself as a cardinal or even being recalled to the Vatican to a senior post in the curia.

Mullins knew enough about the history of his Church in the 1940s and 1950s to know it had been involved with some very unsavoury regimes and causes. He knew there were still too many skeletons waiting to fall out of innocent-looking cupboards. Was this one of them?

It would be bad enough having a financial scandal, but now maybe a political one as well. Now that Pius XII's wartime behaviour was under such hostile scrutiny, no reputation was safe.

So what would he do?

He would have to tell old Archie Bowe at some stage. Bowe was an honest man who would have the best interest of the Church at heart but, for some reason, Mullins did not feel comfortable with him. He was too rigid and a little too self-righteous. He was certain that Bowe already suspected all was not above board about the bishop's last will and would be sceptical about the small amount of residual money. Bowe almost certainly knew that Concannon's life had been lived in different compartments and that he had never been fully in the bishop's confidence. Bowe had hinted at as much to Mullins. Yes, he would have to talk to Archie Bowe. But reluctantly, and not just yet.

And what then?

He could call in his senior priests and make it a matter of diocesan responsibility rather than his alone. But the truth was that, apart from Nestor, he did not trust any of them and he knew they resented him. They would have little of use to say and their main concern would be to see how they could get their hands on some of the loot and embarrass him into the bargain. The thought of Gilmartin among them, and the potential it would give him for further gossip, closed – and closed emphatically – that particular option.

Nor was there any good reason to look to his 'brother' bishops for help. He liked some of them but deeply distrusted the archbishops. No reason to expect any collegiality. It would all be referred to Rome and, if need be, he would be hung out to dry.

So why not go directly to the nuncio? He realised he barely knew Valetti's name and had never met him. His bishop colleagues instinctively distrusted the nuncio and saw him as a spy in their midst. Still, it was a possibility – he would need to find out a little more about Valetti – but it was not an immediate option.

There was only one thing for it. He would have to mend his fences with O'Donnell and come clean. He would have to show him all the files and financial records. Apart from Nestor, O'Donnell was the only person he could trust, but he now had a problem with O'Donnell trusting him. He pondered what might happen if it emerged he had brought in an outsider to help him. Should he go to the police? He quickly dismissed these thoughts. It was still, he thought, a matter for canon law, not civil law – but he had a doubt that O'Donnell would share this view.

All in all, O'Donnell was the least worst option he had.

He picked up the phone and called Trinity College.

18

....

Heather Ruddock had left a message that 7.30 at l'Ecrivain would suit her fine. O'Donnell's first reaction was that this would prove to be an expensive evening, especially since he no longer had an expense account. But at least the food would be good and the wine even better.

And so they proved to be, when Heather finally turned up. She was late and made no effort to apologise for her lateness. O'Donnell was on his second Campari and soda, sitting alone at the bar surrounded by a babble of bankers and beginning to feel irritated. That irritation quickly disappeared when he saw her – in her discreetly low-cut dress, she seemed taller and even more imposing than when he met her in her office. Her presence had temporarily silenced the bankers and O'Donnell could see that, whatever her age, men looked a second time at Heather Ruddock. And maybe even a third time.

She ordered a glass of champagne for herself and then got straight to the point.

'I agreed to meet you this evening for two reasons – and maybe even three. I know a great deal about you from Louise – although I rarely see her anymore. It's as if I'm part of a past she wants to forget. And given her position, I don't blame her. But that doesn't stop me being curious – about you, about what happened between you and Louise, and why it ended so abruptly, especially since she was so very fond of you. I'm also curious about those rumours that there was a plot against her husband. There was never much about it in the papers.'

She paused, as if to gauge his reaction. It was clear that this sort of directness and this topic was not what O'Donnell had been expecting. But before he could begin to answer she went on.

'You can tell me to mind my own business. If you do I won't be pleased but I will understand and we can have a pleasant chat, a good meal and talk about anything you like – except of course my grandfather.'

Again she didn't wait for O'Donnell to reply. She indicated to the barman to refill her glass. O'Donnell felt two Camparis were enough and changed to champagne. Since he would be paying, he might as well enjoy it.

'I'm a trader. I'm good at it. I trade in information. I give and I take. I can assure you I want to know about Louise only for my own curiosity. I always like to know the full story. I want to know why Louise dropped so suddenly out of my life. You can check around, but you'll find I'm a person who keeps her word. I like Louise and wish her well and will never, ever hurt her. But I would like to know.'

O'Donnell was still playing for time. He had never spoken to anyone about Louise and never thought he would. Would this be a betrayal?

Suddenly Heather was smiling 'Don't look so panic stricken. It's genuine curiosity, maybe even a womanly curiosity. I have absolutely no ulterior motive. And I'm curious about you too. Louise talked about you and I can see why she fancied you – and I might even get to see why she liked you so very, very much. So, over to you.'

O'Donnell did not hesitate long. He wanted the information Charlie Ruddock might have had, but he realised too that he would like to know more about Charlie's granddaughter. There was a hint of danger about her and he began to sense that this was what was missing from his life. He made an instant decision. He would trust her.

'What do I get in return?'

'Let's go to the table. I'll tell you over dinner.'

Clearly Heather was well known in l'Ecrivain – as O'Donnell had been in his expense account days as government press secretary. They had the corner table and, even though the booking was in O'Donnell's name, the sommelier asked Heather about the wines that were chosen, without reference to him or to the fact that he would be picking up the tab. O'Donnell was taken aback and not happy to be treated in an offhand way, but was beginning to sense that he was dealing with somebody who knew what she wanted and was used to getting it.

'Now, the second reason for my agreeing to meet you is that I'm curious about what my grandfather did or might have done. I'll tell you what I know about him and, if I'm happy with your response or you needing to know, I'll give you the files – copies, not originals of course – which I now have in my apartment. These cover Henry Alsop and his business with us and the one note I found on your bad bishop. But it's over to you now. I want to hear the full story about you and Louise.'

By now the wine was being poured and, with less reluctance than he might have anticipated, O'Donnell began to tell the story of his relationship with the Taoiseach's wife – how it began when Taoiseach Jack Mulcahy discovered his wife was living dangerously, frequenting night-clubs and mixing in questionable company. The Taoiseach's real concern, of course, was the possibility of a scandal. So he asked his trusted friend and press secretary Peter O'Donnell to look after her, to keep her busy on various projects. And then, as O'Donnell explained it, one thing led to another and the relationship had developed.

'When did you first go to bed with her?' Heather clearly wanted some specifics.

'It was in Boston. She had just spoken to some emigrant group there and we ended up back in the Bostonian Hotel and, well, it just happened.'

'I'm sure it just happened. These things do, but go on.'

O'Donnell explained that, to both their surprise, each felt in love – a situation normally avoided by the commitment-averse O'Donnell.

'It was intense and frankly reckless. But that was it. We were prepared to take the risk until...'

'Until what?'

'Until some journalist became suspicious or was tipped off. I don't know who it was, maybe even one of her friends. I certainly never told anyone but it was probably inevitable and it certainly shook me.'

'And Louise?'

'Strangely, she seemed oblivious to risk. Told me not to be such a faintheart.'

'That's one of her words all right. Do you think the Taoiseach suspected anything? Did he know?'

'Never that I know and not now. But then it may have suited him not to know. Politics always came first, middle and last with him.'

'So what happened?'

'Well, as you mentioned there was a plot within the parliamentary party to unseat the Taoiseach. A few bad by-election results gave two of the ministers the chance they'd been waiting for. Peadar Cannon in particular began to scratch around, drumming up support among some of the younger crowd with the help of some of Mulcahy's old enemies. It's all history now, though most of it never came out. Anyway, we got the dirt on

Cannon over a dodgy share deal he was involved in. Eventually, Mulcahy steamrolled his way through them all. It all fizzled out and Cannon resigned from the Cabinet, though he's still lurking in the shadows. But it was a close-run thing and, if the story about Louise had broken, it could have been fatal to the Taoiseach.'

They were now on to dessert. She probed him about more detail – did he think there was any other man involved, had they a hideaway 'love nest'?

He assured her – though he could never really know – that he was the only man, certainly after they met, and he felt she had not strayed since the affair ended. This sort of detail seemed to be important to Heather.

She seemed disappointed when he told her the only 'love nest' they had was his apartment in Percy Place, which did not seems to impress her greatly.

'And why did it all end?'

'The plot brought us both to our senses – me much more than her. I realised and she accepted the consequences of us being outed. She thought we could brazen it out, but in the end I had to insist.'

'You mean you ditched her.'

'I suppose you could put it that way. I told her that in our different ways we both loved Jack Mulcahy and we could end up destroying him. That's the truth and, shortly afterwards, I left politics and went back to Trinity.'

'And would I be wrong to say the excitement was wearing off for you and maybe you fancied a younger, not-so-high-maintenance model.'

That was closer to the truth than O'Donnell cared to admit and his denial was less than convincing, but he could sense she had all the information she wanted – at least for the moment.

By now they were at the brandy stage.

'Okay I'll tell you about my grandfather and then we can talk about the files.'

It was straightforward.

'Charlie graduated in law in the class of 1913 from UCD. He was a good student, getting third in the class just behind Arthur Cox and John A Costello. He was the only Protestant in the class and served his apprenticeship with William Fry. It was a family firm and he felt he'd never get very far there and so he set up his own one-man practice in 1918, moving to Mount Street a few years later. By the 1920s he was well-established, specialising in business and company law. He did well, my father joined the practice in 1944 and I joined in 1977. All very straightforward. A few mergers along the way brought us to Ruddock Molony Enright as you saw it yesterday.

'My grandfather had been a Home Rule supporter in his student days, but after 1916 he drifted to Sinn Féin. He was never a fighting man but close enough to some of those who were. He was involved in the Sinn Féin courts and acted as a judge for a while in the Midlands. He had his stories of 'rough justice', as he called it, from those years. He went with de Valera in the Civil War but, from what I can recall, he kept on good terms with the Cosgrave crowd as well. He was great friends with Seán Lemass, who used to play cards in grandfather's house. After Lemass became minister for industry and commerce in 1932, grandfather got a great deal of business looking after new industries.'

She paused and called for a brandy top-up. It was her second, but seemed to have no effect on her.

'It was through Lemass he met Henry Alsop, who had come to Ireland with money to invest. I don't think he actually invested very much but he and my grandfather seemed to get on well, at least in the early days. From what I could see, all of that is in the files. I remember grandfather talking about him when I was young – it was an unusual name, which is probably why I remember. What I remember my grandfather saying was that he was a man who had money when nobody else had, he knew how to make money and could have helped Ireland if his head had not been turned by what my grandfather called 'that un-principled scoundrel' Bishop Concannon. My grandfather sim-ply loathed him. A mention of his name was enough to set him off. I think he hated all bishops but Concannon was the *bête noire*. In fact, he was the one man of whom he spoke only ill. He was never bitter about his political opponents – in fact he used to boast that he briefed Costello more than his own crowd did. But Concannon! You'll see what I mean from the files.'

By now they were the only people left in the restaurant.

'And when will I be able to see these files?'

'Tonight if you wish. As I told you, they're in my apartment on Pembroke Road.'

O'Donnell was surprised but pleased.

'You never asked me the third reason I agreed to meet you.'

But before O'Donnell could respond, she continued: 'I want to see for myself if you're as good as Louise always said you were.'

19

....

Apparently, she was happy that he was.

O'Donnell was back in his own apartment, reviewing the events of the evening. The files he had brought with him as he slipped out of her apartment at 3.30 am were on his desk. They would have to wait a while longer.

Meanwhile he thought about Heather and the evening they had just had. It had been an energetic encounter. She told him in her direct and unadorned way that she was married and securely so. Her husband, a retired partner from a major accountancy firm, lived in the family home in Rosslare, where he contentedly gardened and golfed. Or so at least he told her. Rosslare, she said, bored her.

She enjoyed her work and was proud of the firm she headed and, she said, she made good money. She also told him very directly that she enjoyed the occasional, as she called it, recreational sex, which was one of the reasons she had been so friendly with Louise Mulcahy because they could each give the other 'cover'. But, she added, Dublin was a treacherous place and she had to be careful.

That was the extent of what she told him and O'Donnell was relieved there was no story of an unhappy marriage or a husband who did not understand her. The only reassurance she needed was that 'she was still good at sex' – a reassurance that O'Donnell could very honestly give her. He half expected her to ask if she was as good as Louise, but she didn't. And to his great West of Ireland relief, there was no post-coital tristesse, no exchange of endearments or pledge of any sort.

Two hours after he arrived, she told him it was time to go – she had an early meeting and needed to sleep, and that was that. When he somewhat tentatively asked would they meet again, she simply said 'Of course' and, with that, he was left to find his way out.

As he walked down a deserted Northumberland Road, passing the lone garda sentry at the Israeli embassy, he told himself he would not be required to fall in love this time, but nonetheless he had greatly enjoyed the evening. And he had the files. Life was looking up.

After a few hours' sleep, he decided he needed a good breakfast. He brought the files with him to the Berkeley Court and treated himself to a 'full Irish'. There were only seven shortish documents in all, mostly in the form of 'attendances' Ruddock had written of meetings he had or instructions received. There were no bombshells but plenty of what he regarded as good background.

Charlie Ruddock had been recommended to Henry Alsop by the minister for industry and commerce in de Valera's government, Seán Lemass. Lemass had called Ruddock into his office in Kildare Street in September 1936, where he described Alsop as a man of great wealth and commercial experience who had no Irish roots or background. He had come to Ireland and was interested – for some reason Lemass could not fathom but saw as genuine – in supporting Lemass's efforts to establish new industries in Ireland. Lemass wanted Ruddock, who he obviously trusted, to act as a 'go-between' with Alsop, away from the too cautious civil servants.

Ruddock had recorded this in an attendance written after his meeting with Lemass and this was followed by a series of meetings with Alsop. The first such meeting was in the Stephen's Green Club, which Alsop had joined since coming to Dublin and where each was comfortable to meet. Alsop made clear that he had considerable funds at his disposal, but he was only interested in serious projects that had a realistic chance of being sustainable and he would not have any tolerance for what he called 'airy-fairy' schemes. Alsop made the point, more than once, that he was serious and in a hurry, but that he was also a hard-headed realist. Failure, he said, would help nobody and bring their efforts into disrepute. He was not a man, he said, who had ever tolerated sloppiness or failure. It was Ruddock's job to find schemes he could invest in.

There followed over the next two years a list of potential projects. It was a long list and Ruddock had done detailed background notes on the schemes and their sponsors. But one by one they failed to find favour. There was the new battery-driven cars invented by Professor Drumm of University College Dublin. Plans to modernise the coal mines in Arigna and make them exporters, plans to mine ore in Avoca, plans to set up new leather and shoe factories, plans to establish a private hydro-electric scheme on the river Lee, plans to have ship building on the Liffey, plans to have meat processed in Ireland rather than exported on the hoof. And there were more. But one by one, for different reasons, they were rejected.

The rejections were never brusque or peremptory. Alsop examined all of them carefully, writing detailed critiques on costs, marketing, availability of skilled labour, shortage of managers and, in spite of Lemass's backing, the inflexibility of the civil servants –it seemed to O'Donnell that the civil service and paucity of managers were the stumbling blocks.

Ruddock was sent back time after time to get more details and he must have been growing frustrated, though the fees he earned would have been some compensation. But O'Donnell had the strong impression that Ruddock wanted to help Lemass and Ireland as best he could so his frustration at the slow rate of progress was genuine.

O'Donnell noted the records of occasional phone calls from Lemass, expressing his own impatience but urging Ruddock to keep Alsop engaged. Lemass said he saw hard times ahead and he reckoned Alsop's American and British business connections could prove helpful in getting scarce supplies in the event of the European war Lemass was convinced was inevitable.

By late 1938, in a note to Lemass, Ruddock noted what he called a worrying change in attitude on the part of Alsop. His earlier enthusiasm for economic development was seriously on the wane. Finally, he told Ruddock he had found no project that met his criteria. He had no fault with Ruddock. He had found his services first class and he trusted him. He would like him to act as his Irish solicitor but his own focus was changing.

He told Ruddock to arrange for a generous bequest to the engineering department at UCD, where he admired the innovative work of Professor Purcell in trying to modernise Irish industry, but that his priority now was on helping strengthen the Catholic Church in face of the mounting threats from fascism and communism. Ruddock was at a genuine loss as to what was happening. When he questioned Alsop about the specifics of what he intended doing, the response was vague, if not evasive.

Lemass was annoyed to be told of Alsop's change of mind. He wondered aloud to Ruddock 'which of those bloody blackbirds have got to him'. Not for the first time, Ruddock realised that Lemass had little time for bishops. He asked Ruddock to keep up his contact, believing Alsop might come to his senses. Ruddock doubted this, but he had grown to like the taciturn and abrupt Alsop and, of course, there was always the possibility of future business.

There was a gap of almost a year before they met again and Ruddock was not prepared for the double shock that lay in store for him. It was autumn 1939 and Ruddock was alarmed at the physical deterioration in Alsop's condition. He was gaunt and emaciated. He wasted no time in telling Ruddock that he was dying and had important business to transact and not much time to do it. As Ruddock recounted in his attendance:

> He instructed me to draw up his will and that any previous documents were null and void. With the exception of his house in Lansdowne Road and his flat in Kensington, and allowing for the payment of outstanding debts and expenses, the residue of his estate, inclusive of all shares, was to be left to the Bishop of Kilderry, Dr Thomas Patrick Concannon, to be used at his sole discretion and to achieve the ends they both desired and on which they were in total agreement. His house and apartment were to be left to his business partner and friend from schooldays, Sir Edward Ralph Hoare.

That was the gist of the will. Ruddock noted that he urged Alsop to reconsider but was told that his mind was made up – 'my intentions are clear and not open to discussion and my soul is at ease'. Ruddock received further instructions, which he accepted as binding. These involved the transfer of the bulk of Alsop's cash assets, amounting to £100,000, in to a No 1 deposit account in the name of Bishop Concannon in the Munster & Leinster Bank in Dame Street and a further £10,000 in a No 2 current account in the same branch, also in the name of Bishop Concannon. Alsop would retain a current account in his own name and all expenses, including Ruddock's own fees, were to be paid from this after his death. Any residue in that account, Ruddock was free to leave to any charity of his choice.

There were a few other notes in the file. The most significant was an attendance on the meeting in Alsop's house on October 10, which tallied with the version O'Donnell had read in the bishop's journal. Ruddock's note was cold and factual, including the handover of the stocks and shares, the 'gift' of the valuable desk to Concannon and the confirmation by Alsop that the banking transfers had been effected to the benefit of the two new accounts in Concannon's name. Ruddock's distaste, indeed contempt, for Concannon jumps out of his cold legal words, but the note makes clear that, before the bishop's arrival, Alsop had insisted he was not changing anything and nothing Ruddock could say would change anything.

Alsop died a month after this meeting on November 9 1939 in St Vincent's hospital. His will, exactly as stipulated to Ruddock, was in the file along with an obituary from *The Times* with a brief outline of his career.

The final note in the file was a curt communication from Concannon – 'Dear Ruddock' – informing him that his services would no longer be required and any outstanding matters would be dealt with, and here Concannon named a country solicitor of whom Ruddock had never heard. There was no word of thanks for services rendered, not even a perfunctory nod in that direction. Ruddock was offended by the discourtesy, but not surprised. What did surprise him, and he noted it in the letter, was why Concannon was using a solicitor so far from his diocese and why he had not used the firm – a reputable firm in Ruddock's view – that had handled the affairs of Kilderry for over half a century.

Why had Nathaniel Bowe been cut out of the picture? Ruddock clearly had his suspicions but was helpless to do anything

– but it was a question that Charlie Ruddock would undoubtedly pursue further.

It had taken O'Donnell four coffees to get through the file. But he was pleased with himself and felt he now knew enough to ask the people back at Kilderry some hard questions. He would head down there tomorrow and demand total access to all the files.

Meanwhile, he began to wonder when he would meet Heather again. And, a little to his surprise, realised he very much wanted to.

20

....

Archbishop Valetti was beginning to feel pleased with himself. He was making progress in his quest to get the story on Bishop Concannon and the missing money. It was hard work with no index to guide him, which meant he had to plough through a mass of papers, most of it of no real relevance. And he was also under pressure.

The £20,000 that was coming to him in Concannon's will had not yet arrived, but news of it had been enough to placate his increasingly insistent bookie. But only for the moment. The early warm tones of the bookie were fast changing and a note of menace was creeping in. It was as yet only a hint of what might be in store if his debts were not settled, but the menace was real enough and Valetti knew to take it seriously.

Serious enough to think of going back to his Sicilian cousins, who had made it clear there would always be a useful role for him in their organisation. Just as there had been in the past. But it was not a chapter in his life he wanted to re-visit.

His first document of interest this morning was based more on a whim that it might be useful than on any hard information. It was a record Robinson made of a meeting he had with a man called Henry Alsop at Alsop's request. It was dated July 1938.

> Henry Alsop came to see me at the nunciature. He was introduced to me last year by Fr McQuaid, the President of Blackrock College. McQuaid had described him to me as 'a pious man, a devout and faithful Catholic, an ardent

and proud convert from the Church of England, who wished to help the Faith in any way he could'.

McQuaid indicated to me that Alsop was close to the government and was anxious to help establish some new industries here. But according to McQuaid, these efforts were not meeting with much success, even with the support of Mr Lemass.

Alsop, he said, was a man of considerable wealth and influence, and was prepared to put some of his money towards the propagation of the faith. Fr McQuaid was somewhat vague as to what this might mean, but I did note he stressed the 'Faith' and not the 'Church'. McQuaid is careful with words. He chooses them with care.

Robinson then made a note of the meeting.

I met Alsop as requested. I found him formal and courteous in a very reserved English way, but also very intense. He spoke at some length without saying anything very new about the dangers posed by fascism and communism, and seemed to me to be confused in his prescription for dealing with these threats. He was, he said, prepared to help individual causes in what he called the 'institutional' Church, which he felt was ill-equipped to defend itself in the dangerous times ahead.

I gave him my full attention but fear I had little to say by way of practical proposals. I could see he was disappointed with my response, but he accepted my invitation to come to dinner here sometime soon, where I was sure there would be a full discussion of the issues he raised.

Valetti made a careful note of the name Henry Alsop. He would check him up in the old volumes of *Who's Who*, which he had noted in the library and obviously dated back to the time of Paschal Robinson and had not been added to since then.

What he found provided a few clues. Alsop was born in 1870. His full name was Henry Albert Ernest Alsop. He was the only son of H.H. Alsop, the Vicar of Esher, Surrey. He married Catherine, the only child of Hector Munro of Edinburgh in 1899. She died in 1928 and they had no children.

It was his career details that Valetti found of greater interest. Alsop had been educated at Epsom College and at Downing College Cambridge. In 1896 he moved to Rhodesia, where he worked with that country's mines department. Two years later he returned to London to work with the Nobel Dynamite Company. In 1905 he moved to the US to work for a petroleum company in Texas. He eventually owned his own company, which he sold to Standard Oil in 1922. He returned to London that year and, before long, had been offered directorships in BP and in De Beers diamond company. Several other directorships followed and in 1935 he moved to live in Dublin, although he retained an apartment in Kensington and his membership of the Athenaeum Club. His address in Dublin was given as Lansdowne Road and his club the Stephen's Green Club.

Valetti read all of this with interest. Clearly a man with money and no close family to inherit it. There was no mention of his conversion to Roman Catholicism but then, thought Valetti, such a Protestant institution as Who's Who would be unlikely to mention something like that.

The first reference to Concannon since his appointment as bishop also included a reference to Alsop. It was a note written by Robinson after a dinner he hosted in the nunciature in November 1939. Apparently it was his practice to write a summary after all such quasi-official gatherings as part of his information gathering duties. He meticulously noted the names of all his guests with a short note on the views expressed by each of them.

He noted that Concannon spoke with considerable erudition and knowledge on the situation in Europe generally, but on Spain and Portugal in particular. He saw potential developments in each of these countries, new movements and that sort of thing, which could potentially strengthen the Church.

His note on Alsop was short: 'He seemed impatient of discussions on general principle and clearly impatient with the philosophising of the professors. He was eager for specifics. Believe he is unwell and impatient to "do something". Apart from Concannon, there was, it seemed, little enough to interest him.'

Valetti poured himself a glass of his favourite Sicilian wine and lit a Toscanello. He sat back and looked at the stacks of papers still to be read. It would take time but he would be patient and careful. And it beat parish visitations any day.

21

....

When he had finished his study of Charlie Ruddock's papers, and put thoughts of Charlie's granddaughter out of his mind, O'Donnell realised he had a midday meeting of the economics department and had promised his friend and department head, Teddy Dooley, that he would be there. It was going to be a difficult meeting and he knew his support might be needed.

When O'Donnell first joined the department, meetings were rare and the department trundled along, its members bound together by a strong bond of 'live and let live'. Everyone more or less did their own thing along well-established and comfortable routines and practices. There was no talk of corporate identity or of being in competition with other universities, and that had suited O'Donnell very well. But like so many other things, that was changing. Now there were three different factions seeking to control the direction of the department, and an atmosphere of suspicion and antagonism had begun to develop.

The battle was ostensibly about academic direction but, like most academic battles, it was also about personalities. As in most such battles, one group wanted not just the status quo but a return to what it saw as the traditional aloofness of the university from anything outside its walls. Strangely, O'Donnell noted, the leader of this group was also the youngest member of the department and not even a graduate of the university whose traditions he so strongly espoused. The second group was led by an econometrician just back from post-graduate work at Essex who had little tolerance of anything outside his own narrow range. While in the centre, Dooley had to try to forge a middle way.

The meeting was bad tempered and self-indulgent. O'Donnell supported Dooley and, in the process, had to endure some snide comments about his own lack of serious publications and the amount of time he spent on outside consultancy work. He reflected to himself that it was better no one knew how he was really spending his time at present.

The meeting seemed to O'Donnell to go on forever and, of course, came to no real conclusion. He realised just how bored he was and what a small contribution he was making in the academic world. Time to look elsewhere? But where?

He found it easier to think about Heather Ruddock. He thought about phoning her after the meeting but hesitated – in part because he feared rejection, but in part too because he felt a little exhausted. So instead he phoned his friend Tommy Newrie and invited him to join him for dinner in Nico's, which O'Donnell reckoned was the best Italian restaurant in Dublin with the best scampi anywhere.

O'Donnell had a good reason to want to talk to Tommy. He needed to stand back and reassess his situation and clear his mind. Too much had happened too quickly and he was becoming confused. He needed a good listener with a cool forensic mind. Tommy was that man.

Tommy was an old drinking pal of O'Donnell's since their student days. Tommy had taken his time going through medical school and had never been accused of being over-ambitious or careerist. But he was the best doctor O'Donnell knew – an instinctively good doctor with uncannily accurate diagnostic skills and, most of all, he was a listener with a patient and tolerant understanding of human nature.

He would tell Tommy everything – right up to that last night with Heather. Tommy would not be judgemental, even if a trifle envious. These things didn't happen to men their age all that often.

Through a very good meal and two bottles of the house red, Tommy listened. He wanted O'Donnell to tell him everything from the start. By the time he had finished, they had reached the Sambuca.

'Let's be clear about one thing from the start,' began Tommy. 'This is about money. An awful lot of money. Keep that clear in your mind and be prepared for it to turn dirty, very dirty. And don't trust anyone – even those on your own side.'

Tommy was on his fifth Benson & Hedges.

'Let me give you the bad news first. From what you have told me, Heather Ruddock has probably given you all she has on her grandfather. She may be a great ride but, unless she finds some new papers, forget her. She could become a distraction. She is a bit player and has played her part.'

This was not what O'Donnell had bought a good dinner to hear. Reluctantly, he saw Tommy's point – but doubted if he would follow the advice.

'You came in to this cold and you have made some mistakes. Telling that stockbroker was a mistake. I know him. He is a 14-carat shit. He smells money. He knows you are still close to the Taoiseach and thinks you still have some power. He will want to know where you got the money or, more likely, who you are working for. He will be asking about your background, your friends and your family. He will know by now that your uncle – your only real relative – is a senior cleric in Kilderry.'

O'Donnell had long-regretted speaking to Mr Pickwick, Sigerson Keane.

'And now the bishop tells you your uncle made a right pig's ear of it by blurting what he did to that parish priest. Those guys don't keep secrets, They're a crowd of old women. One way or another, this will get back to somebody in Rome or to the papal nuncio. If the focus is on Kilderry, they won't take long to start looking at Concannon and there are bound to be files somewhere. The Church is a bit like the Nazis and the Communists – they keep records on everything and everybody. And one thing is clear about Concannon. He will have made enemies.'

Another pause as Tommy lit a cigarette.

'So you don't have much time. If the heavy guns in Rome get involved, your bishop will cave in. They always do. An obscure Irish bishop is in no position to stand up to them. The Church and the mafia are close cousins.'

'That's all very depressing,' said O'Donnell, who was beginning to look as depressed as he felt. 'Are you saying they might as well hand it all over to Rome at this stage and let them sort it out?'

'Absolutely not,' snorted Tommy. 'You're not beaten yet. I've more to say. Let's go and have a pint in Smyth's.'

When they had settled in the front snug with two pints before them, Tommy continued.

'It's too early to be depressed. The important thing is you are ahead of the pack. You've been handicapped up to now because that bloody bishop has not been straight with you. He has to give you total access to everything. Simple as that. And I think he has no option but to do that.'

O'Donnell reassured him on this point.

'And I think you've been too narrow in just going after the stuff in the archive. There are plenty of other sources of information. There'll almost certainly be an office diary for the diocesan office, which the bishop's secretary kept. It will have a record of all his appointments – the usual stuff; confirmations, ordinations, funerals the bishop attended, but also very likely meetings and appointments in Dublin and even Rome, meetings with other bishops and ministers. It's amazing how much you can find out and at least get a framework to work within.

'And then there's the folk memory. The people who knew him. He had a big staff in those days – cooks, a gardener, almost certainly a driver. He will have been a big figure in their lives. All these names will be easily found. Most may be dead, but almost certainly not all of them.'

'But how do I find these people?'

'You find them by asking your uncle. He was the bishop's secretary at one time. He'll know everybody. If he's not helpful, go to the pubs.'

'What pubs?'

'The pubs in Kilderry, of course. The right pubs.'

'There's one other thing. You mentioned that first nuncio, Paschal Robinson.'

'And?'

'Well I've heard a fair bit about him. And I think he might be the key to finding out more about the money Concannon got. He might be worth following up.'

'How?'

'I've heard more than I ever really wanted to know. I have a patient, a retired diplomat. He served in the Vatican. He knows everything about the Church. He loves an audience and he doesn't really have one these days. He was a young diplomat in the war years, but the Church is his real obsession. Not a great fan, but knows a huge amount.'

Newrie went on to talk about his diplomat friend and O'Donnell encouraged him. But O'Donnell's mind was on Tommy. He was just the sort of person to back him up. Tommy was a moocher. He could sniff around and get people to talk. He was a sharp observer. He could make himself unobtrusive. And people liked him.

'Tommy, what are you doing on Friday?'

'I have a day off. Thinking about the races, Gowran Park. Why?'

'You're coming down to Kilderry with me. I'm phoning the bishop in the morning. You are now my assistant on this investigation and he can take you or leave me'

Tommy was not hard to persuade and the bishop made no objections. In fact, O'Donnell thought the bishop was beginning to panic a little – or maybe a lot. He had had a call from the nuncio's office asking if it would be convenient for the nuncio to visit Kilderry in the near future. This had never happened before and Mullins was around too long to see it as a coincidence. He would put off the visit as long as he could and, meanwhile, try to fend off some of the rumours in the diocese, which he attributed to JJ Gilmartin.

As far as he was concerned, there was now a real sense of urgency and if Tommy Newrie could help, he had no difficulty with that. He was not sure how he might help, but all help was welcome – wherever it came from.

22

....

O'Donnell and Newrie left Dublin early on Friday morning. They agreed on the way down that the key years were almost certainly the war years, especially from very early 1940 after the death of Henry Alsop and the handing over of the cash to Concannon. Whatever plans he had for the money dated from those years.

O'Donnell took up the story.

'We know that the cash was lodged in the Munster & Leinster Bank, but we've no idea what happened to that money or what shares were cashed in. We need to find out who Concannon was meeting in those years. He must have had some collaborators so, if we can find his diary for that time, we can start making progress. Whatever he was going to do, he had to get others involved. So who were they – other bishops, bankers, diplomats? And where were they – Dublin, Maynooth, Rome, Madrid?'

These were just some of the questions. They agreed that O'Donnell would demand to see the full journal – not the bits already selected for him – and Concannon's full system of filing cards. Newrie would see what he could find in the official diary for those years and try to find out if any of the old staff were still around.

Bishop Mullins had breakfast waiting for them. Greasy as the fry was, they both welcomed it. O'Donnell saw immediately how worried Mullins was.

He had received a letter that morning from one of Dublin's

most litigious legal firms, couched in icily polite terms, acting on Richard E Murdock's behalf and seeking details of all Concannon's financial affairs. There was a strong hint that if this was not provided, and provided quickly, an injunction seeking discovery would follow.

The bishop's instincts told him that, in spite of the bullying tone, they had no right to this information. But he was not too confident how strong his position might be if it came to the test and was certain Murdock was both reckless and determined and would have no problem in going public – the last thing Mullins wanted.

That was not his only worry. He had not yet spoken to his own lawyer, Archie Bowe. Archie would not be pleased that he had been kept in the dark – indeed, ignored on a matter he would have regarded as very much his business as lawyer to the diocese. That, said Mullins as he lit his breakfast pipe, was also a mistake – Archie almost certainly knew a great deal and about things of which they had no knowledge. It was a question now of getting him on side and, to do that, they would have to tell him everything.

There was no question now of O'Donnell not having full access to everything and Mullins accepted Newrie as part of the team.

They sat down to work in the bishop's study, a room dominated by the great desk Alsop had given Concannon to the great annoyance of Charlie Ruddock.

Newrie had been right. There was an annual diary of the bishop's engagements. It predated Concannon, with volumes going back well over a century and included one for every year of Concannon's long reign. It was mundane stuff detailing confirmation and ordination ceremonies, visits to parishes, the four-yearly meetings of the bishops in Maynooth and all official functions attended by the bishop. But it also included meetings he attended and, most significantly, some of those he met.

Newrie saw very quickly that Concannon was methodical and, in the early years at least, an energetic and hard-working man. He was one to delegate, visiting every parish on a regular basis, summoning priests to see him and seeking to control every aspect of the life of Kilderry.

Newrie decided to concentrate on the war years and the period after his meeting with Alsop in 1939 up to 1946. He saw straight away that, in spite of the petrol rationing, Concannon visited Dublin on a very regular basis and was particularly busy in 1940, with frequent visits to the Spanish embassy on Shrewsbury Road. He also saw regular meetings with a number of names with no addresses or titles, which meant nothing to him but which he noted, and one recurring address, 51 Lower Mount Street, with no name attached. The entries simply said 'meeting' and the time. Clearly the bishop was a stickler for record-keeping but, unusually, here he was keeping the information about the nature of these meetings to himself.

Newrie also looked through the list of 'lay staff and servants' as they were described for those years. What a feudal organisation that still described staff as 'servants' and still used that strange term 'lay' to those not part of the clerical caste. It was actually a short list and the name that immediately caught Newrie's interest was that of John Ryan, who was described as gardener, driver and general handyman and who remained as Concannon's driver right up to the bishop's retirement. He immediately asked O'Donnell to find out what there was to be known about John Ryan from his uncle.

Monsignor Nestor was surprised by the question but was forthcoming.

'John Ryan. He always went by the name of Johnny Flower-pot. I don't know why. I think it went back to his school days, but he never took offence. It could be because there were a couple of families called Ryan in the area. He was only 18 when he came to work here as a handyman in 1939 but he could drive, which not many could in those years, and he loved cars. Before long he became the bishop's driver. The bishop himself never drove – that would be beneath the dignity of a bishop in those days. He clearly found Johnny reliable and I think he genuinely liked and trusted him. In fact, he even left him a decent bequest in his will.

'As it happened, Johnny was not as discreet as the bishop thought, especially after a few drinks. But no word ever came back and Johnny stayed until after Concannon retired and the new bishop had no use for a driver – in fact, he hated the very thought of being driven around, sitting in the back of a big car. I should say the old bishop loved a big car. I think he felt it was appropriate to his status. Anyway, that's Johnny Flowerpot for you.'

'Is he still alive?'

'Very much so. The bishop gave him a decent pension and he drove a hackney car until recently. He lives close to here and I'm told he spends most afternoons in Hickson's pub, reading the *Evening Herald* – it used to be the *Evening Press*, seeing as he was always a Dev man, but that collapsed a few years ago so now it's the *Herald* – and talking to anyone who will listen.'

Newrie had all the information he needed and he felt like a pint. Within the hour, he was sitting in the small comfortable snug of Hickson's bar. He had no difficulty in finding his man. He was the only other person there in the middle of the afternoon, reading his *Evening Herald* and looking as if this was his second home. He was delighted to have Tommy Newrie's company, especially when Tommy arrived with a pint.

They talked a bit about racing. Tommy told him he was a doctor and, after a short while on that subject, Tommy asked about Johnny himself. It was not long before Concannon was mentioned and Tommy mentioned his own interest in history. He told Johnny he had an interest in Concannon and realised very quickly he would have no difficulty in getting Johnny going on the subject.

Concannon had clearly been an important part of his life and he was delighted to have a new audience for old stories – stories the pub regulars had long tired of hearing.

The gist of his story, as recounted by Newrie later to O'Donnell, was that indeed he had been the bishop's man – 'a powerful man, a strict man but fair. I drove him everywhere. He had this great big car, a Bentley first and then a Rover'. Johnny detailed how he had got the Bentley, buying it second hand from the Archbishop of Dublin, who preferred French cars, Citroens, to English ones.

'Ah the Bentley was a great car, hard on the fuel but getting petrol, even in the war years, was never a problem for his lordship and it always made a great impression, especially when he turned up for confirmations in some country parish or visited one of them embassies in Dublin. The bishop used to say to me it was important to give the impression of power, people liked to see their rulers that way. He always saw himself as a ruler. He was never a man who went in for the humility.'

Newrie noted fairly quickly that Johnny was not in the habit of buying his round or maybe he thought he had met a soft 'touch', but he was enjoying the chat and was prepared to put the next three pints down to 'necessary expenses'.

Johnny was only too happy to tell him about the war years, about the embassies – the papal nuncio, the Spanish, the British – about frequent dinners and lunches in the Stephen's Green

Club, but Johnny was quick to say he never saw any sign of drink on the bishop. Nor did he ever tell Johnny who he was meeting, but Johnny usually knew from the doorman at the club, who liked to talk hurling with him. No, he couldn't remember the names but there was an editor of the *Independent*, someone from the Department of Justice, a fellow with black corrugated hair from External Affairs, businessmen, professors. He promised Newrie he would try to recall some of the names and Newrie, not wanting to raise any suspicions by pressing too hard, let it rest.

He also told Newrie they used to visit some private houses. He remembered two of them, one in Mount Street and the other on Northumberland Road. When this happened, the bishop did not want the car parked outside, so Johnny would be told to come back in a few hours. Johnny never knew who was in these houses and never dared ask.

It was now five o'clock and Johnny was showing no sign of having drunk four pints, but declared abruptly that he had exceeded his quota and the 'war office would be waiting for him at home'. However, he had no difficulty accepting what he called 'a bang of the latch', which he nominated as a large Powers. Newrie took the opportunity to ask for a few more questions. Did Johnny ever meet any of the important people who might have called to visit the bishop in Kilderry?

There was one visit in particular he remembered – Éamon de Valera, or 'the chief' as Johnny called him. 'I even shook his hand as he was leaving,' he recalled fondly.

'To tell the truth, he wasn't expected but he was speaking at an election meeting in a nearby constituency and he called in on the way. It was 1940, a bad year for us. The funny thing is the phone call saying he was coming arrived only an hour or so before his visit and it was a short enough visit. The bishop never mentioned it to me. I just happened to be standing around and, while Dev was civil to me, I felt he looked a bit cross and we had no chat at all.'

Johnny drained his Powers and stood up to leave.

'You know, quare things happened during those years. There were a few other visits that I only heard about from the house-keeper. Big cars were rare enough in the war years and any big car arriving attracted plenty of attention. I'm told there were a few, including an early morning visit from an army car, maybe even more than once.'

Johnny had never asked Newrie his full name –Tommy was enough for him – nor asked him why he was so curious about the bishop. For now, it was enough for Johnny that he had an afternoon of free drinks and a new audience. But Johnny had a suspicious nature and a keen eye. He decided that a man who had bought him many a drink in the past might like to know of this new-found interest from a stranger in his uncle's past. He had a phone number for Richard E Murdock and might give him a ring. But not tonight. He would have trouble enough at home as it was.

And that was not the only call he would make.

***

O'Donnell's afternoon had been neither as productive or as enjoyable. He had gone over Concannon's entire journal and had come to two conclusions. Bishop Mullins and his uncle had not held back anything of real significance. There were a couple of entries that might be of use and he would look at them again when he got home.

His second conclusion was more worrying. He was now certain that the journal for the wartime years, from about the time of Alsop's death in 1939 until 1946, were incomplete. They were devoted almost entirely to local or Church events – meetings of the bishops in Maynooth, discussions with the cardinal in Armagh, pastoral letters he had written, speeches he had made, sermons he had given, priests he had to discipline. But there was nothing about any meetings with the nuncio or de Valera's visit, and nothing whatsoever about the implementation of Alsop's ambition.

O'Donnell reckoned this could not be accidental. The only person who could have removed these references was Concannon himself and, given that all entries were loose leaf, there would be no question of any tinkering with the text.

The more he thought about it the more convinced he became that Concannon, a compulsive and obsessive person who kept meticulous records of all his activities, would have kept a careful record of what he regarded as a 'sacred responsibility'. But clearly it was so sensitive he had been careful to keep it separate from all else. But where was it? Mullins and his uncle had no knowledge of it. It was not among the files retrieved from the bishop's safe or from his house after he retired.

O'Donnell was certain it had to exist. It would be out of character for Concannon not to have recorded these events. But where should he start looking?

He had absolutely no idea.

23

....

Valetti was looking at the letter he had received that morning from the Bishop of Kilderry. It was formal and proper, but certainly not friendly. Unfortunately the bishop's schedule was extremely busy at present, especially with pastoral duties including confirmations, and it would not be convenient to invite the nuncio at this time. At some later date perhaps, but no such date was specified.

Valetti was not surprised. It was exactly how he would have responded had he got something to hide. But there were more ways to skin a cat. And thinking of cats, he was immediately put in mind of a neighbouring bishop of Mullins – Dominic Irwin, a sleek feline man who, Valetti had been told (by JJ Gilmartin actually), was not too popular with his fellow bishops. Irwin saw himself as a social radical, but lived in some style and was widely suspected as the source of leaks to the media of stories from the Maynooth meetings.

Irwin would welcome a visit from the nuncio, even if it might be tedious for Valetti. Irwin was big into liturgical renewal, a subject that deeply bored Valetti, and he would probably arrange a High Mass and invite the nuncio to preach a sermon. Well, he had a secretary who could whip up a sermon for him. It would be neither elegant nor memorable, but a High Mass here and there was part of his job specification so he could put up with it.

From what he had heard, Irwin would be only too pleased to give him any gossip there was on Kilderry, Concannon and the present bishop. It would allow him to get a fix on John Mullins, the man who might be the biggest obstacle in getting to the missing money.

He also thought it was time he got his own mole within the ranks of the bishops and Irwin would probably jump at the prospect. But it would not be as crude as that. Flattery was the only bait he needed. Strange, he thought, how vanity can be such a clerical vice. Probably because there were no wives or children to puncture any latent pomposity. Vanity, he reflected smugly, had never been a problem for him.

He had his secretary phone Irwin's office and, as he expected, his offer was warmly accepted.

He went back with relief to the Robinson archive.

He opened the file for 1940. He was looking for references to Kilderry and Concannon. The first document for that year was lengthy and had no reference to either, but Valetti's instinct told him it might be significant. It was an account of the annual new year visit of the diplomatic corps for the presentation of credentials to the President of Ireland. The nuncio, then as now, was Dean of the Diplomatic Corps – a small enough body in those days with only 10 ambassadors in all – and the event was seen as a formal, routine affair. However, this was no routine meeting as Robinson's note, with his journalistic eye for detail, made clear.

That year the ceremony had not taken place in January but in February. Robinson made a note of his colleagues in attendance. Ambassadors or high commissioners from Britain, Belgium, Canada, France, Germany, Italy, Spain, Switzerland and the United States. Valetti knew from an earlier note that Robinson did not like his fellow American and near neighbour in the Phoenix Park, David Gray.

He had wondered why a man with such little sympathy for Irish nationalism and such affinity with the Anglo-Irish had been appointed by Roosevelt. To Robinson, Gray personified what the Irish in America most resented about what they had experienced in the US – the bigotry and exploitation of a superior caste. He had no doubt Gray's appointment, apart from being a cousin of Roosevelt's wife, was due to the anglophile State Department, which took a dim view of de Valera's neutrality. It was an open secret that Gray and the US ambassador to London, Joe Kennedy, did not get on – old money looking down on new, Robinson had noted.

The report seemed to be an *aide-mémoire* to himself. Robinson began with a reflection on the president's residence, now called Áras an Uachtaráin.

> The building is quite like my own – bigger and grander but with a drab, shabby unlived in look and a pervasive smell of dry rot. Like my own house, it needs money – and lots of it – spent on restoration but, like my own residence, I doubt if this will happen for some time to come.
>
> This is the first coming together of diplomats since the outbreak of the war. Mr de Valera attended in his role as Minister for External Affairs and, in spite of President Hyde taking precedence, the occasion was dominated by de Valera. I don't think President Hyde, a scholarly, genial and somewhat abstracted man, either noticed or minded though his civil service 'minder', Mr MacDunphy, was not so relaxed about this breach of protocol. But he too was clearly in awe of de Valera.
>
> I was very conscious of the tensions beneath the smooth exteriors of my diplomatic colleagues. Eduard Hempel, the German, is a courteous and affable man with

none of the strutting bravado one associates with the Nazi regime. I am told however that, in spite of being a traditional diplomat, he is a committed Nazi who showed an early loyalty to Hitler. He is tenacious and not to be underestimated and I'm told has some very nasty louts working in the embassy, especially a man called Thomsen, an out-and-out Nazi.

Curiously Hempel seems to have a workmanlike, if strained and formal, relationship with Sir John Maffey. I find Maffey warm – for an Englishman – and essentially decent. He is clearly anxious to persuade de Valera to help the Allied cause in every way possible.

Relations between Maffey and his French opposite number, M. Riviere, are not good. Frankly, I found the Frenchman somewhat difficult and always ready to take offence. But, in truth, his situation is a difficult one.

The Italian is a bit of a buffoon and it seems a doctrinaire anti-cleric, which more or less reflects the views of his Duce. The Spanish ambassador, the Count of Arparza, is new and I have yet to form a view of him but, from his haughty demeanour, I doubt if we will become close.

All in all, we are a small and disparate group in this far-away isolated island – an apparent oasis of calm in a world gone mad. In a sense, this is what de Valera said when he spoke. It was strange that de Valera was addressing us since the event was hosted by President Hyde, but it reflected the political reality in which we find ourselves and provided de Valera with an opportunity which he felt he needed.

De Valera is a poor speaker with a plain, flat accent. There is neither eloquence nor elegance in his words but he does have a powerful sense of presence and of real authority. He is all powerful in his own party – in reality a benevolent dictator, and some would say not always that benevolent. Not a man to be crossed.

He spoke very directly about his country's commitment to neutrality. It was absolute and had the backing of the overwhelming majority of the people and all the political parties. It would be defended in every way necessary. He hoped it could be defended peacefully but, if tough measures were needed, his government would not hesitate to take them. And then he made the point he clearly wanted to drive home to us. Any external threat which would jeopardise this policy of neutrality would be dealt with severely and with determination, no matter where it came from. As he said this, I could detect a note of pure steel in his voice. He was giving due warning and this is the message he wanted to go back to the chancelleries of Britain, Germany, Italy and France tonight.

He was listened to in silence. There could be no ambiguity about anything he said. This was not the de Valera of studied ambiguity or verbal casuistry. This was a man in deadly earnest.

We were offered a glass of very indifferent – possibly even corked – wine afterwards and, somewhat to my surprise, de Valera beckoned me aside. For one normally so cordial – indeed we usually exchange pleasantries about the irony of my being born in Dublin and he in New York – there was no warmth today. He was cold and I quote him directly here.

'I am serious when I say I will not see our neutrality jeopardised from any quarter – belligerent or otherwise. It is based on fragile foundation and threats can come from many quarters. Sometimes from surprising and unexpected sources. I can deal with internal threats, whether it comes from ill-advised and wrongheaded politicians – and you know of whom I speak – or from the IRA, which I will crush. But what worries me is that some other sources give an excuse or a pretence to one or other of the belligerents to misrepresent or misinterpret our neutrality and to put unwanted pressure on us – even to the threat of an invasion. That, your Grace, represents a much greater threat than the ones we know. The unexpected is difficult to prepare for and we will not allow it happen.'

He then softened his tone, enquiring after the health of the Holy Father and assured me of his and Ireland's great fidelity to the Holy See. He reminded me in particular of the special position he had given to our Church in his recent constitution.

It was a warning and a worrying one, but about what I do not know. Clearly the Holy See is not his concern. We have our own neutrality to protect and have no desire to interfere in the politics of this country.

No. He must be concerned about some developments within the Church in Ireland. But if so, why speak to me, not to the cardinal or to the Archbishop of Dublin?

I need to make some enquiries as a matter of urgency.

As Valetti noted, there was no reference to Concannon or Kilderry. But as a betting man, he was prepared to wager that there must be a connection.

24

....

Archie Bowe was furious. Never before in the 50 years as a solicitor had he been angrier. He sat at the desk his father had bought him all those years ago when he joined the practice. He was on his third cigarette of the morning and had told his secretary he was not to be disturbed.

He had long suspected that all was not well with the finances of the diocese of Kilderry and that he, Archie Bowe, who with his father before him had served Kilderry so faithfully and honourably for over half a century, was being deliberately excluded from information that should rightfully have been his. There had been too many surprises.

He had been surprised when, a few months before his death, Bishop Concannon had made a new will, drawn up by another solicitor and which replaced the will Archie had witnessed many years before. Archie had only learned of its existence after Concannon's death, when he was obliged to make it public. And though he hid his feelings, he saw it as a personal humiliation.

That was his first surprise, the first of many. He had been astounded at the small amount of money left in the new will. He knew from the first will that the bishop was a wealthy man and he had serious investments in stocks and shares. There was no mention of them in the new will. He did not know, nor had Concannon ever told him, of the source of this wealth.

He had been forced to assume the bishop had wealthy benefactors, especially since the finances of the diocese had always been properly audited. He had no idea who these benefactors might have been, but realised how carefully Concannon had kept this part of his life hidden from his own legal adviser.

He knew well that Concannon had powerful friends in Dublin and in Rome. He remembered Concannon as a man of power, energetic and ambitious, and around whom there was always an element of mystery.

Bowe had in mind the younger Concannon, not the frail, querulous Concannon of old age. Tall, imperious, always formal in dress with well-cut suits and vestments specially tailored in Rome, speaking with great precision, an accent from which the raw vowels of his humble background had long been elided and a voice that always exuded authority and the rightness of his own views. But most of all, Bowe remembered him as a clever man who was calm and measured and very conscious of his own intellectual superiority.

He was what a bishop should be, reflected Bowe, who had approved of the pomp and power that surrounded Concannon. Not like the present scruffy and very ordinary bishop who, it had been reported, even occasionally visited pubs. Bowe had thought in those days that Kilderry would be merely a staging post for the young bishop on an ecclesiastical career that could end with a major archdiocese and even a red hat. He suspected Concannon thought so too.

But then something happened to stall his career. Bowe had no idea what but, as the years passed, he felt the bishop knew this too. Not that they ever discussed it. In fact, Bowe realised, they had actually discussed very little.

Bowe's first reaction to the new will had been to wonder about the whereabouts of the shares that had been in the orig inal. And the second question had been why Concannon had excluded his family as beneficiaries. Bowe had long regarded the funds gifted to the family of Concannon's sister as a potential scandal, but had never worried much about it. In those days, a bishop was effectively supreme in his own diocese, not answerable to his fellow bishops, remote from Rome and immune to scrutiny from press or public.

But now the family had turned nasty and had virtually accused Bowe of some malpractice. He had hidden his own surprise at this development by taking some pleasure in the discomfiture of the outraged family, whom he had long despised. That had been a mistake. The family immediately assumed he had been in some way complicit and was holding back information. It had been unseemly and very unpleasant for a man who hated any show of emotion or hostility. And the worst part for him was that he was as puzzled as the family, but was obliged to hide his surprise.

And now this morning he had received a letter from one of Dublin's most litigious law firms asking some very impertinent questions about Concannon's estate. They could wait for a reply and they would not be the first snooty Dublin outfit he had seen off. But it was deeply annoying for a man who – rightly as it happened – saw his reputation as being beyond reproach.

An even bigger surprise was when he learned the diocese was conducting its own enquiry in to the whole business without doing him, as he saw it, the courtesy of letting him know. He had not learned this by accident. He had been making discreet phone calls to a number of old and well-placed friends in Dublin. And it had paid off. On his seventh call, this time to the daughter of his old acquaintance Charlie Ruddock, he hit the jackpot.

O'Donnell had not asked Heather to keep the matter confidential – he merely assumed she would. As indeed she probably would except that, when she got a call from her father's old apprentice asking if she had heard any stories or rumours about Kilderry of late, she had no hesitation in telling him about O'Donnell's research into Concannon and his interest in Henry Alsop. Alsop was a new name to Bowe, but he would soon know more.

And as for Peter O'Donnell, Bowe had no difficulty in linking him right back to Kilderry. He had heard his good friend Monsignor Nestor talk from time to time of his nephew Peter, who worked so closely with a Taoiseach of whom Bowe resolutely disapproved.

Nestor was a different matter. He was a priest after Bowe's own heart and he had hoped he would succeed Concannon – not that scruffy priest with no academic background who had got the job. Bowe felt justified in feeling angry with Nestor for not confiding in him and he resented whatever role O'Donnell might have.

But Bowe was, most of all, a professional. He would never lose sight of the bigger picture – his first loyalty was to the diocese of Kilderry and its bishop, whoever he might be. It was time for him to talk to Mullins and Nestor and see how the situation could be rectified. There would be some straight talking.

But in a time of surprises, the biggest of all had landed on Bowe's desk yesterday, six weeks to the day after the death of Thomas Patrick Concannon. It was a large envelope sealed with wax that carried the imprint of the episcopal ring always worn by Concannon. It was hand delivered by a lady who insisted on handing it over personally to Bowe – a fact he appreciated when he saw the contents.

The lady – buxom, red-faced and middle aged – introduced herself as Mrs Brigid Byrne. She was a staff nurse at the Tranquillity nursing home where Concannon had spent his last six months. The bishop had given her the envelope shortly after his arrival and asked her to help him seal it with his ring. He asked her to keep it safely until six weeks after his death and, under no circumstances, let anybody else know.

'He was a nice man, very courteous to the staff and no trouble at all. He even gave me some money in an envelope to thank me for being so kind to him – and it was a decent amount too.'

She stopped for a moment and looked Bowe directly in the eye. 'In my job, I see death all the time and different people face it in different ways. I won't say the bishop wasn't a somewhat troubled and restless soul. He was and, while he was not afraid of death, he was in no great hurry for it to happen and he fought it to the end. To tell the truth, I thought that at his age he would have been anxious to meet his God, but that was not the case. Oh well, in my experience no one – saint or sinner – dies easily. Anyway, I'm here to keep my promise to him.'

When Bowe asked her if others knew of the envelope, she said somewhat sourly only her husband, who was too busy with his farm to pay any attention to her or her stories from the nursing home.

Bowe thanked her and asked her to keep the matter confidential. It was what the bishop would have wanted. She agreed and Bowe carefully checked the seal. It was intact. That at least was a relief.

There were two documents in the envelope. The first was a letter from Concannon – no longer written in his strong distinct calligraphy. The writing was spidery and written with a less-than-steady hand. But it was clear and readable.

My dear Archie,

I write this letter at the end of my life. Soon I will enter that eternity of bliss promised by our Saviour – or maybe not. I have been fortunate to have had ample time to prepare myself for the journey and scrutiny ahead. I realise I have been even more fortunate so late in my life to receive a gift – a cruel gift maybe – of a quality I now realise I lacked through most of my earlier life, the quality of humility.

It is in the spirit of contrite humility I write this letter. May I acknowledge the lifelong loyalty of you and your family to the diocese of Kilderry. Never once have I had reason to doubt your probity, judgement and loyalty during all my years as bishop.

Sadly, I was not as loyal to you as you were to me. I concealed matters from you where I should have kept you informed. For this I offer my sincere apologies but, in so doing, I want to explain to you why I felt obliged to take this course of action and, having done so, to ask of you one final favour. A favour, if you will, from beyond the grave.

In 1939 I was entrusted with what I saw as a grave and sacred trust to help propagate the mission of our Divine Church. In hindsight, what I saw as a sacred responsibility may have been a rash and foolhardy adventure. I know now and have known for years that my actions caused grave perturbations in Church and State and the unfinished business from this matter, now that I am dead, may cause difficulties not just for my successor – a simple man but I believe a good one – but for the wider Church I have served all my life.

I know too that with the passage of time and with the opening of State archives, my mission will be examined in a manner hostile to me and to the Church. Believe me when I say my reputation matters little to me at this stage of my life, but that of the Church must be protected at all costs.

I have taken the trouble to provide an honest account of this episode insofar as my memory allows. Only when you have the full facts can a judgement be made.

I hope you will see that my motives were – at least so I was convinced – in the best interests of the Church in which we both believe.

The account I have written is in a sealed envelope. Unfortunately, much of what I recorded at the time I felt obliged to destroy because of the possibility of its falling in to hostile hands. I felt at the time the consequences of what I recorded could be misinterpreted and used against the Church.

The envelope is only to be opened after my death and in the event, and only in the event, of any controversy or dispute arising from this matter entering the public arena.

You alone, dear Archie will be the sole judge of when or if this envelope should be opened. It is a huge burden of responsibility to place on you but I know you will not fail me.

Yours in Christ Jesus Our Lord
ThomasPatrick

† Kilderry.

Bowe's first reaction was to believe Concannon was concerned – even from the grave – as much about his own reputation as that of his beloved Church. But that was a matter for another day.

And he was shaken. How could he or his father not have known about any of this. Even with the passage of 50 years, Bowe sensed this story was sensational and possibly damaging. He would wait until he spoke to Mullins before opening the envelope. He would abide strictly and to the letter of Concannon's wishes.

But it was time for some very direct talking to Mullins and Nestor. As he was about to make this call, his secretary came in to tell him the bishop needed to speak to him as a matter of urgency.

Archie Bowe looked forward to it.

25

....

February 1 1940

Colonel Dan Bryan was worried. And when he was worried he blinked even more than usual. It was the first thing people noticed about him and it gave him the slightly distracted appearance of an amiable academic, though his moustache added a military touch. It would be easy not to take him seriously.

But that was a mistake Éamon de Valera never made. He did not much like Dan Bryan, who was on the other side in the Civil War – and not just on the other side but regarded as the leading intelligence operator in undermining his Republican forces. More than that, he had been a trusted confidante of Cosgrave in the bitter years of the 1920s and a key figure in the Free State army. He was seen by some of de Valera's people as a man to be purged, along with David Neligan of the CID, when they came in to government. De Valera might have encouraged such talk but he was never part of it.

And more to the point, de Valera rarely let revenge take precedence over his political instincts. When the change of government came in 1932, Neligan went but Bryan stayed in place, knowing that de Valera did not like him and that, under de Valera, he would never get the top army job he so wanted. However, he also knew that de Valera saw him as the best intelligence expert the country had and that his first and only loyalty would be to the State he had helped establish.

So he had continued to be one of Ireland's top spies. His relationship with de Valera had lost some of its frostiness and the shared objective of protecting Ireland's neutrality had brought them together in a common purpose. In fact, it was Bryan's clear-headed appraisal as early as 1936 that had engaged de Valera's attention.

Alone among the army chiefs, Bryan anticipated a major European war. He thought it might happen as early as 1938 but, one way or another, he believed Ireland's defences were utterly inadequate in the event of any invasion. He wanted serious rearmament to start there and then – but it didn't and, when the war broke out, the country had no navy, three training aircraft, an under-manned and under-equipped army and a chronic shortage of military supplies. Bryan argued that the country would fight if it had to, but the only sane policy was to stay out of the war if at all possible.

De Valera agreed, but both men knew that any policy of neutrality was vulnerable and every effort must be made to avoid provoking – even marginally – either of the belligerents. In de Valera's view, Bryan would be a key player in protecting Irish neutrality.

Bryan was a man who understood irony. And it was not lost on him that some of his spying these days was on old comrades and senior civil servants, men regarded as pillars of the establishment but seen now by Bryan as potential threats to the sacred policy of neutrality. The IRA and its bombing campaign in Britain was the obvious threat, but it was not the only group flirting with the Nazis.

Bryan's files told another story, a story he hoped would never need to be told. Nobody else, and certainly not de Valera, had ever seen the full files, but they contained the names of senior civil servants, including some in Justice and External Affairs, a few senior army officers and policemen, a journalist or two, university men and more than a few clerics, mainly from the religious orders who not only had strong anti-British sentiments but had members who were actively prepared to work for a German victory – or at least to lend a hand in the event of a German invasion.

Dear God, thought Bryan, there was even his old colleague and friend from the earliest days, Eoin O'Duffy, who had lost the run of himself completely ever since his fiasco in Spain. He seemed to Bryan to be auditioning these days for the role of Gauleiter should the Nazis invade. And O'Duffy was only one such.

It was Bryan's job to spy on these people and to ensure that de Valera knew everything. Or at least that he knew all that he needed to know. Bryan always believed that a good intelligence chief had to keep some information in reserve.

But the bottom line was that Bryan had to ensure the British were not given any excuse to launch a pre-emptive invasion through the actions of any pro-German group in Ireland. He knew that the fragility of Ireland's neutrality was very real. He knew Churchill detested and distrusted de Valera and blamed him for the split after the Treaty negotiations. He knew there were powerful voices in all parties in Britain who itched to invade Ireland and get their hands on the Treaty ports. He knew he had to keep up his good relations with the British secret service and to ensure they accepted his good faith. No provocation could be risked and, as Bryan well knew, provocation could come in many forms and from the most unexpected places.

It was Bryan, and not the Department of Justice, who de Valera first consulted when an old friend – a priest of course, since most of de Valera's friends were priests from his days in Rockwell and Blackrock – had warned him of rumours of close links between the Spanish embassy and some unnamed bishop and some unnamed civil servants. It was all very vague and just one among *the many rumours and tip-offs relayed to de Valera on a regular basis. De Valera took all of these stories seriously and asked Bryan to check it out.*

And Bryan, from a standing start had made some small progress. What he had found so far – and it was little enough – was enough to persuade him that it should be treated seriously.

It had not been easy to get hard information and he did something he did not do all that often – he sought the co-operation of the Commissioner of the Garda Síochána. He trusted few enough people in the Department of Justice but there was one exception, Michael Kinnane, a hard and tough man, a former British civil servant and, like de Valera, a former student of Blackrock College, although Bryan did not know whether Kinnane even liked de Valera. In fact, he suspected not, but Kinnane was a man who always put his duty first.

Before long, the Spanish embassy on Shrewsbury Road was put under surveillance, its phone tapped, and comings and goings at the embassy noted. It was a sleepy and joyless place where very little seemed to happen but, as Bryan looked at the daily reports, a few facts emerged.

Two bishops had dined at the embassy. The first was the Bishop of Elphin and his visit could be easily enough explained. He was one of Franco's loudest supporters during the Spanish Civil War and he rarely issued a pastoral without some reference to the historic ties binding together the two great Catholic countries. But he was now 86 and feeble, and Bryan doubted if he was up to much, if anything at all.

The other bishop was a different matter altogether. Concannon of Kilderry. Bryan's contacts told him Concannon was a vigorous, strong-willed and ambitious man, seen by many as a future Church leader. In fact, he would have been Archbishop of Dublin had de Valera not intervened to put his own man in. But one way or another,

Concannon was the coming man, with strong Vatican support and a wide web of connections in Dublin. He was a man who did not do things by accident or by chance.

Bryan recalled he had seen Concannon in the Stephen's Green Club. He already had his source in place in the club because de Valera was keen to know what James Dillon, the only serious opponent of neutrality and a member of the club, was saying behind closed doors and who he might be meeting. As it turned out, Dillon was much more careful what he said about political matters and usually dined at the members' table, except when he was meeting with the editor of the Sunday Independent or the singer John McCormack.

Bryan's club contact had no difficulty in getting him a list of all those with whom Concannon dined. It was an impressive list – all eminently respectable and, in some cases, powerful men, all noted for their strong Catholic credentials. On an individual basis, each meeting could be explained but, taken as a group, Bryan began to see a vague pattern emerge – a senior banker from the Munster & Leinster Bank in Dame Street, a high-ranking army officer, senior officials in both the Departments of Justice and External Affairs and, most curious of all, the First Secretary at the Spanish embassy, a Señor Sánchez.

It was not much to go on. There was no indication of what had been discussed. It could all be very innocent indeed.

And there was one more titbit from the club. Bryan's contact was in the habit of chatting to the doorman and the bishop's driver, a man called Ryan, was also very friendly with the doorman. Apparently, they had a shared interest in hurling and both were strong de Valera supporters. The doorman recalled the driver telling him he was up and down to Dublin every week, there were so many meetings – and he had no idea how the bishop had managed to get so many petrol coupons. The curious thing was that the driver, who knew so much else about his boss, had no idea whatsoever who the bishop was meeting. The bishop never told him, just instructed him not to park his car outside whatever house it was, and to come back in an hour or two. The driver did say the meetings were usually in the Ballsbridge area and sometimes even closer to the club.

De Valera had no difficulty in agreeing with Bryan that something might be afoot. He was suspicious and cautious by nature and liked to cover all the possibilities.

Up to now he had not considered a link with Spain as a potential threat. But he knew full well that while Spain, like Ireland, was neutral, it was not a neutrality of principle like his own but a neutrality of convenience. Given the right circumstances, Franco would happily jump on the Axis bandwagon. Even without that happening, the British could take a very dim view of any Irish involvement with Franco.

However remote this possibility of some plot or other was, de Valera told Bryan he was in no mind to see it developing.

It had been de Valera's idea to raise the matter with the nuncio. He was certain from Paschal Robinson's reaction that he had no inkling about anything untoward. He had always found Robinson to be straightforward and without guile, and would have reacted differently if he had been aware of anything underhand going on.

But he knew Robinson well enough to know that, as a former journalist, he would be curious and would make his own enquiries. And he would want to protect any interest the Vatican might have. If there was something afoot, the Vatican would move quickly. It had enough problems as it was without creating new ones.

And herein, thought Bryan, lay their best hope of finding something. If Concannon was scheming, the person best placed to find out might be the nuncio. And if he found out, he would act.

But they had no certainty this would happen and they needed to redouble their own efforts to sniff out what might be happening. It was a question of covering all the angles.

26

....

Archbishop Valetti soon found that de Valera's hunch, about which he knew nothing, was right –Paschal Robinson wanted to find out for himself the reason for de Valera's hostile tone at the diplomatic reception. Not that Valetti knew about this hunch, had only recently heard of de Valera and knew nothing of Ireland's wartime neutrality. But where his own interest was concerned, he was a quick learner and he believed he had found an important file in Robinson's papers.

Valetti was beginning to appreciate and even admire the range of Robinson's contacts at the top levels of Irish society. Valetti had never bothered to make any contacts of his own – Irish politics bored him and interested his bosses at the Vatican so little he saw no point in making the effort.

Robinson clearly had a very different approach, seeing it as part of his job, and Valetti had to admit he was good at it. The file Valetti had in front of him was little more than a series of notes Robinson had compiled after his meeting with de Valera. The notes were no more than excerpts compiled after a series of conversations Robinson had and where he sought to conceal the main purpose of his curiosity.

Valetti had already established that Robinson had remained close, both in spirit and socially, with his Franciscan confrères. Valetti had seen a note where Robinson commented on the strong nationalism and pro de Valera stance of his Irish brethren. Some of their nationalism he had noted was 'chauvinistic and narrowly blinkered' and at times 'distasteful'. That

however – as he noted – was none of his business since the religious orders were all independent entities, answerable only to
their own superiors and not to the Irish bishops or, indeed, to him.

Robinson had noted on his last visit to the Franciscan House
of Studies in Killiney the strong support from a number of the
younger friars for Franco's new regime in Spain – a view he
did not share – and their annoyance at de Valera's reluctance
to endorse that regime and, more particularly, to recognise the
Catholic Church as the 'one, true Church' and to give it real
power rather than the 'window dressing' of Article 44 of the
constitution.

Robinson had heard all of this before and had little time for
it. He had an American belief in the separation of Church and
State but, what he noted now, was the cryptic utterance of the
friar Sebastian, a young man of red face and zealous intensity.
'That will soon change. Things are happening now in Spain
that can and will make a difference here.'

Robinson had tried to pursue this topic a little further, but
Brother Sebastian had clammed up and none of the other friars
was willing to elaborate. Robinson had the strong impression
he had said something he now regretted and may have embarrassed his confrères. But what? What could possibly happen
between Spain and Ireland? What indeed?

The next note was a record of a conversation he had with
Professor Pádraig de Brún of Maynooth. Robinson knew and
liked de Brún. He was a man of great flair and learning, worldly wise and unique among Maynooth professors in having no
ambition to become a bishop. In fact, he had told Robinson that
being a bishop would bore him to death and, as a scholar himself, Robinson believed him.

Robinson knew Maynooth to be a hotbed of clerical gossip,
not always reliable and usually tinged with a spice of malice.

Visiting bishops felt it a safe place to let their guard down and never more so than after one of Maynooth's celebrated dinners with good beef and better wine.

De Brún had no difficulty in opening up to Robinson. Yes indeed, the bishops were divided on Spain. All had supported Franco in the Civil War – some, in de Brún's view, especially the cardinal, were intemperate in their support for the ill-fated Irish Brigade. But now that the war was over, most wanted to move on. They felt that the future of the Church was secure but there remained a small number who believed Ireland had much to learn from Franco about the proper role and respect accorded the Catholic Church in a modern state.

De Brún had little patience with this view and did not think it had much support. Curiously, he felt there was more support for what Salazar was doing in Portugal, where an authoritarian state with traditional values provided a privileged role for the Catholic Church. Apparently, some bishops felt this would be a more appropriate model for Ireland.

According to de Brún, few of the bishops knew anything about either Spain or Portugal – or anywhere else for that matter – and, apart from windy rhetoric, he did not think the debate was going anywhere in a hurry.

Robinson steered de Brún back to the question of Spain. When he asked which bishops had the hardest views, he noted a momentary reluctance. De Brún, however, was not much given to self-denial when it came to expressing his views on the bishops and replied: 'The usual ones, predictable really, Armagh, Elphin, Kerry and Ferns. But there is one unpredictable one and probably the most insistent of them all – Kilderry.'

'Why is Kilderry so different?'

'Because it is hard to see what's in it for him. The most ambitious, the most calculating of them all, or so they say. The others are pious windbags, but not Concannon. He is different. Cold and careerist. Sees himself as a future cardinal, though now getting back to Rome would be his target. Dublin would suit him but Dev has it earmarked for his own man. He is a man driven by the urge for power, though he hides it well. He does not do things by accident. His support for Franco must have some ulterior motive and he may even be working to some-body else's agenda. Mark my words.'

Valetti was now looking at the third note – another *aide-mémoire* rather than a record of any conversation.

Concannon is almost certainly the man de Valera had in mind when he spoke to me, though I am not sure if de Valera has any certainty about his identity. But that could change soon. De Valera has good contacts within the clergy and he is a good friend of de Brún – he probably has a good idea by now.

But what exactly is it that Concannon is doing? Speaking at meetings of the bishops where he has little support is not going to damage the policy of neutrality.

I can be sure de Valera is asking these same questions and I am even more sure he is doing something about it. I am sure he is having Concannon's business and social contacts checked out and probably even having him followed. One thing I have learned here is that the Irish State is good at keeping tabs on people it does not trust.

This has the potential to be very damaging for the Church. I need to ask the same questions as de Valera – and get some answers. But who can I trust?

There were three names pencilled in at the end of the note: CM Gerrity, with a Dublin phone number 62745; Professor James Hogan; and Morgan Dannaher.

Valetti had no idea who any of these men were, but clearly Robinson felt they might be of help. Maybe when he got further in to the files, he might learn more.

He was now confident he could concentrate on Kilderry. He needed to know what they knew and he needed to start thinking about how he might make them talk.

Meanwhile, he would have lunch with Bishop Dominic Irwin – the man he had already dubbed his 'mole in Maynooth'. If he knew him a little better, he might have known that Irwin's sense of independence would never allow him become anyone's mole and, when it came to trading gossip, Irwin usually ended up taking more than giving.

27

....

Archie Bowe decided he would let the bishop talk first. Instead of going to the bishop's palace, he had 'invited' Mullins to his office. This had never happened before, but Bowe felt he had to indicate his displeasure. Something that was not lost on Mullins, who agreed with a gruff grunt.

Bowe looked across the desk at Mullins. He noted the same untidy, rumpled and overweight man he could never see as a 'real' bishop, more a rural parish priest who kept greyhounds and did a bit of farming on the side. But Bowe saw too a tired and frightened man who was beginning to look out of his depth. Mullins began to jabber about the danger of scandal, the major crisis facing the diocese, his own desire only to do what was best for the Church.

Bowe cut in coldly. 'There are some matters I have only recently learned. To say that I find them distasteful and up-setting is to put it mildly. To say that I – who have served this diocese with integrity and loyalty all my life – find I have been deliberately excluded from matters which concern me, I find deeply offensive. But perhaps Dr Mullins, it would be better for you to start at the beginning of this story – and remember I am still your solicitor and you are my client. Lest you forget, I am here to protect your interests and that of the diocese of Kilderry, whoever its bishop may be.'

Mullins had calmed down. He took his pipe from his pocket and prepared to light it. Bowe said he would prefer if he desisted from smoking in his office. This had never happened Mullins before, but he did as he was bid.

He then gave a surprisingly coherent account of the files Nestor had taken from Concannon's retirement home, the discovery of bank accounts, stocks and shares, and some elements of the journal, adding that significant parts of it for the year 1940 and later seemed to be missing. He told of the late bishop's confession to Nestor and the sense of panic they both felt.

'And why, pray, was I not informed?' Bowe asked quietly.

'Because I thought we could handle it ourselves.'

'Or maybe because you saw a great deal of money and felt you were best placed to decide how it could be used and, to do this, you had to keep its existence secret. Because, as you must have realised, you had no certain entitlement to the monies – and still do not, I should add – so you decided to go it alone.'

Mullins was taken aback by the directness. 'There is so much that needs to be done. Social services, poverty, church restoration. That was my only thought and I was afraid the family might try to grab it. I thought we could do this quietly and below the radar, but then things began to get too much for us. It was then we sought expert advice.'

'Expert,' sniffed Bowe. 'You mean Nestor's nephew, the Fianna Fáil fellow. You would hardly call him an expert. Expert on what?'

'He's been very helpful,' said Mullins, who had begun to regret following Nestor's suggestion. 'He's found out a great deal for us and he can be trusted. You should talk to him. He will tell you everything he knows.'

Bowe had expected a stouter defence. He was deeply resentful of the intrusion of this 'outsider' in what he considered his exclusive domain, but he was also a realist. He needed every piece of information he could get and if Peter O'Donnell could give him that information he was prepared to swallow his pride. He agreed to meet O'Donnell at the earliest possible opportunity.

Now that he had established and asserted his position, it was his turn to talk. He told of the abuse and misrepresentation he had endured from Concannon's family, including the legal threats from the Dublin lawyers. He told of the information he had got from the other Dublin solicitor – though not mentioning Heather Ruddock by name – and then waited to drop his real bombshell.

Bowe was a good storyteller with a solicitor's eye for the sharp detail. The arrival of Mrs Brigid Byrne in his office with her tale of Concannon's deathbed instructions and the handing over of the sealed envelope, with presumably the bishop's *apologia*, lost nothing in the telling. He noted that, as he spoke, the bishop looked more and more uncomfortable.

Mullins' first reaction was to ask what was in that last letter. Bowe's reply was cool, almost supercilious.

'I have no idea. The bishop clearly stipulated that the envelope was only to be opened in the event of any controversy or questioning of his reputation becoming a matter of public controversy. To the best of my knowledge, but you may know differently, that has not happened. And if all goes well, may never happen. In which case, the envelope will remain safely and securely sealed in my safe.'

'It's too late, too late,' blurted Mullins. 'Too many people know. They're sniffing around even now.'

He told Bowe of Nestor's indiscreet remarks to JJ Gilmartin and of the sudden interest being shown by the papal nuncio, not to mention the reported rantings of the Concannon's nephew. And he reminded Bowe what he had heard from his unnamed Dublin solicitor.

'It can only be a matter of time. We need to know what the story is. How can we defend ourselves or even explain to ourselves if we don't know the full story? And we have that story in your envelope.'

Bowe was more worried than he looked and he agreed with much of what had just been said. But, for the moment at least, he was not for moving.

'I must act in accordance with the late bishop's wishes. Rumours are unpleasant but are not sufficient, at least for now. I am not saying they can be ignored, but I will need something more solid before I can proceed. Dr Concannon may have had good reasons to keep his secret, and unless I can be persuaded otherwise, it will remain so.'

Mullins realised there was no point in arguing and all he could do was to ask Bowe to think again. 'Well, I will not be unreasonable. I want you to understand my first duty will be to the diocese. Let me hear what O'Donnell has to say and then we will look at the matter again.'

He was already coming to the view that, sooner or later, he would have to open the envelope. But he would let Mullins sweat a little longer. He deserved it.

28

....

February 23 1940

Colonel Dan Bryan was quietly pleased he was making progress. Between spies and subversives, he had more than enough on his plate to ensure the British were given no excuse to invade Ireland and, in particular, given no reason to suspect any collusion with Germany and its allies. He was a man who planned meticulously and felt he had covered all of the possible angles, but now he had something he had not anticipated – a bishop clearly hatching some conspiracy involving Spain.

Bryan had no idea what it might be but felt, whatever it was, it meant trouble. And it was his job to deal with trouble before it happened. But Spain? Surely Spain was like Ireland, a neutral country, and no harm could come of that. But Bryan was sure that the British did not see it that way. Franco was a fascist, no lover of democracy and, if he judged the circumstances right, would give his support to Germany. Bryan knew de Valera saw it that way too and there was no value in being wise after the event.

He had to find out what Concannon was up to and he felt he was on his way to doing that. He now had a list of all those Concannon had been dining with in the Stephen's Green Club and he was working on finding out the houses Concannon called to on his Dublin trips.

In fact, Dublin being the small city it was, he found he knew (or knew of) all the names and had started looking for further details about them all.

First on his list was EJ Nolan of the Munster & Leinster Bank. Bryan knew of Ted Nolan and what he knew he did not like. He was a careful, disdainful man who took himself very seriously. Bryan's friend in the bank, Bob Ryan, told him Nolan was noted for his meanness, especially in his dealings with his staff. However, like most office bullies, he was extremely deferential to those above him and liked to boast of his contacts with leading politicians and members of the Catholic hierarchy. He spoke frequently at Chamber of Commerce dinners, where his topics ranged from wasteful public expenditure and the extravagance of government back to wasteful public expenditure. 'A joyless little bugger,' was how Ryan summed him up.

But why should Concannon be meeting him? Looking for money? Money for what?

Then there was FX Grace from the Department of External Affairs. Bryan knew and liked him, even if it was a good 10 years since they last met. He had been a senior clerk in the Indian Civil Service when the War of Independence started. He had given up his job – a secure and pensioned one – to come back and work with Desmond FitzGerald in the Dáil's propaganda department. He was good at it too, reflected Bryan, who remembered Grace as flamboyant and a little on the wild side, with a reputation for drinking too much and a liking for 'loose' women, both of which were frowned on by de Valera but seemed to endear him to Michael Collins.

Grace was one of the first people appointed to the new Department of External Affairs. Bryan had heard he married – for money some said – and had now become very respectable. When Bryan thought about him, which he had no reason to do for years, he found it strange that someone who should be a top ambassador by now was in a bit of a backwater and not likely to go much further. Something clearly had happened to his career.

Bryan was not a man to speculate. He would find out very quickly what had happened but he was curious about him dining with a bishop. He had been one of the few self-proclaimed atheists in the old days.

And Mortimer Buckley. What was he doing on the list? The sourest man Bryan knew. A Kerryman, Bryan recalled, and cute even by Kerry standards. Laid low during the Troubles and then jumped in to a handy job in the new Department of Home Affairs. He liked to portray himself as devoutly religious and something of a moral crusader. He liked 'hard lines', whether it was against prostitution, drink, aliens, jazz, English newspapers, immoral books and films, or whatever the Jesuits were currently against.

But Bryan was not fooled and felt nothing but contempt for Buckley. He had a file – he had many and never forgot a single one of them – from the London police who had apprehended Buckley in compromising and unsavoury circumstances. And not with a woman, mused Bryan. Buckley had managed to get the charges dropped, but not before London Special Branch had sent the file to their counterparts in Dublin, who shortly afterwards handed it to Bryan. Not for the first time a file that might come in very useful. For the moment, however, Bryan wanted to know what Buckley was talking to the bishop about and who had brought them together?

Bryan was surprised to see the name of Eoin O'Duffy on his list. Surprised, but not too surprised. Bryan was a friend of O'Duffy's from the old days. There was a time when he even admired him, especially the way he crushed the army mutiny of 1924 and his early years as chief of police. Then the shine began to wear off as O'Duffy started to lose the run of himself, believing his own propaganda – and boy was he good at drumming up all that shameless self-publicity and believing he knew better than the government. It was Bryan who had persuaded Cosgrave in 1931 to drop O'Duffy if he got back to power. In the event, de Valera did it as quickly as he could – and, in spite of all the opposition outrage, Bryan thought he was right.

As indeed he was, as events quickly showed – the delusional thinking that he could be an Irish Mussolini, the catastrophic adventure in Spain, and even now flirting with the IRA and the Nazis, fancying himself as Germany's Gauleiter in Ireland. Bryan privately felt O'Duffy should be locked up in the Curragh with the IRA for the duration of the war, but for some reason he still liked O'Duffy, seeing him as more a fool than a knave. But dangerous. And what did the bishop want from him?

There were two others on Bryan's list. The first was Professor James Hogan – again someone Bryan knew well. They had been together in Intelligence in the early days. Bryan had always seen Hogan as academically brilliant but short on common sense and political judgement. He knew that Hogan and O'Duffy disliked each other – in fact it was Hogan who had precipitated O'Duffy's fall from the leadership of the Blueshirts. Hogan was obsessed with the dangers of international communism but Bryan could not see him involved in any conspiracy that included O'Duffy – indeed they could barely be in the same room together.

The last name on Bryan's list was the strangest of all. Joe Bradley. Bryan recognised him as a rough diamond, a hard man even by the standards of the Troubles. He was a hitman and some of Bryan's colleagues felt he liked the work he did more than the cause he served. Just before the end of the Civil War, he emigrated without notice to the US and was not heard of for some years. He returned in 1934, seemingly prosperous but with no indication as to the source of his wealth. Of course, there were rumours that the skills he had picked up in the Troubles had been put to good use and there was talk of bootlegging, but there was no proof of anything.

He bought in to an old and failing import and export firm called Goolde and Goolde, quickly got rid of the existing owners and was now one of the richest men in Ireland. It was suspected the firm was a cover for some sort of illegal operations, but no evidence emerged. Now, nearly a decade after his return, Bradley (although not quite an established part of the country's social scene yet) socialised with some politicians, bankers and horse owners – even if many doors, especially at the upper levels, were still firmly closed to him.

These were the people Concannon was meeting, all more than once, with the exception of Hogan. Bryan knew straight away that Mortimer Buckley would be the weak link – a bit of blackmail always helped – but he could wait a little longer. He first had to find out about the houses Concannon visited on his Dublin trips and about his man in the Spanish embassy, Señor Sánchez.

He would only raise suspicions by asking any questions of External Affairs or the Irish embassy in Madrid. Word would get back – it always did – and Bryan wanted to avoid that. He would do what he increasingly did these days – go to his friends in British intelligence and the man he dealt with in their embassy, Norman Archer, with whom he had built up a good relationship on the basis that neither would lie to the other. They would, of course, be curious as to what he was up to, but he knew that, in this particular, world favours were traded, not given and there would be a price to pay.

29

Archbishop Valetti was learning the hard way that ploughing through archives could be arduous and unrewarding, especially when no effort had been made to index the material. Robinson had been neat and ordered, but clearly somebody else – possibly one of his successors or more likely a nosy clerk – had been through the papers since his death and had left them in some disarray. Valetti had no idea what they might have been looking for, maybe nothing at all and it may have happened when the old nunciature in the Phoenix Park was being vacated long after Robinson's death.

His real problem was that his latest trawl had yielded very little. He was looking for a follow-up after Robinson's strange meeting with de Valera. All he could find was a memo headed 'The Church and Irish Neutrality'.

April 1940

Met C.M. Gerrity at the reception in the British embassy. He is the dominant figure in the US embassy but is smart enough not to let Ambassador Gray realise this. I am told from D.C. that the Secretary of State respects his judgement, which is not always the case with Mr Gray. Gerrity disapproves of Ireland's adherence to neutrality and doubts its sustainability, but does not underestimate de Valera and admires his tough policy with the IRA.

I asked what he saw as the main threats to neutrality, apart from the IRA. The only real danger, he said, was

Britain's perception of its own best interest. He said it was clear to him that, if Ireland's neutrality endangered its own security and gave an advantage to the Germans, then Britain would invade and seize the Treaty ports. And to justify the invasion, any excuse will do. He said any evidence of groups in Ireland – and they don't have to have official sanction – who are aiding Germany or harming the British effort would be enough of an excuse to act. He understands de Valera's paranoia and thought he was right to be paranoid. He could not afford any laxity.

I probed him to see if he had any idea as to what sort of groups might fit this bill. 'Oh, the usual suspects,' he said, 'the IRA or one of its splinter groups. General O'Duffy, or one of the variety of crypto-fascist groups or even some crack-potted religious fanatics – as you probably know yourself.'

I was slightly taken aback by this last remark and assured him that, while I was aware of some of these groups, I did not think they amounted to very much and, as far as I knew, they had no support from any of the bishops. I added that, while some of the bishops might be anti-British, they would not get involved with these groups. I then asked him if he had heard any rumours to the contrary.

His answer unsettled me slightly. He agreed that yes indeed some of 'your bishops', as he called them, were anti-British – and maybe especially the cardinal in Armagh – but he did not see any of them as pro-Nazi.

'However, and here may I speak directly, a few of them seem to be warm admirers of Salazar and Franco. All I can say is they must never have been to Spain or Portugal and seen at first-hand what these regimes are like to speak as they do.'

When I asked him what bishops he had in mind, he said he could never remember their names, but added that if he did hear anything out of the ordinary he would let me know.

As always, I wondered if he knew more than he was telling me. They usually do.

The memo concluded with a short note:

Mr Morgan Dannaher is shortly to move to the Vatican. He will visit me in the near future. Have yet to speak with Professor Hogan of University College Cork.

By now Valetti was getting tired of all this archive work. He saw four more boxes lined up for his inspection. He needed a break and, maybe, he now knew enough to do a bit of digging of his own. It was time to get out and about.

On an impulse, he picked up the phone and asked his secretary to get him Bishop Dominic Irwin. Irwin was surprised, but pleased, to get this unexpected call. He was even more pleased when the nuncio told him he would value his advice on a sensitive matter. Irwin said he would be in Dublin in two days and they agreed to meet for lunch.

Valetti reflected on what it was he needed to know. Basically, he needed to know how Concannon had been seen by his fellow bishops, if anything was suspected or seen as odd, and if Irwin was aware of any skeletons in cupboards. Valetti had already read all the obituaries of Concannon, all of which were uniformly respectful and uninformative. Par for the course, thought Valetti. If there had been something untoward, it would have been well and truly swept under the carpet.

If anyone still living knew of any secrets, it would be Irwin. He was the longest-serving bishop – 31 years – which was far too long in Valetti's view, but it might come in useful now.

He had a short biographical note on Irwin on his desk. He was only 35 when appointed in 1966. The Vatican must have seen a future for him to be appointed at such a young age, but clearly that future never came or he would not have been left all those years in a diocesan backwater. Had he blotted his copybook or had he made powerful enemies? One or both was certain. He had better find out and no better source than the fount of all clerical gossip, JJ Gilmartin. 'Maybe I can arrange some sort of papal honour for Gilmartin to keep him sweet. Something meaningless like making him a monsignor,' Valetti mused.

A quick call to Gilmartin gave him a fuller picture. First, he was surprised that Gilmartin, who normally spoke disparagingly about his fellow clerics, was warm about Irwin. 'An absolute gentleman and very good company. A bit obsessed with liturgy but his priests like him. He knows more than all the others put together about the history of the hierarchy. A truly lovely man.'

'Why was he never promoted? Why was he left in that backward place?'

'He made enemies shortly after he became bishop. You remember *Humanae Vitae.*'

Valetti did. Pope Paul VI's encyclical banning all form of contraception. Valetti thought it was crazy at the time and it had caused deep divisions everywhere.

'Well, Dominic spoke out against it and, for once, the archbishops of Dublin and Armagh agreed on something – they came down on him like a sack of spuds. Neither ever forgave him and he was never going to go anywhere after that. And of course, he got no support from his fellow bishops. Most were probably pleased to see this young high flyer shot down and he was under suspicion ever after. The strange thing is he never became bitter, just kept his head down and got on with his job. And he never became pompous. He was a great loss.'

Valetti was surprised to hear Gilmartin so positive about anyone. Irwin was his man if it was information about the past he wanted.

He had his secretary book a table for two in the Lobster Pot in Ballsbridge. No stuffy club for him.

30

....

Johnny Ryan had not been fooled for one minute by Tommy Newrie. He did not believe Newrie was an innocent academic historian doing 'research' on the old bishop. Nor did he think it a coincidence that the visit should take place so soon after the reading of the bishop's will.

Of course, he had been pleased with the £2,000 he had been left by the bishop – but not overpleased. In truth, he had expected a good deal more. Concannon had told him on that last day he drove him as Bishop of Kilderry that he would look after him, that Johnny at least had been loyal to him to the end and that he would make sure the car – by now a Mercedes – could be bought at a cheap price if Johnny wanted to start the hackney business he told Concannon was his great ambition.

In the event, Johnny bought the car and started his business. But there was no cheap price. Bishop Mullins saw Johnny as part of the old gang, the old 'codology' as he called it, and while glad to be rid of him and the Mercedes, he had insisted on 'market value' no more, no less.

Johnny had not been present at the reading of the will and had no inkling that Murdock and the family had been excluded. In fact, he had expected them to be the main beneficiaries – a point Richard E Murdock had made to him more than once. He had never wondered that a bishop could be so wealthy. For him it was just one more of the many 'mysteries' the Catholic Church expected its followers to believe and he had neither the inclination nor the interest to ask questions.

He was also one of the very few people who actually liked Richard. What he did not know, but probably suspected, was that it was a relationship Murdock cultivated. He knew Johnny spent more time in the bishop's company than most and that the bishop liked Johnny. So whenever he came to Kilderry, he made a point of taking Johnny out for a few drinks or occasionally a meal.

Johnny liked free drinks and Murdock liked an audience for his many stories about himself and his exploits. Johnny, who was timid by nature and married to a somewhat fearsome wife, was enthralled by Murdock's stories, especially his main topic – his extramarital affairs, or his 'swordsmanship' as he called it, boasting that 'no woman anywhere, if you get her at the right time and the right place, will say no'. The stories, whether true or contrived, did much to feed Johnny's imagination and for that he was always grateful – and in some awe.

So he had phoned Murdock immediately after Archie Bowe, the old snob, had written to him to tell him the news of his bequest, expecting Murdock would have got his own good news and would be a happy man.

'Well, no more worries. You must be in great form. You had to wait a while, like myself, but I'm sure it was all worthwhile in the end.'

He was not prepared for the vehemence of the response.

'What the fuck do you mean? The miserable old fucker left me nothing. Not even the steam off his piss. Not a mention of me or the family – the only family he ever had and all we did for him. I still can't believe it and there is no way I will accept it. I will fight to the end for what is rightfully mine.'

'So who did he leave it to?'

'That's the fucking point. There was no money – no real money. Just a few bequests – 20 grand to the bloody papal nuncio, the same again to some Spanish crowd and the bloody Irish College, and yourself. That was that. I thought there would be at least a million there. I was not just expecting it, I was fucking depending on it.'

'But he must have left it to someone before drawing up that will. Bishop Mullins maybe?'

'Maybe. Or maybe someone robbed it or got to him while he was soft in the head. I'm going to find out if it's the last thing I do.'

Johnny was certain of one thing. Concannon was never 'soft in the head'. He knew that from the nurses who had looked after him. No one had pulled a fast one, but he did not say that to Murdock.

'What do you think might have happened?'

'I'm certain it was that ignorant bogman Mullins, that fucking imposter of a bishop. And he was probably helped by that creepy arsehole Nestor. It has to be them.'

'What makes you so sure?'

'Two things. The will was not drawn up by Archie Bowe. It was witnessed by another solicitor –Cooney from Cloghan – and only delivered to Bowe on the bishop's death. Bowe was furious and, even though he tried to hide it, he was as astonished at the contents as I was. Secondly, I know files were taken from the bishop's house after he went to the nursing home. It had to be Mullins or Nestor.'

Murdock did not elaborate on how he knew this – and Johnny did not ask. He just said he would keep his eyes and ears open.

So when Tommy Newrie turned up in Hickson's pub, he was not too surprised. He found Newrie polite and pleasant, and free with his money. He made sure not to show any suspicion or even curiosity as to why Newrie should have sought him out. He knew immediately this was part of a bigger game and, for the moment at least, any loyalty he had was with the Murdocks. And he might even get some clue as to what had happened.

What surprised him in looking back at their conversation was that Newrie had made no mention at all of the bishop's reputed wealth and seemed to be interested only in the bishop's politics and visits to Dublin. Newrie must have known already about the money and didn't need to ask. Or so it seemed to Johnny.

Before phoning Murdock, he made one further enquiry. It would be useful to know if there was any connection between Newrie and Bishop Mullins. In fact, he thought Newrie had been very vague about the reason for his interest in Concannon. He said he was interested in history but Johnny could see no academic credentials apart from him mentioning he was a graduate of UCD – but that was in medicine. As far as Johnny could fathom, he was some sort of a bone-setter in St Vincent's. But Newrie had given him a phone number where he could be contacted and he had written it on the *Evening Herald.* It took him another day to find the paper again. Then he contacted Murdock with his story and Newrie's phone number.

It would be interesting to see what Murdock made of it, but it at least reassured Murdock that he, Johnny Flowerpot, was on his side.

31

....

March 4 1940

'*Do the English never learn? Do they never vet their own people?*' *Colonel Dan Bryan asked himself as he read the report in front of him from Daniel Woodman.*

Woodman was one of Bryan's most valued sources in Britain, an assistant editor of The Times and to all who knew him a paid-up member of the Tory establishment. But Bryan had known another Daniel Woodman, a committed and effective member of Michael Collins' staff during the War of Independence.

His name then was Donal Mac Choille and he reported directly to Bryan. Bryan remembered a fresh-faced and very funny young Kerryman with a talent for mimicry and a seemingly disarming candour, which persuaded far too many people – especially women – to tell him things that might better have been left untold. Mac Choille was a journalist with the Irish Catholic – a newspaper not much favoured by Dublin Castle because of its strident nationalism, but not seen as part of the mainstream rebel side.

Mac Choille was a particularly good tennis player, which gave him a ready entrée to Donnybrook Tennis Club, where he had no trouble finding favour with a series of army wives. They tended to tell him more than they should over afternoon tea or occasionally even over a gin and tonic. Bryan knew it often went much further than a gin and tonic and trusted Mac Choille's discretion not to endanger any of his sources.

The information had been useful but Mac Choille, bit by bit, began to feel uneasy about what he was doing. These feelings came to a head when the husband of one of his sources, a woman of whom he had become very fond, was kidnapped, roughed up and shot. Mac Choille knew the information that led to his seizure could only have come from him and he was filled with self-disgust and self-loathing, resulting in a sort of nervous breakdown.

Bryan felt sorry for him but, knowing that a damaged spy was a danger to all, took him off his books just as he was to do with Emmet Dalton after Collins' death. He sent him off to recuperate in Mount Mellary, then had him anglicise his name to Daniel Woodman and got him a job with a Catholic newspaper in Scotland. That was the end of the war for Mac Choille and no record of his role survived.

That was in late 1920 and Bryan had kept up discreet contact with Woodman in the years since. Woodman gradually integrated himself and prospered in his new surroundings. He quickly outgrew the Catholic paper, spent 10 years with the Glasgow Herald and then on to The Times. During that time, he acquired an English wife and an uppercrust English accent, and had been as accepted in London society as his fellow Irishman, Brendan Bracken, with the double difference that nobody suspected his Irish roots and he did not make enemies.

Bryan was not a man to forget a favour owed. When he met Woodman in London in 1935 he reminded him that once a spy always a spy and he would be grateful for any information he might have about the attitudes of the top English politicians, civil servants and business people with regard to Ireland, or 'Éire' as they had taken to calling it. In return, he could depend on Bryan's support and confidentiality. And Bryan had even got Woodman to write a few short articles showing Irish neutrality in a slightly favourable, or at least more understandable, light.

Bryan had Woodman's latest report on his desk. It made dis-

*turbing reading. Some ministers were convinced a German inva-
sion was now inevitable and, once again, pressure was growing
about seizing the ports. 'Those bloody ports' as Bryan called them
– Cobh, Berehaven and Lough Swilly. Woodman reported that
the Admiralty had now advised the War Cabinet that possession
of the ports could add considerably to the safety of their Atlantic
convoys. De Valera would be asked again and the expected refusal would be followed by 'a much tougher line'. There was no
indication what this line might be, but they could expect trouble.
De Valera had no friends and some serious enemies in the British
Cabinet.*

*Bryan's first job this wet morning was to get this disturbing
news to de Valera, who would be neither surprised nor intimidated. Bryan still did not like de Valera, but he did admire his
steeliness.*

*But there were other disturbing reports on his desk and, as soon as
he got back from de Valera, he turned his attention to them.*

*The first concerned his old comrade Eoin O'Duffy. Bryan was
now becoming angry with O'Duffy. Any affection between them
had long disappeared and he viewed O'Duffy's ego as a real
source of danger to the policy of neutrality – the only policy that
mattered as far as Bryan was concerned.*

*O'Duffy had dined the previous evening in the Red Bank
restaurant with Henning Peterson, the key Nazi figure in the German embassy. Peterson was trusted by the Nazi inner circle in
Berlin much more than Ambassador Hempel, who Bryan saw as
an each-way bet man and who de Valera respected. Bryan knew
from other sources that Peterson would have the task of setting up
a 'Quisling' type government in the event of a German invasion
and had been sounding out some civil servants and army officers
– some of them very senior indeed. He asked himself once again if
O'Duffy was auditioning for the role of Irish Gauleiter?*

O'Duffy, what a buffoon but not funny anymore. Bryan had told de Valera more than once to lock him up in the Curragh but Dev demurred. Bryan was sure his reason was party political – he was an embarrassment to Fine Gael out of jail but might assume martyr status if locked up. Bryan's worry was that O'Duffy and his flirtation with the Nazis could give the British a very plausible reason to invade. O'Duffy, after all, was a former chief of army staff, a former chief of police and a former party leader and, it could be argued, he was a person of real consequence. Bryan knew the reality was different – O'Duffy was a busted flush – but it could suit the British to represent him otherwise.

Bryan made a note to increase the surveillance on O'Duffy.

Then there was that bishop. Concannon. Something serious was going on. De Valera's warning to the nuncio had not made any difference. Maybe they should have been more explicit with the nuncio – but then what was there to be explicit about. Maybe he should have a word with him himself and with the only Irish bishop he really trusted.

There had been another meeting of Concannon's group, once again in the Stephen's Green Club and once again in the private dining room. All the usual gang – Ted Nolan from the Munster & Leinster Bank, FX Grace from External Affairs, Mortimer Buckley from Justice, O'Duffy, Joe Bradley and someone from the Spanish embassy. But James Hogan was not present and Bryan found this unusual. Hogan, he knew, was very conscientious about attending meetings. Was he having second thoughts? Well, there was only one way to find out.

That would be his first priority today and he also needed someone he could trust among the bishops. There was only one such person. He would not be too happy but, for Bryan, the stakes were high enough to warrant it.

First he would see what Hogan had to say.

He had known Hogan from the old days. Very clever, a genius in many ways but he had no real judgement, especially of people. Always impatient to change the world, he could be single-minded, even obsessive, and not always alive to the consequences of what he was doing.

His obsession in the 1930s had been 'the Communist threat', which he tended to see everywhere. He even wrote a book Could Ireland Become Communist? The answer to his own question was that he believed it could. And easily enough too. De Valera did not like the book, with its insinuation that Fianna Fáil was 'soft' on communism and that de Valera was a 'Kerensky' type figure.

De Valera got his opportunity when it was discovered that Hogan had based his case to a great extent on files he had been illegally given by former colleagues in Military Intelligence. He probably felt he was safe enough while Cosgrave remained in power, but when de Valera came to power in 1932 some old scores were settled and, for some reason, de Valera had a particular dislike of Hogan. He was brought before a Military Tribunal and charged with treason. The case failed but it was a close-run thing.

Bryan had not been involved in giving the intelligence to Hogan and would have refused had he been asked. It was this which, more than any other factor, persuaded de Valera to keep him on. Hogan for his part believed, wrongly as it happened, that Bryan had some hand in his acquittal. Bryan was happy to let both de Valera and Hogan see it in different ways.

Hogan's next obsession was with the Corporate State, which he claimed was the Pope's blueprint for a modern and Catholic society. Hogan wrote much of the programme for O'Duffy's Blueshirts but when he saw – and he was the first to say so – O'Duffy getting out of control, he quickly jumped ship and, in so doing, mortally wounded the new movement.

Bryan liked Hogan and saw him as a man of integrity and

academic brilliance, but devoid of judgement and common sense.

So he was not fully surprised when he saw his name cropping up on Concannon's list. But what exactly was he up to?

There was only one way to find out.

He looked at his watch. It was 10.30. There would probably be someone on the switch in University College Cork by now. There was, but he was told in a querulous Cork accent that the Professor never came in before 11. He left a message asking Hogan to call him as a matter of urgency.

Hogan was back to him within the hour.

Bryan wasted no time on preliminaries. 'Well James. Some strange company you're keeping. I've had to save you from yourself before – what nonsense are you up to this time?'

There was a silence and then: 'You know Dan, I was half expecting this call. I know very little and am getting out of this nonsense. I won't talk on the phone. I will be in Dublin in two days. I have a meeting in the National University and can meet you then. Leave a note in 49 Merrion Square saying where you would like to meet me and I will take it from there.'

'That's fine – but one more thing. Don't speak to anyone or get out of anything until we meet. That is not advice – it's an order.'

Before he left his office, he wrote a short letter to his old friend Michael Fogarty, Bishop of Killaloe, to tell him he could expect him for lunch in Ennis tomorrow. He was confident the letter would arrive in time. He was not too confident the bishop would be pleased to see him. But that did not bother him one bit.

32

....

March 5 1940

Dan Bryan made an early start for Ennis. It was a miserable grey March day with little or no traffic, but the recent rain had left plenty of surface water on the substandard roads. The bad state of the roads had its own compensations mused Bryan, whoever invades will get little help from them, but he was pleased that all signposts had been removed. But then, whoever the invader is, they will be able to depend on some local help – O'Duffy and the IRA will help the Germans, while the British will have no shortage of collaborators either.

As they passed through Inchicore, his driver handed him the morning papers. Even with his many sources, Bryan felt there was always something to be got from a careful reading. Apart from noting that London had endured another night of heavy bombing with at least twelve fires, and that Church and State, including de Valera, had turned up at Dublin's pro-Cathedral to celebrate the anniversary of the papacy of Pius XII, his eye was caught by a debate in the Senate.

Apparently, two of the small number of anti-neutrality senators, Douglas and MacDermot, had been mildly critical of official policy. For this they had been savaged by two of de Valera's bare-knuckle senators, McEllin and Quirke, who accused them of treachery and worse. As far as Bryan was concerned, what they were saying reflected de Valera's real feelings on the subject, but he had to go no further than a few more paragraphs to get the official line. It was a bland admonishment from Dev's loyal minister Sean T O'Kelly, who warned senators 'they had to walk warily and watch their steps and words so as not to give offence to one side or the other involved in the war'.

And that was it in a nutshell, thought Bryan, and underlined for him the utter importance of his task. Whatever it was Concannon was up to could tip the scales the wrong way. He had to find out what it was and stop it in its tracks. If that meant being rough, then so be it.

Most of the traffic he encountered was horse-drawn and there were few enough people about. Naas was deserted, Abbeyleix a little busier, but at least Portlaoise offered some sign of life.

As he drove through Durrow, a few miles from his native Kilkenny, he allowed himself a few memories – growing up as the eldest of 12 on his parent's farm in Dunbell, heading off at age 16 to study medicine at UCD and then, after 1916, finding himself in the Volunteers, where his talent for intelligence work was quickly spotted. He eventually assumed a key role in the new army, right up to the present moment. And hopefully it would go further. For a farmer's son, just 40 years of age, he had not done too badly.

His first stop was in Nenagh to have a cup of tea with the owner of the Hibernian Hotel, an old friend from the Troubles and a man well placed to give him a good assessment of the popular mood.

'Very uneasy' was how his man in Nenagh saw it.

'Radio Éireann gives no news, the papers even less and the government seems very remote from the people. Maybe the government has no choice but, in the absence of real news, all sorts of rumours abound. If you believe all the rumours, the Germans have landed in five different places. There was even a landing in Bansha! And, of course, there are spies everywhere. The unlikeliest people have been named as spies, including a German priest

over in Rockwell. As harmless a man as you could find, but it was nasty for him – especially since it emerged the rumour started in the college itself. There's a lot of that sort of thing around and it could turn nasty yet.'

'And what about the heroes. Any sign of a stir from that quarter?'

'Quiet enough since you opened up the Curragh for them. They don't come in here, but I'm told they still have some support in the Boherlahan and New Inn areas. But since all the IRA leaders are locked up, it's mainly armchair generals and, from what I hear, they are mainly in Dublin.'

Then on to Limerick, sleepy damp and shabby, with little evidence of much commercial activity – or activity of any kind. The Limerick-Ennis road was the worst yet, but Bryan arrived at the bishop's fine house, Westbourne, on the edge of Ennis in time for lunch.

Bishop Michael Fogarty's welcome was polite, but not overly warm. Bryan knew why. They had once been close friends and Fogarty had been a real help in calming some of the more anti-Sinn Féin bishops during the War of Independence. Bryan liked to think of him as his spy in Maynooth, but he knew Fogarty would have been offended at such an appellation.

There had been a coolness on Fogarty's part since 1932 and Bryan knew it was because he was now working for de Valera – if there was one man Fogarty hated, it was de Valera. The hatred was simply enough explained. Fogarty believed de Valera could have prevented the Civil War but did not do so, for which he could never forgive him.

The hatred was made all the more implacable by the fact that de Valera was the local TD for Clare, heading the poll in every election and adored by his followers, who far outnumbered all other parties. That was a particularly bitter pill for Fogarty to swallow since de Valera made a point of befriending many of the younger priests and charming the nuns in the many convents in the diocese. As Bryan liked to remark, Dev liked his revenge served cold.

Bryan had been thinking about this on the way down – the way some hatreds and enmities from that time, and it was less than 20 years ago now, had hardened and intensified in the intervening years. If anything, they were worse now and would be brought to the grave. And maybe passed on to the next generation.

Bryan reckoned, he himself had plenty of reasons to be bitter but, like many others, he just got on with it, adopting a live-and-let-live attitude. His own relationship with de Valera exemplified this. He would never like him, but he would never be less than fully professional.

Fogarty's welcome was civil but with little warmth. 'Well Dan. Still working for the Long Fella. Rather you than me.'

'No, my lord. I'm working for Ireland. I don't like de Valera any more than you do, but I am loyal to this State. I helped set it up and will serve loyally whoever the people elect.'

Fogarty allowed himself a wintery smile.

'Ah fair enough Dan. You were always straight and I suppose you could be called a survivor. Willie Cosgrave speaks well of you and that's good enough for me. I told him you were coming down and he said I could trust you.'

Fogarty was an old-style bishop. He had already been in Killaloe since 1904. Looking at him, it was clear to Bryan he would be there for many more years to come. He was a generous host. Bryan knew little enough about wine and was regarded as a teetotaller, but on occasion allowed himself a quiet drink. He knew enough to know the white wine that accompanied the poached salmon was the real thing. Not for the first time he noted that being a bishop had its own compensations.

He got to the point of his visit quickly.

'The country is in very real danger of being invaded and, if we are, there will be bloodshed. We will have to resist but we will not last long. Or maybe we will, but one way or other there will be bloodshed. And we will have our own traitors settling scores. We've seen that once in our own lives and neither of us want to see it again.

'My job is to ensure that neither side, British nor German, is given any excuse to invade. Any suggestion that our neutrality is not even-handed would be enough so there must not be the slightest suggestion of that. That is why the IRA is locked up and why there will be executions.

'But the IRA is not the only danger. There are powerful people who would welcome a German invasion. Your old friend O'Duffy is one such, flirting with Franco and canoodling up to the German embassy. We have a few buckos in the army and civil service who are behaving strangely. I think we have them all covered.'

'I understand that very well. But why are you here? I wish you well, but what has it got to do with me?'

'There's one other group I am concerned about – and it involves one of your brother bishops.'

For the first time, he had Fogarty's full attention.

'A bishop? Surely not. Some few might be intemperate in their views, injudicious even in the case of Killala and my neighbour up the road in Clonfert is radical, a bit cracked even, but certainly not a danger to the State.'

He paused and thought for a moment.

'You could have a point about some of the religious orders. A few of them were very unsound back in the '20s and would still be supporters of the IRA. But not a bishop. You must be mistaken.'

'No. I am not. Let me be specific. Concannon.'

'Kilderry. No, you must be mistaken. He's far too shrewd and ambitious. He is not going to damage his own upward ascent. I've known him since he was a student at Maynooth. He's too calculating to get involved in anything like that.'

'Maybe he feels this will help that ascent. Let me tell you what I know.'

He filled Fogarty in on what he knew and what he suspected, with special emphasis on the links with the Spanish embassy.

'We have reason to suspect there is a conspiracy afoot which, whatever the motives, has the potential to blow our policy of neutrality out of the water. It will give the English the excuse they are looking for to invade. It is as serious as that, and you of all people know I was never an alarmist. I have always been a man for hard facts.'

Fogarty invited him to leave the dining room. It was a gloomy room and Bryan wondered once again why clergymen rarely tolerated bright colours or cheerful surroundings. And the study was just as drab, but at least the deep leather armchairs were comfortable and the bright fire fought the general atmosphere of gloom.

Two cut glasses were produced and Fogarty poured generous measures of Hennessy. Pipes were lighted.

Fogarty seemed depressed.

'I have to accept what you are saying. But I am an old man now and have no idea what you want me to do. Maybe you should have gone directly to Armagh or Dublin. They carry more authority than I do.'

'I came to you because I trust you. I know you are straight and I believe you will see the bigger picture and do the right thing.'

'So what do you want?'

'Two things. I want everything you can tell me about Concannon and I want you to keep your eyes and ears open for anything that might help us find out what is happening.'

'You mean you want me to be a spy for you?'

'It wouldn't be the first time I asked you. And you never let us down.'

'Try and tell that to the Long Fella. Well, so long as it is for you, I will do as you ask.'

'No, my lord, it's for this oul' country of ours.'

And with that, they got down to business.

33

....

March 12 1940

Bryan told Professor James Hogan that he would meet him in Larry Murphy's pub, just up the street from the National University. He knew Hogan was a bit sniffy about pubs and wanted to meet in a hotel, but Bryan didn't trust hotels – too much possibility of chance encounters – and preferred the privacy of a quiet pub, especially if the publican would leave them undisturbed during 'holy hour' when pubs were obliged to close.

Hogan arrived on time; lean, highly strung, and full of energetic intensity. He looked none too pleased at being dragged away from a university meeting on matriculation standards, which had at least two good hours left in it, but he had worked too closely with Bryan in the past to ignore his urgent summons. And he knew he owed Bryan a debt.

Bryan respected Hogan, indeed was in awe of him in all respects except one – his political judgement. Hogan had been an active soldier in the War of Independence and yet had time during this period to publish his first book on medieval history, which won him the Chair of History at University College Cork at the age of 23. He had worked with Bryan in military intelligence during the Civil War before heading back to Cork and a life of exceptional scholarship.

But not all of his interest stayed in the safety of medieval Ireland. He had made a profound study of communism, which per-

suaded him it was a threat to all democracies and, in 1935, had written Could Ireland Become Communist?

The book, allied to his espousal of the Pope's social policy in an encyclical, landed him in political trouble. He had greatly annoyed de Valera and his government, and the fact that the book was based on secret intelligence reports supplied to him by still-serving former colleagues in Army Intelligence, landed him before a court martial. He was acquitted, but only on a technicality.

Since then Hogan had stuck to academic matters but, when Bryan saw his name on Concannon's list of conspirators, it had come as a shock. In Bryan's world, a shock can sometimes become an opportunity, which was why they were now sitting in Larry Murphy's comfortable snug.

'Dan, you know I don't like pubs. Never go near them. Most of them are low dives as far as I can see.' Hogan had always been on the fastidious side.

'Well if it makes you feel any more comfortable James, this building used to be a sort of seminary for gentle ladies training to be nuns. So you are in no danger of contamination and maybe even some of the stored-up sanctity in the building might rub off on you. And Larry Murphy is a man you can trust.'

Bryan went straight to the point. 'James, I thought you had learned your lesson. I told you to get out of politics. You have no head for it. You are too intellectual, too full of theory and you are no judge of people. You might have eventually brought O'Duffy down, but you were the one who brought him in. You should know all that by now.'

Hogan looked offended, even sulky. People in University College Cork did not speak to him like that. But he did not challenge what Bryan had said. He remained silent.

'For a start, I want to know exactly how involved you are with Bishop Concannon and that motley shower he has around him.

You know us well enough to know we wouldn't miss that sort of goings-on. And we haven't. Have you no idea what you are getting yourself in to?'

Hogan remained silent.

'James, last time round I was helpful. This time I will be merciless. This is the security of the State – our State, yours and mine – that I am talking about. This is not some academic fantasy game. This is real. And this time I am on de Valera's side.'

Bryan knew that Hogan was fair-minded and essentially reasonable. Or at least he had banked on him being so.

Finally, Hogan spoke. 'You know Dan, I believe you are right and I am wrong.'

Bryan was surprised at the speed of the capitulation.

'I've been asking myself how I got involved. Mary has eaten the head off me and told me not to be such a fool. In fact, I've only been to one meeting and had decided not to attend any more. I missed the last one.'

Something Bryan already knew.

'I've decided not to attend any more. I will write to Concannon tomorrow to tell him I am out. I don't know how he will take it. He won't like it, but I agree with you. There is something about the group I do not like or trust.'

But Bryan had only started. If Hogan thought he could get back to discussing matriculation regulations and compulsory Irish he was mistaken. Bryan wanted every detail he could get and it took a few glasses of Larry Murphy's good wartime whiskey before Hogan would get back to a meeting that might well have ended.

Hogan explained he had first met Concannon at a meeting in the papal nuncio's residence. He had been impressed by Concannon's informed defence of the Pope's encyclical, his admiration for Salazar and, to a lesser extent, Franco. He was particularly impressed that Concannon had made a clear distinction between corporatism and fascism. Hogan recounted that the nuncio had been dismissive, seeing Salazar as 'dangerously authoritarian', while James Dillon was scathing in his condemnation.

Hogan, however, had found much sense in what Concannon was saying, but felt it was never going to get off the ground in Ireland. He found Concannon an imposing figure but was struck by the quiet enthusiasm of another guest, an Englishman whose name he had forgotten, for what Concannon had been saying. All he knew was that the man was a convert to Catholicism and reputed to be very wealthy.

He had particularly noted the passionate intensity of the Englishman. 'Tall, yellow faced – indeed sick looking – but when he spoke, his eyes lit up.'

He hadn't said very much but his main point, according to Hogan, was that the Church, including the Church in Ireland, was unprepared for the battles ahead. The Church needed its own 'shock troops' – Hogan had remembered this phrase in particular – well-trained young people, men and women, drawn from elite groups, who would be highly disciplined and able to fight the masons and Communists at their own game. They would be especially good at infiltrating all key levels in society, including politics.

He told them he was not talking about some vague theoretical possibility. Just such a group of shock troops as he described existed in Spain. Franco found them useful and Pius XII had given them his blessing.

'Had they a name?'

'Yes, let me think. Yes, yes, Mysterium Fidei or something like that, but I am not certain.'

Concannon repeated almost word for word what Hogan remembered the Englishman saying except that he had not mentioned this group specifically at the meeting. He said he would fill them in on details later, but he could assure them that, thanks to an unnamed 'benefactor', ample funds would be available. Hogan suspected it might be the Englishman.

Hogan claimed he had become uneasy at this point, but said nothing. He had decided to get out and did not attend the next meeting, but did not say why not to Concannon. Just university business, he said.

Bryan had a few more questions before he let Hogan back to his matriculation regulations.

'Is there any other bishop or senior cleric involved?'

'No. Concannon said they must remain a small, self-contained group, each member selected because he had a particular role to play – so someone from Justice, External Affairs and the bank. They would have help from inside the Spanish embassy but, apart from that, nobody else would be involved.'

'One last thing, James. You are not going to resign. You will stay in the group and you will report to me everything you learn. Everything. Is that clear? Otherwise I'd hate to see you in trouble. You are too good a historian for that.'

But he was not quite finished.

'I must report all this to de Valera. I'm doing this because I have to, but also to ensure he has no bad thoughts about you.'

Hogan knew he had no choice.

'So, I'm a spy again.'

It was the second time in a week Bryan had heard that said.

With that, Hogan headed to a dreary Kingsbridge and the slow, cold train back to Cork. Matriculation regulations would have been more fun, but he would do what Bryan asked him.

34

....

'You know, I have no idea how I ever slipped through the net.'

Bishop Dominic Irwin and Archbishop Valetti had reached the brandy stage. Irwin had made a good choice in picking the Lobster Pot. In fact, Valetti decided this would be his restaurant of choice from now on – discreet and with the best fish he had eaten out of Sicily.

'How do you mean slipped the net?'

'How I ever became a bishop. I actually believe in Vatican II – still do – but no Irish bishop, with the exception of Willie Walsh, has been appointed since the arrival of the present pope, who believes in it. Your predecessor saw to that.'

Valetti himself had no particular liking for Vatican II and generally distrusted its supporters but, as he told himself, he did not care very much either way. He liked Irwin and had enjoyed his company, but he still had to get to the point of their meeting.

He had done some research on Irwin and knew he had been regarded as a fine scholar, but he had gone offside on the *Humanae Vitae* issue and had been severely out of favour both in Rome and with the leaders of the Irish Church ever since. He was depicted as 'unsound' and too soft on dissident priests, too protective of them to be trusted. Valetti knew that much worse was said in clerical circles about Irwin – unsubtle hints that he 'liked fine dining too much' and 'was friendly with political radicals like Conor Cruise O'Brien and Michael D. Higgins'.

None of this bothered Valetti. He could see the portly and cheerful Irwin liked his food and was a good judge of wine.

As far as Valetti was concerned, these were good points in his favour and he was prepared not to be judgemental.

Irwin was not surprised when Valetti raised the name of Concannon.

'Yes, I heard there's a bit of a problem there. Money I believe. Well it is at least old-fashioned and makes a bit of a change from the child sex abuse cover-ups so many of my brother bishops have got themselves in to. I can only hope I have no skeletons in my own diocesan cupboard.'

Valetti detected a flicker of sadness, and maybe even fear, on Irwin's face.

'Yes, it's a sad, sad story that, but the full story will probably never come out. For the Church's sake, I hope it doesn't, but it does us no credit, no credit at all.'

Valetti had no desire to go down that route. Partly because he knew too much about it from his days in Rome and had his own dark memories, but mainly because it deflected him from the question of Concannon's money.

Valetti told Irwin his only concern was a possible financial scandal that might damage the reputation of the Church. He wanted to do everything within his power to avert such a scandal, but was getting no help whatsoever from Bishop Mullins. He did not mention he had not yet spoken to Mullins and had no hard facts to put to him.

'I need some background information on Concannon. I believe you served as a bishop with him for 15 years. What can you tell me about him?'

'I felt I knew him long before I met him. My old mentor during my student days in Rome was Professor Semple. He described Concannon during his Rome years as the most single-minded and ambitious cleric he had ever met. Ambition defined his every breath. Kilderry was to be his first step to the red hat. Rome rated him highly and it was widely accepted that, after a few successful years in Kilderry, he would get the first available archbishopric, possibly even in Armagh.'

'So what happened?'

'Hard to say exactly. He never lost his position of dominance, his self-confidence never flagged and when he spoke everybody listened. As a young bishop, I was in awe of him, but he always treated me with courtesy. When Dublin and Armagh were giving me a hard time over my stance on *Humanae Vitae*, he defended me. He was the only one who did. But we never became friends. No one ever did.'

Irwin seemed crowded by memories. But he was clearly enjoying them.

'Great haters, some of the bishops. Some of the rivalries dated back to slights – real and imagined – from seminary days. Celibacy has a lot to answer for.

'But back to Concannon. Dominant as he was within the hierarchy and prominent as he was in taking on the politicians, the promotion never came. He remained in Kilderry and clearly it bothered him. He never really became resigned to not being the leader and I think it haunted him. I could see it in the scornful way he dealt with the archbishops, all of whom feared him.

'Nothing ever became public, but on a visit to Rome after I became bishop, old Semple – who was obsessed with Concannon – told me that something funny had happened during the war. According to Semple's story, which he claimed he got from an Irish diplomat in the Holy See, there was some question of Concannon getting involved with Franco, though I never saw that published anywhere. Apparently de Valera had been furious and made his views known. And you know as well as I, Rome listens to politicians when they make promotions and appointments. Anyway, whatever happened, Dev was livid and never forgave Concannon. By the time Dev left office, it was far too late.'

Irwin stopped for a moment and took an appreciative sip of brandy.

'The funny thing is that what Semple told me never surfaced here. No bishop ever mentioned it to me and you know what gossips we are. I saw Dev and himself together at various functions and their relationship seemed cordial and proper, so I paid no attention to Semple's story. But then, they were both old professionals.

'Looking back on it, I should have been more curious and, if I thought about it at all, I probably felt he was a victim of bad timing – the right vacancy never came up at the right time.'

Irwin continued: 'Secrets are strange things. Not all remain buried forever, as too many are finding out today to their cost. Who knows what secret has come back to haunt Concannon's underwhelming successor in Kilderry. I would lay an even fiver with you that this secret has to do with the reason Concannon never got promotion.'

Valetti was about to accept the bet, almost out of sheer force of habit, until he reminded himself this was something he wanted to give up.

Irwin was now very alert.

'But surely you are in the best place of all to get to the bottom of this story. Your predecessor, Paschal Robinson, must have been up to his elbows in whatever was going on. He knew whatever Rome knew and he almost certainly knew what Dev knew. Dev always stayed close to the priests and I'm told Robinson was a scholar who kept good records. But I am sure you know all that already.'

Irwin was sharper than Valetti anticipated. One of the reasons he was having lunch with Irwin was precisely because there was no trace of any such files in his office. But Irwin had hit the nail on the head. There had to be files. But where?

Valetti felt Irwin had told him all he was going to tell. He had no doubt he knew more, maybe much more, but it would have to wait. In spite of his impatience, he felt confirmed in his certainty that the file which could unlock this mystery was missing. But why was it missing? Was it so explosive that Robinson put it in a secret place and who was he hiding it from? Or had it been stolen – and, if so, why and to whose benefit?

In spite of this, he had enjoyed his lunch.

Bishop Irwin had enjoyed himself too. His curiosity had been aroused and old memories revived. This, he thought, could be a bit of fun. He knew that his old friend Morgan Dannaher would agree. Especially, since that wily old diplomat might know what happened the file de Valera must have had in External Affairs. That must still be around somewhere.

35

....

Morgan Dannaher had long discovered that being a retired ambassador offered little by way of lifestyle. He had known it since his return from being ambassador to Luxembourg. Living back in Mount Merrion was a comedown after years of fine residences, official cars, obedient underlings and helpful domestic staff. There was all the difference in the world between being an ambassador and being a 'former ambassador'. One invited deference while the other earned indifference. What was even worse was that the people you had known were, by and large, retired or dead. And when you did meet up with the few that were still alive, they had little enough to say that was fresh. It was extraordinary, he thought, the extent to which people depended on their jobs to give them a sense of identity and purpose.

Most of his former colleagues felt much as he did but, as he told himself, he at least was not stuck at home with a nagging wife who felt the loss of status and perks even more keenly. In fact, he told himself he lived well – a decent pension, a nice house, active membership of the University Club and, most important of all, a mind that was still sharp and retentive.

He had to admit that he was lonely and it was for this reason, more than because his knee was giving him trouble that he found himself in the waiting room of the outpatients department of St Vincent's Hospital. He had come to enjoy the company of the doctor who had looked after him on previous visits. He had at last found a doctor who not just looked after his ailments but liked to hear his stories.

Dr Tommy Newrie knew well that there was little wrong with Dannaher's knee. But Newrie was a doctor who liked his patients and always saw them as real people, often with a good life story to tell. Or so he liked to tell his friend Peter O'Donnell, who occasionally teased him about the amount of time he was prepared to spend with individual patients. 20 minutes with Morgan Dannaher might not do much in medical terms, but would ensure the patient left in a better state than when he came in.

But Newrie had another motive today. From previous visits, he had picked up a great deal about Dannaher's earlier career, the highlight of which seemed to have been the years 1940–45 that he had spent in the Holy See. Not that his career after that had not been exciting, including spells in Washington and Bonn, though never as ambassador, and a major part in preparing the Irish case for entry to the Common Market before finishing off in the relative calm of Luxembourg. He knew too that Dannaher had a very special interest in the Catholic Church and greatly enjoyed the arcane politics of what he called 'that most fiendishly devious of institutions'.

After his visit to Kilderry, there was a point to Newrie's interest. He had intended making contact with Dannaher but here he was in front of him. After a quick reassuring inspection, Newrie told his patient that he had a coffee break coming up and invited him to join him.

As they sat smoking and drinking bad coffee in the drab basement coffee area of St Vincent's, Newrie took a good look at Dannaher. Rotund and owl-like, he still looked young for his 80 years. In some ways, he struck Newrie as having a priestly air about him. Newrie was a fan of G.K. Chesterton and Dannaher reminded him of Chesterton's great creation, Fr Brown. Whatever about the physical resemblance, this was especially true about the sharpness of his mind.

'You know,' Dannaher began, 'the hardest thing I ever had to face was retirement. The worst thing about it is you stop doing things, stop meeting people, stop having problems to resolve. In other words, you stop mattering. You have to fall back on your memories and, before long, people begin to regard you as a bore. No, no, don't tell me this is not so. I see it in myself, in the club, every conversation beginning "I remember the time" and in seconds eyes start to glaze over.'

'But you had a good career. Surely you get satisfaction from that. I've heard it said you were one of the best minds ever on our foreign service.'

And in truth Newrie had heard that.

'That's very kind of you. Very kind. But all in the past. All past, no future. But stop me. I am a self-pitying bore. Please forgive me. I do have much to be thankful for.'

'You started in Rome?'

'Yes, 1940. I was just in to the service, early 1939 in fact. Cadets they called us then, but I had fluent Italian and good Latin and the minister to the Holy See, Leo Macaulay, needed some help. I was expendable and off I was sent. Wet behind the ears and the journey out was an adventure in itself. Five dangerous but wonderful years.

'There were just three of us. Leo Macaulay left as I arrived and my boss was TJ Kiernan, a lovely man, CJ O'Donovan and myself in a nice little villa on the Via San Martino della Battaglia. Because we were such a small team, I was involved in much of what went on – though not all of it. I think I was trusted, which made life very agreeable. And of course, some of the Irish priests were great sources of hospitality and gossip, as was Dr Kiernan's wife Delia – a great singer she was too.'

Dannaher described some of his later appointments, ending up as ambassador to Luxembourg.

'Have you ever thought of writing your memoirs? They would be fascinating.'

'Well, that sort of thing is frowned upon. We all signed the Official Secrets Act on joining up and as, you are probably aware, no Irish civil servant – certainly no one of any consequence – has ever published a memoir. Some may have left extended notes and papers to be deposited in various archives or with their families, but only to be published after a fixed period of time. It is probably illegal.'

Newrie knew when to be silent and after a pause Dannaher continued.

'Have you a particular interest in this area. I have not met many young people, including our younger historians, who have – and more's the pity.'

'I have. You may have seen reports in the papers a few weeks ago the death of Bishop Concannon. You may even have known him. Well – and I can explain to you if you wish – I do have an interest in him.'

Suddenly, there was a new alertness about Dannaher.

'Well now, that's a coincidence. Only yesterday I had a phone call from the one bishop I know and trust among the present crowd. He is a decent man – so decent in fact he has been sidelined these many years. He told me the papal nuncio, Archbishop Valetti, took him to lunch – and it was a good lunch in the Lobster Pot. No nuncio had ever entertained him before so he was suspicious and he doesn't trust Valetti – Sicilian blood, he says.

'It didn't take long to discover the reason for the lunch. Valetti wanted any information he had on the very same Bishop Concannon. He told my friend it was about some possible financial irregularity concerning Concannon and he wanted to protect the Church from scandal. My friend says he humoured

Valetti, but gave him very little. Now he's more than curious as to what it might all be about. And now, out of the blue, you mention this long-forgotten name.'

Newrie was taken aback and, being taciturn by nature, decided to remain silent.

'One thing I have learned over my career is to be very wary of coincidence. I don't hear about Thomas Patrick Concannon for 13 years. I was one of the last people to visit him in his nursing home – about a year before he died – and now I hear his name twice in two days.'

But if Newrie thought Dannaher might be censorious or disapproving, he could not have been more wrong. Dannaher was chuckling to himself.

'This might be fun and I don't get much of that these days. So maybe you can tell me a little more.'

Newrie took an instant decision. He would trust Dannaher, at least up to a point. He owed no loyalty to Kilderry, only to O'Donnell. And Peter O'Donnell had asked him to help solve a problem. He was genuinely curious.

Without going in to much detail, he told Dannaher about O'Donnell – Dannaher already knew who he was – being asked to deal with issues concerning Concannon's legacy, the existence of large amounts of money and even more mystery. He himself had become intrigued and he felt Dannaher would too.

And he confessed his coffee invitation had not been accidental. If he had not turned up today, Newrie was going to contact him.

Dannaher looked 10 years younger. His malfunctioning knee was giving him no more pain. Newrie could see he was fully engaged and wondered for a moment if he could trust him. On balance he felt he could – and what other option did he have?

'Look, I have to go back to work. Luckily it's a slack day, but I've been away now for 40 minutes. A very useful 40 minutes,' he added.

'Would you join Peter and myself for dinner tomorrow evening and we'll tell you all we know. My instinct tells me we can trust you – that is if it's okay with you?'

There was no hesitation. 'Of course it is. This could be fun. You've cheered me up no end. And I should add I know the Holy Roman Church too well and have met too many dodgy bishops to be in awe of any of them. I knew Thomas Concannon very well, or at least as well as anybody knew them. I respected and liked him, and I felt he returned the compliment – though he was never a man to be effusive.'

Dannaher invited them to dine in his club but Newrie did not like clubs and suggested Nico's. Dannaher immediately accepted. Nico's, he said, had many happy memories for him.

'Dr Newrie, you have made an old man very happy. And you have put a spring back in my step. I may even have a surprise or two of my own in store for you.'

36

....

'I love this place. And it hasn't changed in 30 years.'

Morgan Dannaher looked around Nico's with undisguised pleasure.

'Look at those colours,' he gasped as he surveyed the lush all-enveloping purple that had gone out of fashion decades earlier. 'You don't see colours like that anymore.'

And Dannaher's pleasure was even greater when a grizzled bear of a man hurtled himself across the room and embraced him with wet kisses on each cheek. It was Emilio, the owner.

'Morgan, dear Morgan. Where have you been all these years? I thought you were long dead and buried.' Soon the pair of them were off in voluble streams of Italian.

When O'Donnell and Newrie finally got him seated, he was still on a high.

'You know I love this place. It has so many great memories. I was afraid to come back after I retired in case it had changed or for fear that nobody would know me.'

Whether they wanted it or not, he was going to reminisce.

'I first came here as a student and I can still taste their chicken *cacciatore* – five and six it cost, a fortune for a student but it gave me my first taste of Italian food. And then in the late '60s when we were applying to join the Common Market, my job was to persuade the journalists to be as supportive as possible. And what better way than over long, long lunches. Those boys could drink; Mike Burns, Raymond Smith, Sean Duignan, but they were good journalists – at least my bosses thought so and that was fine with me.

Newrie was pleased to see Dannaher – technically his patient – so happy and looking so well, but he tried to steer him back to the business they were here to discuss. He thought it best to start by getting O'Donnell to tell their side of the story. For the second time in two days, O'Donnell did just that. And once again it was the full story.

Dannaher was a good listener, asking a few very relevant questions, but listening mostly with a quiet intensity.

'Right, gentlemen. Where do I start? At the beginning, I suppose.'

He had entered the Department of External Affairs as a cadet. De Valera was his minister and remained so throughout the war. He was one of the second batch of recruits in the short history of the department. He spent his first 12 months in Dublin, but when Leo Macauley, the minister to the Holy See, asked for an additional junior, his fluency in Italian and his degree in Latin from UCD made him an obvious choice.

'I had to wait around for several months before I got to Rome but, in that time, I made a point of getting to know the papal nuncio, Paschal Robinson. An extraordinary man, totally forgotten now. Because he was American, I made the rather dangerous assumption that the best way to meet him was to go the direct route. So I wrote to him and he invited me up – I think he was quite lonely – and we became good friends.

'Nobody in Iveagh House knew of my approach and the boss, Joe Walshe – not a nice man, at least not nice to me – would have disapproved had he known. He would have regarded my initiative as insubordination. Anyway, he never did know.'

Dannaher would visit Robinson in 'that mausoleum of a house he had in the Phoenix Park'.

'He may have had an ulterior motive of getting some gossip from External Affairs, but I never felt I was being used. He was very American, very egalitarian and I think he lived his friar's vow of humility to the full. He was never at ease with the pomp of so much that surrounded him.

'He told me about his early memories of Dublin, living at Percy Place, of the parish priest of Haddington Road Church, which was still his favourite Church in Dublin, and then of his father having to emigrate. He was a scholar and often talked to Eoin MacNeill about the efforts to replace some of the medieval documents lost in the Four Courts fire during the Civil War. But most of all he had the sharp eye of the journalist. And he was also a good listener. He would sound me out on my views on Irish life and the politicians and, of course, at that age I had views on everything.'

Dannaher described his long and dangerous journey to Rome via Lisbon and how he corresponded monthly with Robinson while there.

'I came back in late 1945 and stayed in Dublin until 1950. I visited him several times before his death in 1948.

'That is just background. Now to Concannon. Robinson told me in early 1940 that he had a disturbing conversation with de Valera, who implied that somebody in the Church, and probably in the hierarchy, was involved in activities that could seriously damage Ireland's policy of neutrality. Dev was not specific and Robinson suspected he was on a fishing expedition. But, he also knew Dev well enough to know no conversation was ever accidental. Dev was warning him to find out what was going on and to put an end to it straight away.'

The meal was long finished. Emilio had already sent over two rounds of Sambuca and was happy to look after his guests in to the small hours if necessary.

'Dev of course knew what he was doing and clearly I was only one of the people Robinson consulted. It was a strange and jittery time. No one knew how the war would go. Pro-German or anti-English feeling was stronger than people later cared to remember, and that included people at the highest levels of all walks of life. Everyone spied on everyone else – Military Intelligence spied on senior army officers as well as on top civil servants; Special Branch spied on journalists and politicians; the Department of Justice spied on External Affairs; and Joe Walshe, my boss and a man who had his own secrets, spied on everybody.

'Anyway, I got a whisper in External Affairs that Military Intelligence had a special interest in a bishop. There was no reason given and it was just one of many rumours at that fevered time. Most of the rumours had little or no foundation. But then, late one evening in O'Neill's pub in Merrion Row where the Justice fellows used drink, I heard a mention of Bishop Concannon. It was only that, a mention, and it came from a fellow who had too much drink on him. A fellow who usually had too much drink on him. But, I always saw him as a fellow who knew things.'

Another Sambuca.

'Anyway, I cycled up to the Phoenix Park the next evening to tell the nuncio. It would not have been safe to phone or write and everyone cycled everywhere in those days. When I told Robinson, he was flabbergasted. "Concannon – the last man I would have suspected." He was very grateful to me and I never knew until much later just how useful my tip-off had been for him.'

Dannaher explained that Robinson trusted him totally from that point on and returned the favour many times during Dannaher's stay in Rome.

'It also made me very curious about Concannon but nothing more happened while I was in Ireland. I'm sure Robinson passed on his name to de Valera – it was not his job to protect the Irish bishops from their own mistakes and he knew most of them greatly resented his presence in Dublin, seeing him· as some sort of spy. Robinson told me he protected his source, but I suspect he may have spoken well of me to de Valera, who always made a point to being very kind to me – something Joe Walshe noted and did not like, which made me all the more glad to get to Rome.'

By now Dannaher, who Newrie noted was a skilled storyteller, was tired.

'When I got to Rome, I decided to find out what I could of Concannon. I found far more than I expected. And since by now I fancied myself as a trained diplomat, I made careful notes of what I learned.'

He paused – rather too long for Newrie.

'And all those notes are now buried deep in Iveagh House?'

'Yes, they are. But you mentioned yesterday about me writing a memoir. I was not fully frank with you. I always thought that what I was involved with at any given time was the most important thing in the world. It's an occupational hazard for all bachelors, or so I am told, but I did think about a possible memoir some day. For that reason and because I am a squirrel by nature, I made copies of many of my notes and kept many of the papers, which I intend to donate to the UCD archives – but only after my death.'

O'Donnell wondered if this would be twice in two days that valuable information would be withheld because of some scruple or other.

But he need not have worried. Dannaher felt himself once again at the centre of events. He was relishing every moment of it.

'I will need a day to sort out those notes that are relevant and then perhaps, if it is not too much trouble, you might come to my house in Mount Merrion.'

They had one more Sambuca and put Dannaher in a taxi. Newrie and O'Donnell retired to Smyth's for a pint. Last orders were being called as they arrived and they settled themselves in the front snug. O'Donnell, for the very first time, began to feel a little of that confidence he had talked to Archie Bowe about.

And he had re-established contact with Heather Ruddock – something he did not tell Newrie. An expensively perfumed note had arrived that morning asking him to call her tomorrow. Two good things to look forward to.

37

....

It was less than five minutes after opening time and Richard E
Murdock was sitting at the bar of the Lazerian Hotel. It had become a daily ritual but today, in addition to his usual hangover,
he had further bad news to handle.

The first bit of bad news was his wife. How had it come to
this? He thought he knew her and that she was happy to be the
wife of a well-heeled and prominent country solicitor. He had
not been mean with money and he reckoned she had no real
interest in sex – how long had it been? – and was happy with
her golf, her bridge and her lunching friends.

That at least was how it seemed to him, and he could hardly
be blamed if he looked elsewhere. He knew now he should have
been more careful, but drink tended to make him take risks and
he was genuinely surprised when she set a private detective on
him. He blamed that busybody friend of hers, Margot Forrest,
bloody social worker, ugly harridan and probably a lesbian. He
conceded he might have been more restrained when she confronted him with her findings. He hadn't meant to hit her so
hard, but by God he had been sorely provoked.

Now he had even more evidence, she was flaunting her in-
fidelity. The apprentices were bad enough but this time it was
with a teacher – a fucking national school teacher at that from
a nearby school. And she was not attempting to hide it. In fact,
flaunting it at him seemed to be part of her game.

They barely spoke anymore and, to make matters worse, this
seemed to make her even more contented. A separation would

cost him dearly, both financially and reputationally. And the money she would screw him for. Holy Jesus, could it get any worse?

As he thought about it, he began to realise she had changed without him even noticing. She had lost weight, been to various stylists and found new friends. He had to admit, the frumpy, joyless wife he had known had become a new person and a very presentable one at that.

Sally was the least of his worries. The Law Society were sniffing around his practice and it was only a matter of time before he faced an audit. He knew that this was being whispered among his colleagues and he expected no mercy from the Law Society.

On top of that, he received a letter that morning from his expensive Dublin solicitors, enclosing a copy of Archie Bowe's reply to the letters the Dublin solicitor had written to Bishop Mullins, who had passed it on to Bowe to deal with.

Bowe would never have used the term, but Murdock saw it for what it was: a 'fuck off' letter. He was not entitled to any of the information sought, it was entirely a diocesan matter, all proper procedures had been followed. If he was not happy, he could go to the High Court but they would vigorously contest the matter.

It was clear from the accompanying letter that his costly Dublin solicitors, while happy to pursue the matter if instructed, saw some difficulties and recommended a further consultation.

'Consultation my arse. Another grand on the table to be talked down to and told nothing I don't know already. Fuck that,' thought Murdock to himself.

He was in deep trouble and he knew it. And this realisation sobered him up. This was a time for a clear mind, a steady hand and, even if he had neither, he reminded himself there was one game he had played well and that was poker. It was time to resurrect those skills, see what cards he had left and play them as best he could.

He surprised the barman by refusing a second drink and ordering instead a strong cup of coffee.

But what cards did he have?

He had thought little in the past about the source of his uncle's wealth. As long as it was there was all that bothered him. He assumed that having money and not being accountable was what being a bishop was all about. On reflection, he could see that Kilderry was not a particularly rich diocese and that Archie Bowe would not have countenanced any irregularities in its financial affairs – extravagances such as the Bentley and fine residence maybe, but not much more.

There had to be some other source that Bowe knew nothing about. In fact, there was much that Bowe might not have known about. That might explain his grumpiness at the reading of the will and the fact that it had been drawn up elsewhere.

So where did the money come from? For the first time in his life, Murdock asked himself this question. And it was not idle speculation.

But who could help him find out? Knowing the source of the money might be his only hope of getting his paws on some of it.

Certainly no one in the diocese would help him.

What about that fellow, the nuncio who had been left 20 grand? Why had he been singled out? Who the fuck is he anyway? Why should he help me? Can I get anything on him?

And this other crowd – what are they called? He had written it down: *Mysterium Fidei*. Never heard of the fuckers, but why were they left 20 grand as well? Was this just another bequest or were their snouts in the trough all along?

He was ruling out one avenue of approach after another. He reluctantly realised the only other individual actually mentioned in the will was Johnny Ryan, Johnny Flowerpot himself.

Johnny was one of the few people Concannon liked. He had been with him all those years he had been bishop. Johnny had driven him everywhere. He knew where he went, who he met and maybe even more. And he had been good to the old boy after his retirement and continued to drive him on the rare occasions he wanted to go somewhere. Johnny was there, especially in the early days. And Johnny had a great memory.

Why had he not thought of this before? It was staring him in the face all along.

He took out the telephone directory. It was 11.30 and Johnny would almost certainly be in Hickson's pub.

He was. Murdock reckoned he could drive the 70 miles to Brannocksbridge in under two hours. He asked Johnny to meet him for lunch in the Brannocksbridge Arms.

Johnny, in fact, had been expecting a call and had a fair idea what it might be about. Tommy Newrie's visit had made him suspicious. Something was up and he was going to enjoy it, and maybe even make a few bob out of it for himself. And a free lunch was a free lunch – he would have the steak and onions, and plenty of whiskey. He had never been a man for wine.

It was good to feel wanted again.

38

....

Archbishop Valetti looked at the list in front of him for the fourth time. It was a chore, but he had to do it.

It was the day of the annual embassy reception, an event set in the calendar and on which he had no discretion. It was part of the work of every embassy and there was no getting away from it.

He looked again at the guest list.

The four archbishops were invited. Dublin would send a junior bishop, Armagh would ignore the event, while, for some reason, Cashel and Tuam never missed a chance to come to the capital.

All the other ambassadors, including the Russians and the Chinese, had been invited. He had also invited the Taiwanese, which meant the Chinese would not turn up – a piece of intentional mischief on his part designed to cause offence.

Most of the European embassies would send the first secretaries, but all of the African ambassadors would attend – they attended everything – and would liven things up. He did not blame his fellow ambassadors for not attending. He hated these events himself and rarely attended, usually sending his number two, that obsequious little Peruvian monsignor who loved these occasions.

Then there was the usual mix of embassy-goers, especially the 'friends of the Holy See', most of whom he knew to be far more Catholic than he was, and who would expect pious platitudes from him. Well, he would be on his best behaviour.

There were also a few former ambassadors to the Vatican and some diplomats who had served there. Most of them would be elderly and glad of a rare day out. He decided he would spend some time with them. If he was lucky, one or two might be able to help him in his quest. It was a long shot, but worth trying.

He had also invited Dominic Irwin, because he liked him, and JJ Gilmartin, because he knew it would please him. Gilmartin would have told every priest for miles around of the 'personal invitation' he had received from the nuncio, and no doubt Bishop Mullins would have heard by now. Good, he thought –Mullins would know he had his own source of information within the diocese.

Irwin had mentioned that Concannon had a number of very rich friends among Catholic businessmen. The most prominent of these by far was Joe Bradley, believed to have once been one of the richest men in the country and who had died in 1977. Irwin said Bradley had been a controversial figure, not well regarded in Dublin society and, in Irwin's view, he had flaunted his friendship with Concannon as a badge of respectability.

Valetti had also discovered through Irwin that Bradley's son, 'Junior' Bradley, was a very wealthy man, a successful race-horse owner and a quiet supporter of Catholic charities. Jeremy Bradley would be coming to his reception.

Before meeting Junior, he needed to find out about old Joe Bradley and he knew exactly where to go – Sebastian Madden, his bookie. He still owed Madden a few thousand, but their relationship was cordial.

Madden was nobody's idea of a bookie. He came from an 'old' Dublin family. His father was an eminent cardiologist who was appalled with his son's choice of career – until he saw how much money he was making. Madden had a degree in philosophy; a calm, self-deprecating manner; old-fashioned courtesy; and the sharpest mathematical brain in Dublin. Valetti had been told this slight, bald and gentle-seeming man knew everything there was to know about the leading citizens of Dublin – almost as much as he knew about the racing form book.

Madden told the story simply. Old Joe Bradley was a man people either loved or loathed, mainly the latter. He was engulfed in rumour, with every known fact of his life disputed. What was known with some certainty, Madden spelled out to Valetti.

Bradley had a fearsome reputation during the War of Independence and there were some who hinted he had been more trigger happy than was necessary. In the Civil War he had opposed the new government. He had been a wanted man after the burning of a house led to the death of a young boy.

He disappeared after the Civil War to the general relief of both sides and was next heard of in the US. The years that followed are short on facts, but Madden believed Bradley was involved in bootlegging, in which he allegedly made a great deal of money. He moved to the West Coast, where he bought up some distressed property in the Depression and sold it back later for a great profit. That, at least, was the story he told when he returned to Dublin, where he often used to boast that he had been in the film business – a claim that was not generally believed.

He came back to Dublin in 1934 a rich but not generally respected man, just 40 years of age. Most of those who had known him were wary of him, but he bought a number of established businesses, married in to a respectably impoverished Dublin family in 1938, bought a large house in Dalkey and lived there in some splendour until his death in 1977.

'The rumours never really went away and there was always an element of mystery about the source of his money, not just when he came back but throughout his life. It was felt his businesses were not making much money so how did he manage to spend so much. There are always rumours like that in Dublin and that is all they ever were. The other thing people noticed was he craved respectability, acceptance into Dublin society, such as it was, but never really got it.'

'That's fine,' said Valetti, 'but where did Concannon come in to this. What was the connection there?'

'Having a bishop as a friend was one way in. Concannon was new and apparently the coming man, and Bradley clearly cultivated him. Unusually for an Armagh man, Bradley could have great charm, and it seemed to work on Concannon. He even baptised their only child in 1940.'

The only other information Madden had was that the friendship seemed to peter out in the 1940s, but nobody knew why.

Valetti had at least got a new lead. Junior Bradley was coming to his reception and, in the absence of Robinson's missing files, he at least had something to pursue.

He had Madden's conversation in mind as he prepared to welcome his guests. He was always careful to present well and, even though he was overweight, he cut an imposing figure as he greeted his guests in his Roman-tailored soutane with its purple cummerbund and gleaming pectoral cross.

Junior was one of the first to arrive. Valetti noted the chauffer-driven Rolls Royce, which was parked at a discreet distance.

Old Joe Bradley might have been a rough-cut diamond, but his son was the epitome of languid elegance. Tall, slim, hair tossed to a precise degree of tonsorial insouciance and with a real sense of presence. Valetti was impressed, even more so when he noted the expensive cut of the light-grey suit and the handmade brogues.

To his surprise, Valetti found Bradley warm and open. He had not expected the English accent spoken with a slightly arrogant drawl.

Hard as he tried, Valetti had always found it difficult to be charming or to make small talk. He immediately began to talk about the only thing that interested him at that moment – Joe Bradley.

'I've heard some great stories about your father. What a wonderful supporter he was of the Church and how he was helpful on so many occasions. I know my predecessor Dr Robinson thought highly of him and, indeed, I've come across references to him – all good I must say – in Robinson's papers. I really would like to know more about him.'

If Bradley was surprised he did not show it, but Valetti detected a wariness, a sudden coldness in his attitude.

'Strange. I never heard him mention a Dr Robinson. I have to confess my father was not universally loved. He was a strong man who made some enemies in the War of Independence and there were some things he would never talk about. Indeed, the fact he – a lifelong republican – sent me to school at Ampleforth and then Oxford told its own story.

'He wanted to give me a fresh start and didn't want me involved in Irish politics. I never questioned this – I had no interest in politics anyway and hard experience has made me wary of people who come looking for information about my father.'

Valetti felt he had been stopped in his tracks. This was as near to a brush-off as made no difference.

Bradley noted his reaction and quickly added: 'I'm talking about journalists and the so-called academics of course. There have been a few nasty pieces written, inaccurate and malicious I am certain, and I have no intention of helping them. Forgive me, but of course I am not including you in that.'

He paused. 'What is it that interests you?'

There was no warmth in the drawl.

'Well actually, my main interest is in Bishop Thomas Patrick Concannon. I'm told he was a very close friend of your father.'

All warmth was now gone.

'Yes, I believe he did know Concannon, although he is little more than a vague memory to me. Why don't we have lunch and you can tell me just what it is you want to know. I will be in touch. I don't want to monopolise you with so many others waiting to pay their respects.'

Shortly after that, he made his farewells and left the reception.

With a growing sense of boredom, Valetti went through the motions for another hour or so – and then his luck turned.

He had been talking to a number of retired diplomats when he was introduced to an owlish-looking, small man.

'I'm sorry I did not catch your name ... Morgan Dannaher?'

Suddenly Valetti was alert. That name rang a bell. Where had he come across it.

The elderly man told him he was a retired diplomat and had known every nuncio since Paschal Robinson and how glad he was to add Valetti to his list.

'So you knew old Paschal. Quite a guy from what I hear. 20 years they left him here.'

In truth, the fact that Robinson had never been 'promoted' out of Ireland struck Valetti as strange. Surely, if he was as good as people said, he could have done better than Ireland. Had he also blotted his copybook in Rome?

He was only half listening to Dannaher when suddenly he remembered where he had seen his name. Before he could think, he had blurted it out.

'Holy God – now I remember. I came across your name on one of Robinson's papers. He seemed to know you well.'

This was not the time to probe, but a seemingly energised Dannaher took the initiative.

'Oh, you are going through his papers. Have they been archived? I have a deep interest in diplomatic history.'

Valetti was angry with himself. 'No, they are not archived and they are in a bloody mess. Half appear to be missing.'

'What a shame. Do you have any record of who oversaw the removal of his papers from the old nunciature in the Phoenix Park before it was demolished in 1982? They might have been mislaid. I doubt if they have disappeared.'

Valetti had regained full composure. This boring little man could be helpful yet. It was at least worth a lunch.

And so they parted. Dannaher happy he had a story to tell his new friends and Valetti with some glimmer of hope.

39

....

Johnny Ryan was well ensconced when Richard E Murdock arrived at the Brannocksbridge Arms. A pint in front of him, the *Evening Herald* open at the racing page and with that cheerful openness that had always been his hallmark. But also with that hint of impudence which said that, while he might be in service, he was always his own man.

'Well, Mr Murdock, that's some right mess we seem to be in.'

'It is Johnny and I can't make head nor tail of it.'

Murdock asked for a gin and tonic, a menu and a quiet corner table.

He had little appetite, but Johnny ordered a prawn cocktail followed by a T-bone steak, well done, with onions and chips. Murdock ordered consommé and an omelette.

'Johnny, I'll tell you what I know, you tell me what you know and maybe we can make some sense of it.'

Murdock began. 'The Bish always had a shitload of money and he was always generous to me and my family. He never left us stuck for anything, but that changed about two years ago. He began to refuse our visits and never answered our letters or took our calls. I was worried but felt he was going soft in the head. I thought he wouldn't last long and then we'd get what was rightfully ours.'

Johnny might have asked by what right they should expect to get it at all, but he didn't. He enjoyed his steak and let Murdock continue.

"Then he changed his will without even consulting that little prick Archie Bowe. But there was no money there. None for us, none for the diocese, just those bequests for that fucking Spanish crowd, the fucking nuncio – and I know and you know too he never had any fucking time for nuncios. And then that bequest to the fuckin' Irish College he left 60 years ago. The only bit of decency he showed was to leave a few bob to you and, to tell the truth, it was a mean little sum, not nearly as much as you were entitled to expect.'

'What else do I know? Well, someone snuck into the house after he went to the nursing home. Remember he had a bit of a stroke and was moved sooner than he might have expected. We even thought for a while he might die. The strange thing, all that was taken were those files and the strongbox he had taken when he left the palace. It was no ordinary break-in and the only people I suspect are Mullins and his sidekick Nestor. But I have no proof and, when I asked, they told me to fuck off. And then we had this fellow – Dr Newrie you said – claiming he was a historian and doing some research on the bishop. I hope you didn't tell him too much.'

'No, boss. You can rest assured on that. I drank his drink and told him nothing. But I can tell you for a fact he is no more a historian than I am. He's a medical doctor and works in St Vincent's Hospital in Dublin – that was the number he left me and when I rang they told me he was not available. I didn't leave any message. I heard later he was up at the bishop's palace with Nestor's nephew, who I'm told is now a frequent visitor. And there's something funny going on with the bishop. He's even more distracted than usual. And that, as they say, is all I know.'

'That's fair enough Johnny and I don't doubt you for one minute. But clearly they think you have some information that could be useful to them, some information that you mightn't even know you had. And I think they could be right.'

Johnny bristled. 'Are you saying I'm holding back, that I am not straight up?'

Murdock knew from past experience that Johnny could take offence very easily. 'Not for one second, Johnny. There is nobody I trust more than you and nobody I would be happier to see right if we can sort this out.'

Johnny did not look particularly mollified.

Murdock continued. 'Let me explain. None of us ever wondered where all that money came from. No bishop goes hungry, but not many bishops are wealthy either. I know. I've made my own enquiries. That's a fact.

'So where did the money come from? And why did he get it? If we can figure that out then we have some chance of getting back what is rightfully ours.'

Murdock was perspiring even more than usual and he had forgotten his gin and tonic.

'From what you told me about this fellow Newrie, he was asking about who the bishop used to visit and who called to him, especially in the earlier years. That right?'

Murdock looked Johnny straight in the eyes. 'You're sure you told him nothing?'

'Nothing worthwhile. A few things here and there, but I'm not sure I know very much anymore. The old memory is not what it used to be. Too many things have happened since then.'

'Shite, Johnny, shite. You know it's shite. I don't believe you told this fellow anything, but Johnny you remember everything so don't give me any of that old nonsense.'

If Johnny was taken aback by this outburst, he did not show it. 'I'll have another pint.'

'I remember many years ago you told me you had got a good business training from the bishop. He was a perfectionist – the car always had to be gleaming, the engine checked so there would be no breakdown, the tank full. All of that. He trained you in punctuality, in never taking a drink and, most of all, in knowing when to shut up. But he was a controlling man. He had to know everything and he insisted on you keeping a log of every journey made – date, time destination and person visited. True Johnny?'

'Yes it's true and, to tell the truth, the training I got was a great help when I set up my own business.'

'I'm glad to hear that, but that's not the point. Let me be clear.'

There was a new coldness in Murdock's voice, but had he been looking more carefully he would have seen the beginning of a smirk on Johnny's face.

'I believe the full story of where the money came from and possibly why it was given can be put together from your logs. Johnny, I know you kept them and I want them.'

'Ah now, Mr M. You're putting me in a tough spot. I'm on a small pension, the missus is not well and times are hard enough. The problem is this fellow Newrie told me there would be hard cash for what he called any documentary evidence that could help his research.'

Murdock knew this was a lie. But he was around long enough not to be surprised by the turn the conversation had taken. His relationship with Johnny had never been one of friendship, merely one of convenience. Johnny knew that too and there was no way he would be bought off with vague promises of seeing him right.

'How much did he offer you?'

'Two thousand pounds.'

It was more than Murdock expected.

Should he call Johnny's bluff and walk away? Or should he try to beat the price down? And just suppose Johnny was telling the truth. If he rejected Johnny's offer, his last hope was gone.

He made a quick decision. 'How soon can I have them?'

'As soon as I see the money.'

Murdock took out his cheque book. 'There's a cheque for two thousand here as soon as I can see and verify the logs. How soon can that be?'

'Right now.' Fumbling in the large rucksack he brought everywhere, Johnny drew out five neatly bound volumes.

'His lordship liked to get all his records bound in volumes. He said it was essential for quick reference, whatever that means. Anyway, I took these just before he retired. He had enough on his mind then and he never even noticed. I thought they might come in handy some day. And so they have. I hope they will be as helpful to you as they were to me.'

With that he stood up and examined the cheque before carefully folding it. As he prepared to leave, he thanked Murdock for what had turned out to be a very expensive lunch.

As he was leaving he turned to Murdock. 'By the way, if you need more information on any of the people mentioned in there, I'll be happy to help. No fee.'

And with a tuneless whistling of 'Kelly from Killane' he was off.

40

....

Peter O'Donnell had a long phone conversation with his uncle. Monsignor Nestor told him the bishop was both impatient and fearful. The legal threats from Murdock had unsettled him, Bowe was still acting the prima donna and he could not figure out what the nuncio was playing at – but felt that whatever it was, it meant bad news. Indeed, Nestor had begun to fear that Mullins was not far off a nervous breakdown.

For his part, O'Donnell expressed his impatience with Bowe.

'It's time for him to put up or shut up. I know he has been nosing around asking questions about me in various legal offices in Dublin. I'm bloody annoyed with him and it's time he got over his sulk. I've been fully upfront with him, but all he's done is badmouth me. Can you do anything to put pressure on him? He has to know more than he's telling us.'

O'Donnell had been careful not to mention that his source on Bowe was Heather Ruddock. She told him that Bowe was making enquiries in some of the older legal firms in Dublin and that this had sparked some gossip about Kilderry. Not much because there were no hard facts, but that vacuum would soon be filled with gossip and speculation.

He phoned Heather to bring her up to date and mentioned the meeting Tommy Newrie had arranged with Dannaher that evening. She said that, since she was now 'fully on board', he should drop over to her place no matter how late and fill her in.'

It was his first bit of good news in some time.

***

Dannaher had invited O'Donnell and Newrie to his house in Mount Merrion. It was the house of a man who liked order – books stacked and catalogued, neatness and precision everywhere, soft pastel colours and pictures that all featured Dannaher. One with Pius XII, one with de Valera, another with Jack Lynch in Brussels and, in pride of place, the gold medal he had won for Latin in UCD in 1937.

He greeted them with a formal welcome and the absence of food or wine made it clear that this would be a business meeting. O'Donnell was pleased, Newrie less so.

It was a very focussed Dannaher who began and clearly saw himself running the meeting. It was almost as if he was back in harness – an ambassador again.

'I've been through all my papers and I've made notes in chronological order of events that may be of interest or relevance. I think they will be.'

He consulted his first set of notes.

February 3rd 1940

Meeting at his request with Nuncio. Clarence Hotel 11 am.

Dannaher stopped and smiled. 'As a junior I was not entitled to leave the office unless instructed. I had to invent an urgent funeral. I checked the *Irish Independent* and found one in Adam and Eve's on the quays. Then I had to go to Walshe himself to get away. Fortunately, he believed me and I was given two hours.'

He looked back at his note. 'Robinson was worried about his conversation with de Valera at the Áras about the dangerous behaviour of a bishop. He had no idea who it might be. He asked me to keep my ears open.'

March 5th 1940

Cycled to Nuncio's Residence after work to inform him
of rumours I had heard indicating Bishop Concannon
as being under investigation. Stressed it was only a rumour but thought to be reliable. Nuncio troubled but very
grateful to me.

'There is nothing much of relevance after that as I left for
Rome a short time later. Some journey that was, but that's for
some other time.

'When in Rome, I made my own enquiries about Concannon. TJ Kiernan was no great admirer but didn't know him
well. The Vatican in those days was a very small place, totally
Italian dominated, often a spiteful, self-important place. The
British were particularly unfriendly to us –they even tried to
stop us having our own embassy and went out of their way to
be unhelpful.

'My main source was Professor Semple of the Irish College.
Like me he was a Latinist and we got on very well. He told me
Concannon had not been much liked by the Irish community,
whom he seemed to avoid. It was somewhat different with the
British and he had been one of the few Irish clerics invited to
events at the British embassy. His great friend was a Ramiro
Marcone, a Benedictine priest who later became papal nuncio
to Croatia and who had taught at the Angelicum.'

O'Donnell was beginning to feel impatient. This was going
nowhere.

Dannaher seemed to sense his impatience.

'Be patient. Marcone was significant. In spite of being a
humble monk he was close to Cardinal Secretary of State, his
Eminence Eugenio Pacelli and had real influence in the Vatican.
It was he who gave Concannon his inside track.'

He took another sheet from his desk and read.

May 1940

Message from Dublin. Unconfirmed British rumours of possible Irish intervention in Spanish politics. Unnamed bishop suspected of involvement. Please investigate.

'We did try but we could find nothing apart from the earlier rumour that it might possibly be Concannon. The feeling in the embassy was that, if there had been any complaints about Concannon, Marcone would have intervened on his behalf. But that was only speculation on our part. We had no evidence and it was a time of all sorts of wild rumours, so we had to tell Dublin we had no information.'

Dannaher was now lost in his own thoughts.

'I wrote to Paschal Robinson about this and he suggested I get to know Marcone, whom he already knew. He wrote me a letter of introduction. It took some time. Ramone had been appointed Papal Legate to Croatia in 1941, but visited Rome frequently. Rome was a small place then and I did eventually get to meet him. My excuse was my interest in medieval studies and we had a good chat. He was a genuine scholar and happy to talk to me.

'Eventually, I steered the conversation to Ireland. He spoke warmly about his good friend "Tomazzo" Concannon and expected him to be the next leader of the Irish Church when either Dublin or Armagh became vacant. He thought it would be Armagh and said it was a shame that Tomazzo's great plan to help the Church with new Spanish methods had been frustrated. I immediately asked "What plan?" I realised as I was asking that I had become over-eager and Marcone was immediately on his guard.

'His attitude changed and he brought our conversation to an end. He was not unfriendly but he ignored my attempts to meet again and, apart from confirming for myself that Concannon had a Spanish connection, I was none the wiser.'

Dannaher was not finished.

'Marcone was now an archbishop and served as nuncio in Croatia, with no great distinction but with the full support of the Vatican, turning a blind eye to the terrible atrocities carried out in the name of Catholicism. A bad affair that, but he seemed very pleased with himself – though in fairness, he did help some Jewish children escape to Turkey. The next I saw of him was at the end of the war when he became a strong supporter of the Catholic Action movement. He was active in helping Luigi Gedda set up the new Christian Democrat party to combat the Communist threat in Italy and it was rumoured too that he was involved with some resistance group in Croatia. But they were only rumours.'

Dannaher then recounted his last meeting with Robinson.

'It was late 1945. He was tired, even thinner and gaunter. He seemed quite depressed. He told me he found the Irish bishops tiresome and difficult. He sought consolation in his scholarship and his friendship with other scholars, especially Dan Binchy. I thought he was a bit obsessed by the bishops. I remember his exact words: "They are authoritarian and take the people's loyalty for granted. They may come to regret it – and they will if they continue to treat the people as if they were moral infants. In any event, they don't like me. They see no need for me and most of them ignore me."

'I asked him about Concannon and the rumour I relayed to him in 1940. He told me there was definitely some substance to it but he never got to the bottom of it. In fact, he told me the whole thing may have begun at his own table out of a conversation between Concannon and a very rich and very ill Englishman. They both seemed very taken with this extremist Spanish organisation *Mysterium Fidei* and, whatever they were planning, probably involved this crowd.'

Robinson then told Dannaher that, whatever the plot was, Dev moved quickly. Not a word appeared in the papers, there were no rumours and Concannon continued as bishop. All that could be said was that he seemed to be pretty subdued for a while.

Robinson then said it must be a coincidence that they were now talking about Concannon because only yesterday he had a phone call from Concannon asking to come to see him as a matter of urgency. Robinson said he would see him next week and would ask him then.

'That was my last meeting with Robinson and I never got to know what Concannon had to say –if anything. Maybe, indeed probably, Robinson left a note of that meeting.'

A sudden thought occurred to Dannaher. He did not share it.

'I then asked Robinson about Marcone. His reply was very definite. "A bad one." He felt there was something soft about the Benedictines but always found them to be good people. But not Marcone. His support for the Ustaše was outrageous and, when he came back to Rome, he was up to his neck raising money for Catholic Action and meddling in politics. But the Pope – and his judgement of people is far from infallible – thought highly of him. He continued to be influential and maintained a close friendship with Concannon.'

Dannaher had little more to add. He still had some further papers to sort out, but was convinced Marcone held the key to their puzzle about the money.

Newrie was sceptical, but this turned to concern when Dannaher told him of his invitation to lunch with Valetti. He had been delighted to accept and told them he could probably get a little more information about what the nuncio was up to.

Newrie was uneasy. He had begun to like Dannaher, but the man was a gossip and who knows what he would let slip.

On that note, they parted company. Newrie to Smyth's for a solitary pint or two. O'Donnell went to meet Heather Ruddock.

41

....

Richard E Murdock was in an angry mood when he left the Brannocksbridge Arms. He had been bested by Johnny Ryan, the ungrateful little fucker. And to think of all the pints and meals he had bought him over the years.

But now at least he was in a position to find out who it was his uncle had been meeting all those years ago. From that he hoped he would discover the source of the money and maybe even why it was given. And if he knew that, maybe he was halfway there. Or so he told himself.

As he worked his way through the notebooks, he had to admit Johnny had been well tutored by the bishop. And he wondered again at the bishop's need to control every aspect of the world around him.

Each page recorded every journey made by Johnny – date, time of departure, time of return, mileage, place visited and in most, though not all, cases the name of the person visited. Johnny had neat, old-fashioned writing, which made it easy to get through the pages with relative speed.

Most of the visits were routine – parish visits, confirmations, ordinations, the occasional funeral and wedding – including Murdock's own wedding. There were meetings in Maynooth and meetings of the Committee on Church Renewal, which Concannon chaired, and meetings with the Department of Education in Marlborough Street.

All of this was to be expected, but Murdock could not help being impressed by the sheer energy and impressive workload of his uncle. He had often been described as dynamic and Murdock could well believe it.

He decided to concentrate on the early years and, before long, he felt a pattern was emerging. The entries for 1939 yielded little except perhaps a flurry of meetings with some fellow called Alsop and a solicitor called Charlie Ruddock. Ruddock. He knew that name and vaguely remembered a firm of that name was still in business in Dublin. He would check that out, but from what he knew it was mainly in the corporate world – about which he knew little.

And Alsop? Well he could answer that. The bishop presided at his funeral in Haddington Road church in Dublin in November 1939. But that did not rule him out as the source of the loot.

The notes for 1940 proved more productive. A series of meetings with named individuals, all one-to-one meetings and, with one exception, always in the Stephen's Green Club. That exception was with a Joe Bradley and the meetings were apparently at his residence in Dalkey. Ulverton Road to be precise.

He made a note of this and also of the other names – a Professor Hogan, a Ted Nolan, Joe Bradley, FX Grace, Mortimer Buckley, Eoin O'Duffy (where had he heard that name before?) and a Spanish name that meant nothing to him.

There followed a series of almost weekly dinners in the club over a period of six weeks in 1940, which ceased almost as quickly as they began. After that, the only name from that list that Concannon kept in contact was Joe Bradley. A quick perusal of engagements for later years showed regular dinners at Bradley's Dalkey house up to 1945, when they ceased abruptly.

Murdock had already decided Bradley could be the main lead and realised he knew nothing about him.

He also noticed something else. In 1939 and 1940 there were frequent visits to the papal nuncio. These stopped abruptly in mid-1940. Only one further visit was noted, but that was not until the end of 1945. Why? He had never heard of Paschal Robinson. Was he relevant?

There was one further point of interest. A series of meetings at a house in Northumberland Road. Always in the afternoon and clearly all Johnny Ryan knew was that he was a 'Spanish diplomat'. Or maybe the actual name was too complicated for him.

After a few hours trawling through the details, Murdock realised he was not much wiser. There was only one person who could help him. Fuck it, he thought. There was only one place he could go – back to Johnny Ryan. The stakes were high and, if he had to eat a bit of humble pie, then so be it.

He acted on impulse and phoned Hickson's pub. It was not long after opening time, but Johnny would already have been to the bank that morning and cashed the cheque.

Johnny replied almost as if he had been expecting the call.

'So you're still talking to me?'

'Of course I am Johnny. I might have done the same myself if our roles had been reversed. But you drove a hard bargain, so you did.'

'And you're back now because you need more information. I've done well and I'll give you any help I can.'

***

Murdock pulled up outside the Brannocksbridge Arms just as the Angelus bell was ringing. This time there was no talk of lunch. It was pints and straight down to business.

'It was a great job to have. Your uncle liked cars, although he never learned to drive. His first car was a Dodge and then the Bentley. Great cars to drive and they always made an impression, which is what he wanted. I know I was only the driver, but sitting behind the wheel of a Bentley could give you notions.

'The bishop always sat in the back seat. He had a reading lamp and was either reading or saying his Office. I'll say that for him – he said his prayers. But he was considerate to me. He had the cook Mary Kielty make up sandwiches for me, real sandwiches with roast beef and ham, and a flask of tea. Better food than I got at home.'

Murdock was going to remind Johnny that it was rumoured that Mary Kielty gave him more than sandwiches, but decided to cut through the reminisces.

'The names, Johnny. Can I start with Henry Alsop?'

'I only saw him once. It was back in 1939 before the war, but not long before it. He had his house on Lansdowne Road, just up from the rugby ground. The bishop came away looking very happy. The next time I saw him was at his funeral in Haddington Road a few months later.'

No progress there. Maybe *Who's Who* might be of help.

Johnny went through the names of the people the bishop had been meeting. He had little to add. Hogan was 'aloof and stuck-up – a typical Fine Gaeler', Nolan was a 'rat-faced little fucker who totally ignored me and told me not to park the car outside his house', but that was all he could add.

'There were only two people he called to on a regular basis. The first was a Spaniard. I could never get his name, but I believe he was the number two man at the embassy. The bishop used to say he came from an old aristocratic family, but to me he was arrogant and rude. As far as he was concerned, I was a servant and should be ignored. Sometimes Joe Bradley turned up at these meetings.'

'Anything strange or odd about them?'

'One funny thing. I told you the meetings ended abruptly in 1940 but, very shortly after that, your man, the Spaniard, was killed after falling from his horse in the Dublin mountains. The strange thing is the bishop didn't attend his funeral. I was surprised, but he was very preoccupied and worried at that time. He never told me why.'

'And Joe Bradley?'

'A different kettle of fish altogether. A returned Yank. Seemed very wealthy – certainly had a big place in Dalkey. He had a nice friendly wife and one son I think. I was always brought into the kitchen while the others were talking. I was well treated and Bradley often slipped me a few quid. He was a man who liked people and was always in good humour. Some of the lads told me he had a bad reputation from the Troubles, especially in the Armagh area. But he was always good to me and he was the one person the bishop continued to visit. Up to 1945 and then suddenly I never heard his name again. As abrupt as that.

'Whatever it was between them, it put the bishop in to fierce bad humour. Like a scalded cat he was. I saw Bradley's death in the paper years later and I asked his lordship if we would be attending the funeral. He just looked at me and smiled, a sad smile, and simply said "No Johnny. That was in a different world." That was the first and last mention of him since that day in 1945.'

This time Johnny bought the drinks, which Murdock accepted. He had learned something, little enough to justify the two thousand pounds Johnny had cost him, but enough to keep digging.

42

....

Morgan Dannaher never made it to the top in his department. None of the great postings ever came his way – London, Paris, Washington – even though he felt more than qualified to hold any or all of them. Much of his career had been spent in backwater postings or on administrative work at home.

It was something he resented and tended to put down to his suspected homosexuality. In fact, his bosses had long known of his orientation but saw it as being 'of the harmless variety', and not likely to lead to embarrassment for the department. His friends, if asked, had a different explanation for his failure to make it to the key postings – he was a gossip and a mischief maker. In his own words, he liked 'to stir things up'. He felt it made him 'great company at a dinner party', and it often did, but what amused his friends in the club was seen by his superiors as a serious lapse of judgement and the mark of someone who could not be fully trusted. One of his bosses had told him as much.

When he told O'Donnell and Newrie that he had met Valetti at a reception and Valetti had been interested in his friendship with Paschal Robinson, they were apprehensive. They were even more so when he told them with a twinkle in his eye that he 'might stir things up' a little and provoke Valetti into 'showing his hand'. They were right to be apprehensive.

The nuncio's residence in Cabra had none of the grandeur, faded as it was, of the old residence in the Phoenix Park. It was a functional and charmless building set in the grounds of a former convent.

It was this which gave Dannaher his opening gambit when he arrived. He was able to tell Valetti of his friendship as a young diplomat with Robinson, of his visits to the old residence and then years later how he came to visit Robinson – then ailing – after his return from Rome.

'I always felt he was a bit isolated. Most of his friends were either scholars like Schrodinger or Binchy, or else his fellow Franciscans – though in truth he thought them a rather dull lot. He always felt he was never welcomed by the other bishops and, strange as it may seem, he often asked my advice in those days.'

'What kind of advice?' asked Valetti somewhat sharply – the very question Dannaher had been inviting.

'Again, and strange as it may seem, it was often about how this bishop or that was seen by the government.'

'But why would the government concern itself with bishops?'

'Well it was wartime and they were afraid of anything that might endanger neutrality. It was often paranoid stuff, but it was the mood of the time. Anyway, there were suspicions that one or two, Armagh especially, were pro-German and the government was worried. And there was a time when they thought one of the bishops was up to something or other with Franco. Nothing ever came of it I'm happy to say.'

'Who would that have been?' The question was abrupt.

'Oh, he's dead, long retired and forgotten now. But he was seen as a powerful man then with good connections in Rome. Concannon from Kilderry. Have you heard of him?'

'Kilderry and Concannon. Two months ago, I'd never heard of either but I'm hearing too much of them these days. Strictly between ourselves, I've reason to believe the bishop there – can't think of his name – is up to his elbows in some financial chicanery arising out of Concannon's will. There is talk of large sums unaccounted for. I don't like that sort of thing. It looks bad and reflects on all of us. But they refuse to answer my queries and won't invite me to the diocese. It is worrying.'

Dannaher could feel his worst instincts were asserting themselves. He was back to his old self.

'I don't think your predecessor would have been surprised. He suspected Concannon in 1940 – I tipped him off – but something more serious happened around 1945. He never told me what it was and it never became public, but it ended any friendship he might have had with Concannon. That I do know.'

Dannaher paused. He had Valetti's full attention.

'I looked to see if there was any record of Concannon's activities in the department but found none. I know for a fact, though, that Robinson kept careful records – his old journalistic training I'm sure. He was a stickler for records and kept Rome well briefed on all that was going on. He told me he wrote them all in Latin – Rome liked it that way and he enjoyed the intellectual stimulus of writing in Latin. Indeed, our mutual love of Latin was one of our common bonds.'

Valetti cut in. He saw a point and he wanted to get to it.

'Yes, I know. I've seen all his records up to 1940. That's 11 full years. And yes, I'm a Latinist too and he did write well. He mentioned you in one of the last records I found.'

'And?'

'And I can't find the records for the last eight years of his life. Can they have been destroyed? But who would have done that? Certainly not one of my predecessors – as far as I can see they had no interest in history or records, so who would have destroyed them?'

'And you have searched everywhere?'

'I think so. We have an archive here. Recent and not well organised, and no sign of them.'

Dannaher was silent for a long pause.

'I have a hunch, and it's only a hunch, but it is the only possibility I can think of.'

Valetti was brooding and not expecting anything of use.

'In the early 1980s, your people decided to get rid of the old residence. It was riddled with dry rot and very run down because your people, who got it rent-free, never invested a penny in its upkeep. As it happened, I was one of the government officials, along with the Board of Works, asked to decide the future of the building and to see if the State had any use for it. There was talk of making it an official residence for the Taoiseach, but neither Haughey nor FitzGerald were interested. So the decision was made to demolish it.'

'Yes, yes I know all that – but how does it help me?'

'*Festina lente.* I decided to have one last look around. I had good memories and quite frankly I thought I might find some little memento or souvenir to remind me of Robinson.'

'And did you?'

'What I found was that your predecessor had got there ahead of me. The only really valuable things were the two Gandon fireplaces and by then they were on their way to Sicily. It was theft, you know, and there were Dáil questions, but nobody wanted to know.'

'Indeed,' said Valetti, who knew the story well and would have done the same himself.

'But that is not my point. The rest of the remaining furniture was divided into three lots – stuff that would be useful in the new embassy and this table we are sitting at and the sideboard in the main hall are part of that lot. Lot two was poor quality stuff and was to be sold off at auction.'

Dannaher paused for effect. He had Valetti's attention now.

'And the third lot was a series of boxes and filing cabinets with Robinson's papers and other records. And there was one rather battered desk where Robinson – and I checked this – kept his more intimate papers. They were earmarked to be stored in the basement of the new building until a proper archive could be built.'

Dannaher allowed himself another Sambuca before beaming almost beatifically at Valetti.

'Excellency, if you can find that battered old desk, you have your papers. I am sure it is in some storage space in this very building and has been ignored all these years – all these years since 1981. Find it and you solve all your problems.'

Valetti was thankful but impatient. He couldn't wait to get rid of Dannaher and start his search.

As he sat in his taxi on the way home, Dannaher felt very pleased with himself – a not uncommon happening. He did not feel he had broken his trust with O'Donnell and Newrie or that he had done anything wrong.

He had just done what he had always done. He had stirred the pot and would sit back and see what happened.

43

....

Peter O'Donnell was surprised and more than gratified by the warmth of the welcome he received when he called to Heather Ruddock's penthouse apartment after his less-than-happy meeting with Dannaher.

'I've two surprises for you. I've been doing some rummaging around in a box of my father's papers I found in my attic. The wonder is they were not dumped years ago, but the woman who looks after our records hates throwing anything out. I keep telling her how valuable our space is and to be ruthless, but clearly she pays no attention to me. She was here in my father's time and I think she sees his papers as some sort of holy writ. Anyway, I asked her to look around and within the hour she placed a very dusty box on my desk. Most of it is really of no value but, lo and behold, there is one document that may interest you.'

There was a pause.

'But before I even offer you a gin and tonic, we have other business to attend to.'

And so they had. O'Donnell, who did not lack experience and was somewhat taken aback by the frankness and directness of her approach, soon found himself every bit as enthusiastic as she was and it was some time before the offer of a drink materialised.

As they sat around, she in an exotic kimono and he in what he now realised were very unfashionable underpants, she lit a cigarette and suddenly became serious.

'Peter, there is something I must say to you.'

He froze. He was no stranger to post-coital conversations and experience told him to be wary.

'I want you to know something. I love my husband and under no circumstances will I ever leave him. This may seem strange sitting here now, but I want you to know it. To be honest, I like sex and I need sex. That's the way I am and I know, believe me I know, I can only have good sex with someone I really like and I really like and enjoy you. But I don't want you to fall in love with me and if I think there is any danger to my marriage then I will end it. What I am saying is I can't give commitment.'

O'Donnell was relieved to hear these words, but he knew from past experience that this was not the reaction expected of him so he chose to remain silent.

'Peter, I know how you must feel and I understand it. And I'm not saying we must stop seeing each other. Absolutely not. I love being with you and of course I want to keep seeing you. But please understand my position. All I'm saying is we must be discreet. That is all.'

He decided the only appropriate response was to take her back to bed. It was the right response.

Then they finally got around to discussing the files she had brought to the apartment.

'I was very interested in the story you told me about Concannon and I want you to bring me up to date before you leave tonight. I mentioned to you I had another phone call from Archie Bowe. He told me he was an old friend of my father but the truth is my father couldn't stick him – 'a typical Fine Gael small town solicitor, up his own arse and full of old codology' was how my father described him. I told him as little as I could, played it very vague, but probably said enough to confirm his suspicion that there had been enquiries. I didn't say where they came from and told him we had nothing of interest in our records. I don't think he fully believed me but that was that.'

She pulled over a file from the table.

It was a record, or 'attendance' as it was named, with Henry Alsop in early 1939. The note recorded that Charlie Ruddock had already transferred cash to the value of £100,000 to the account of Thomas Patrick Concannon in the Munster & Leinster Bank in Dame Street.

The note also recorded the details of the stocks Ruddock was to transfer directly to Concannon 'for the realisation of purposes already agreed between Alsop and Concannon'.

Attached was a full list of the stocks and shares.

O'Donnell couldn't hide his excitement.

'Brilliant. Now I can compare this with the stocks and shares he left in Kilderry. That will show us just how much the old codger got rid of.'

And there was more. A note dated late 1940 and based on what Ruddock described as 'a very reliable' source indicated that shares to the value of £400,000 had been disposed of over a three-week period, the American shares apparently doing very well.

A final note dated 1945, and again sourced to 'reliable information', indicated that a further £400,000 of shares had been sold.

Charlie Ruddock had once again been given details of what had been sold – and appended his own estimates. This was in 1945. The sales had been expertly executed by a skilled stockbroker who concentrated on American shares, but he reckoned the remaining shares amounted to nearly a million pounds and would certainly appreciate.

Scrawled across the note Ruddock had written: 'What the hell is going on here?'

'This is brilliant. Now I can go back and check out the rest and get a true value. Your father was a shrewd bloody man and he'd an inside track on the stock exchange. And if there'd been further transactions he'd certainly have been told.'

'He was all of that. But he belonged to a generation that kept their mouths shut. If you hadn't been so good in bed I would never have bothered going after that information. But now I'm hooked and we're going to work this out together. I want to see my father vindicated.'

She was not smiling. The hard edge that intimidated both clients and opponents was there. Whether O'Donnell wanted it or not, he had a new partner. And on balance he wanted it.

'Now, I have a tough case tomorrow. I need my sleep. Get back as soon as you have a plan worked out.'

O'Donnell made the short journey back to Percy Place in a happy mood and slept well. He made an early morning call to Tommy Newrie.

'Tommy, we need to get down to Kilderry as soon as we can. I'll pick you up at the hospital at 12.30 and tell you in the car.'

By 2 pm they were in Concannon's old study in Kilderry checking off Ruddock's old list against what remained. Basically, the details tallied and the 1945 estimated £1million valuation of the shares could be multiplied eight times over in present-day 1997 values.

Bishop Mullins had joined them. O'Donnell was struck by how haggard he looked, his clothes even shabbier and his appearance unkempt.

'What's new?'

'An awful lot. We know Concannon tried to keep whatever promise it was he made on getting the money. Whatever it was, it happened twice – once in 1940 and again in 1945. Nothing we know of happened after that, so they had either achieved their objectives or there was nothing more he could do.'

Mullins met this with a listless shrug of the shoulders 'Great. But how does that help us?'

'If we find how the money was spent that might guide us to the original purpose and maybe help you sort out what happens next. And if we can't do that, you're back to square one and in the middle of a messy legal situation.'

'I should never have opened that bloody safe.'

'Well you fucking well did. And we can't leave things as they are. Too many people know and, as soon as some journalist gets wind of something, you'll find yourself at the centre of an almighty scandal. And you'll be hung out to dry by your bloody colleagues.'

'What can I do?'

'Get up off your fat arse, stop feeling sorry for yourself. Go up to that prissy little fucker Archie Bowe and demand he open that letter Concannon sent him on his deathbed. You're the Bishop of Kilderry. He works for you, not for God as he appears to think. Act like Concannon would have acted. Threaten him if you have to but, one way or other, tell him that if there is a scandal he will be caught up in it too.'

Newrie marvelled at his friend's dressing down of the bishop. But in fact, O'Donnell's words seemed to cheer Mullins up.

'You're right. He has no right to withhold that letter. I'll show him who's boss.'

And suddenly the self-pity and lethargy were gone.

44

....

When Monsignor Nestor arrived in Kilderry the next morning he was astonished at the change in his bishop. Mullins looked 10 years younger. He had shaved and showered and his clerical suit even looked as if it had been dry-cleaned. And more than that, his appetite had returned and he was well into his substantial fry.

'Jimmy, that nephew of yours is a great young fellow. I can see why you speak so highly of him.'

Nestor was surprised. Up to now the bishop had seemed to treat O'Donnell as little more than a necessary but temporary nuisance.

'Why do you say that?'

'He did some straight talking to me yesterday. It was hard stuff, but every word of it was right.'

Another mouthful of egg on fried bread followed by a slurp of tea.

'I hope he was not offensive.'

'Of course he was offensive. And he meant to be offensive. He told me I was a fucking disgrace, that I was supposed to be a leader and here I was full of self-pity, blaming everyone and doing nothing to help sort out the mess. He even said half of the mess was of my own making.'

'That was pretty rough. But maybe he had a point.'

'Of course he had a point and it brought me to my senses. It was the first time anyone spoke to me like that since I became a bishop. Mind you, some of my friends told me that once I became a bishop I would never hear the truth again.'

And back to the rashers and more tea.

'Was there a specific issue that brought on this exchange?'

'Yes, he told me this Dublin solicitor, a Mrs Ruddock, a Protestant by the sound of it, had got more information for us about the source of the money and about how a lot of the original cash disappeared in 1940 and in 1945, but we would never get the full story while – and I use his words – that little prick Archie Bowe sits on his pride and will not open that last letter from Concannon. He told me I was the Bishop of Kilderry and I was entitled to know what was in that letter and, if Bowe would not show me, then I should fire him and go to another solicitor – he even said Mrs Ruddock would be willing to act. And I've to tell Bowe that I will make sure the world knows he was fired.'

Nestor listened in horror.

'My nephew spoke like that?'

'And dead fucking right he is Jimmy. And I agree with him. I've asked Archie Bowe to be here at 12. You can sit in on it if you wish.'

'But John, the Bowes have been solicitors to Kilderry for over 100 years. Think of the scandal that would cause.'

'And that's what Archie Bowe will think of as well. The scandal, the loss of face, the humiliation. And that is why he will do as I ask.'

Nestor was certain the bishop was right. But he was disturbed. This would not be his way.

'And that's not all Jimmy. I drank a half bottle of whiskey last night to help clear my mind of all the shit that has been building up since we discovered that bloody treasure trove.'

Nestor had never known Mullins to be a drinker, but he had been told that a few whiskies at the right time could help a man think more clearly. It was not something he had ever put to the test.

'Jimmy, you know I never wanted to be a bishop. It came as a shock to me when I was asked. It should have been you but you had your enemies. I was running a small parish and spent a lot of my time helping Nurse Martha Keane run her hostel. I still try to get a few hours a week with her and, to tell the truth, it is the only part of my work I enjoy.'

He headed down to the kitchen and came back with a fresh pot of tea.

'I was flattered to be asked to become a bishop, and I accepted for all the wrong reasons. It pleased my parents to have a son a bishop; it got up the noses of my old classmates at Maynooth who regarded me as a second-rater and now I had passed them all out. I'm not very proud of that now and I suppose, in fairness, I thought I could do some good.'

'And you have John; far, far more than you realise. You have been fair and humane with your priests and a true pastor to your people.'

'Maybe,' said Mullins sceptically. 'But I hate it. Anyway, that topic is not for today but I will come back to it when all this mess is sorted out.'

This last bit puzzled and unsettled Nestor. What did he mean 'come back to it'? But it was not the time to pursue the matter.

'What your nephew said yesterday jolted me back to my senses.'

Nestor could see he had more to say.

'We're a funny breed, us priests. We lead a lonely life but we are not meant to be lonely. Christ was never lonely. We have a celibate life and for most of us celibacy is not a normal state. Christ never said a word about it and the apostles never bothered with it. When I was ordained Jimmy, it was faith that bonded me and gave me a purpose. I did want to proclaim my faith in the watches of the night. But you know, Jimmy, as you get older your faith does not burn as strongly as it used to and when that happens you can feel very vulnerable.'

He saw the look of shock on Nestor's face.

'No, don't worry Jimmy. I'm not going to do a bunk, but you know I am right. You're one of the exceptions Jimmy – you are a genuine believer. This whole thing has set me thinking about myself and the effect this bloody money is having on me.'

'But your first reaction was how much good you could do. You were spending it already.'

'True. But it was all about me. It led me on the path to that greatest of priestly sins – no, not sex. Greed. It was all about what I could do. I saw myself at the centre of all that happened and I was becoming arrogant and impatient. Your nephew jolted me back to reality.

'I really do hate being a bishop. I hate those bishops' meetings in Maynooth where the very first reaction when something comes up is not whether it is right or wrong but how can we cover ourselves. It's bring in the big Dublin lawyers and fight everything. They don't see the harm they're doing and it's going to come back to haunt them and they will deserve every bit of it.

'Jimmy, I'm sick of it. We think of everyone but the victim and of everything but the sin. Child abuse, a bland phrase that covers what it really is – rape, buggery, torture, lives destroyed. I try to speak in these terms but I mustn't be doing it well. The cardinal just gives me that baleful look of his and talks about canon law and the guidelines and directives from the Holy See.'

He stopped and Nestor could see he was close to tears.

'I'm sorry, but I had to get that off my chest. And I'm glad I have. To tell the truth, I wouldn't have got to this point if it were not for your nephew and that drop of whiskey.'

'So what now?' asked Nestor, fearing the worst.

'We have a problem to solve. We have to bring this whole mess to a conclusion.'

'And how do you propose we do that?'

'We know now the money was never meant for Kilderry, so we will not pursue our claim. But we are still the lawful custodians of the money. We hold it until we establish the purpose it was given to Concannon. If we can't establish that, we have to find a way in which it is used for the common good.'

Nestor noted that when the usually bumbling Mullins wanted to be clear, he could be very clear indeed.

'We fight off those vultures circling around. For a start that useless, parasitic family have no rights of any sort and we will make that clear.'

'And the nuncio?'

'I've talked to Dominic Irwin about that Sicilian rogue.'

'He's Canadian actually.'

'Sicilian blood, but no matter. Dominic tells me he is tough, tricky and ruthless and Dominic knows what he is talking about. He has been doing his own research and tells me Valetti was involved in a bit of a scandal in Cyprus and sent back to Rome in some disgrace. He knows Rome, does Dominic, and he says Valetti had his protectors there, laid low and was cleared in what was generally seen as a cover-up. That's Rome, Jimmy, but Dominic also sniffed out, and I don't know how, that Valetti has money problems here. We will need a good lawyer – a Dublin lawyer – and I think your nephew has the one we need.'

'You mean you won't use Archie Bowe?'

'No bloody way. I want a Rottweiler, a toughie and preferably a Protestant who would have no fear of the Vatican, or the Knights or Opus Dei or any of that crowd. I will trust your nephew. He knows that world. Jimmy, you and I are mere provincials.'

Nestor could not disagree. The years had fallen away from John Mullins. He knew what he wanted to do and was ready for the fight.

Starting with Archie Bowe in an hour's time.

45

....

Archie Bowe was not expecting anything like what happened. He had thought long and hard about his position. Indeed he had thought about little else since he discovered he had been effectively sidelined by Bishop Mullins in the events following Concannon's death.

To him it had all been a great betrayal, not just of himself but of his father and grandfather. This was a question of principle. He had to make a stand and his mind was clear as to what it would be.

He hadn't been pleased to be summoned to a meeting in such a peremptory fashion and it added to his already overflowing sense of grievance. He would show what stuff the Bowes were made of. He had a century of tradition to fall back on.

He expected capitulation and recalled how distressed and irresolute Mullins had been at their last meeting. Clearly a man under great stress, not fit to be left to his own devices and in serious danger of being badly advised by whatever arrogant Dublin firm he was talking to. He was a man who had to be saved – and the diocese with him – from himself.

That was Bowe's thinking as he arrived on the dot of 12 at the bishop's residence where, to his surprise, he was met by a clear-eyed and business-like Mullins.

'Well Archie, I expect you have brought along the documents left to you by Dr Concannon. You can leave them with me and I will let you know what we are going to do in due course.'

'My Lord, with respect, you don't understand. There were very strict and explicit conditions pertaining to the opening of that particular material and, you may remember, I was to be the sole judge of when these conditions existed – or not, as the matter might be.'

'Archie, it's you who doesn't understand. These are Kilderry papers. I am the Bishop of Kilderry. This is a matter of vital importance for the diocese of Kilderry. I have decided I must see what is in those papers and, moreover, I am fully entitled to overrule you in this matter.'

'My Lord what you ask is most irregular and I can't in conscience allow it.'

'We all have consciences Archie and on this matter my conscience is clear. I want this matter sorted out once and for all and I want it done now. Immediately.'

'Yes, my Lord. So do I. But not by taking shortcuts.'

'Shortcuts my arse Archie. Let me be clear. The bishop, my predecessor, left a great deal of money – after he had also spent a great deal on we know not what. What is left is in stocks and shares, which have not been touched in 50 years. He got that money for a specific purpose but that purpose clearly was not for Kilderry. While he lived, the diocese never saw a penny of it and, unless you have evidence to the contrary, he never intended it for us. In blunt terms Archie, that money is not ours.'

Bowe looked shell shocked as Mullins continued in a softer tone.

'Archie I have to confess when I first learned of the money I became greedy. Greedy for Kilderry maybe, but greed is greed.'

Bowe tried to intervene but Mullins was in full flow.

'Other people are greedy now as well – that worthless family of his, the nuncio who seems to believe he has some hold over the money and maybe there could even be a crowd called *Mysterium Fidei*, who I believe are nosing around.'

Archie again tried to intervene.

'And maybe even your own firm Archie, for all your high-mindedness, will be expecting its cut.'

Mullins had meant to be offensive and Archie was ready to be offended.

'All I'm saying is that the Bowes have been loyal to Kilderry, but Kilderry has been good to the Bowes. I know how much we pay and, in fairness, we seem to get value, but we pay...'

He left the words hanging there.

'Now Archie, this is what I propose to do.'

He paused. He had Archie's full attention.

'I intend to find out first the purpose for which the money was intended. I'm sure the original purpose – specific purpose that is – is no longer relevant and has long ago disappeared into history, but I intend to find a modern-day equivalent and let them have the lot.'

'But there will be legal difficulties, court cases even,' spluttered Archie.

'I don't doubt it, but I will get good and honest advice. It will be my job as Bishop of Kilderry and custodian of the money to make the final decision. After that, *fiat justitia ruat caelum.*'

He didn't need to translate. Archie knew his Latin.

'Meanwhile, I will deal with the family and the other imposters as roughly as I choose – and it will be rough.'

Archie had not prepared for this and his natural caution told him it was time to retreat and regroup.

'Archie, you are talking to a man even more stubborn than yourself. Either those documents are on my desk by 5 pm this evening or I will replace your firm as our legal advisers. I don't want to do it Archie and I was wrong to say I would make it widely known. If I have to, I will do it quietly and discreetly – but I will do it.'

He stood up to leave.

'Oh, one last thing. I am asking a Dublin lawyer with no Church connections to look after us in the resolution of this particular matter – just this matter, at least for the moment anyway.'

He had not done anything of the sort, but he was on the way to doing it and he wanted Bowe to realise the gravity of his own situation,

A shell shocked Bowe – this had never happened to a Bowe in over 100 years – asked the name of the new lawyer. Mullins told him he would know soon enough. He would leave it to O'Donnell to choose the firm but felt he probably had the right person already.

46

············

It was early next morning when Peter O'Donnell got a call from Bishop Mullins.

It was not the morose, negative, and petulant Mullins he had become used to.

'Peter, you have done me a great favour. You told me the truth and it has made me a new man. Now let me tell you what I think.'

He repeated to O'Donnell the analysis he had given Archie Bowe, and with much the same plan of action.

'I've been a fool up to now. Worse, a clerical fool wrapped up in my own canonical world of unreality. That's over now. We are going to get to the bottom of all this and sort it out for once and all.'

He told him in full of his conversation with Monsignor Nestor who, as O'Donnell expected, was nervous and apprehensive but did not disagree. O'Donnell was pleased – he did not want to be disloyal to his uncle.

'And Archie Bowe? Did he give you the documents?'

'No. I had a strange, sad little note from him that arrived at 5 pm precisely. I have it here. Let me read it to you.'

He read from the handwritten note.

'My Dear Lord Bishop,
I would not be truthful if I did not tell you that your attitude yesterday pained and shocked me. I hope you will reflect on some of the harsh things you said yesterday,

and on reflection will realise how unfair you have been to me and reconsider your views.

As to the instructions I received in Dr Concannon's last letter. He said very clearly that, unless his name and his reputation were damaged or misrepresented in some public controversy, I was not to open the documents. To the best of my knowledge, and I have researched the matter as fully as I could, there has been no public controversy and indeed no reference in any of the public prints to the late Bishop or his affairs.

I, therefore, feel bound by this instruction. May I gently point out that *he* wrote to me as *his* solicitor, and it is in that capacity I must and will act. I feel I can do no other and I would ask you to accept my integrity in this matter.

I would also say to you that our firm has never acted for the diocese of Kilderry out of any consideration of financial gain. We feel it a great honour to have acted for the diocese for over a century. Our loyalty is total and the well-being of the diocese is our only concern. I would ask you to accept this.

May I make one last point. I share your impatience to see this matter resolved. I do not take seriously the claims of the family, the papal nuncio or any other body to the monies concerned. I agree with you that the central issue now is to find out the purpose of the original donations, the destination of the monies already disbursed and then to decide what –if anything – in current circumstances would be appropriately done with such funds as will remain after all costs are taken in to account.

To this end, I am prepared to see if anything in our own records will help resolve these questions and I will be happy to assist in any way you deem appropriate.'

'The bottom line,' said O'Donnell, 'is that he still won't give up the document, even if he is eating humble pie. And I notice he is putting in a marker about his costs as well. Once a lawyer, always a lawyer.'

'The threat of losing the account and the shame of it all has given him a jolt of reality,' Mullins observed. 'I don't basically give a shit who our solicitor is and it is probably better to keep him inside the tent –barely inside mind you – for the moment anyway. Now that the gun is to his head, he might come up with something.'

'So, what next?'

'We need a new solicitor to handle this side of things and to speed things up. I do not want one of those Catholic solicitors who see themselves as defenders of the faith. I've seen too many of those boys lately and I don't like them, craw-thumping vultures.'

'So what do you want?'

'Someone who is a good lawyer, tough, irreverent, and with real balls. Preferably a woman and better still a Protestant.'

'Why a woman?'

'Peter, everyone in this case is a man – myself, your uncle, yourself, Tommy Newrie. We are all men. We see, think and talk like men. And that's why we are stuck. In my experience, women think differently, they are more direct, more pragmatic and more ruthless. Believe me, I know. And what's better, clerics and the Vatican hate dealing with women, especially tough women. So Peter, get me a woman.'

O'Donnell was taken aback.

'Why me. Surely you know one yourself?'

'You know more about women than I do. You know the Dublin scene. I want a Dublin lawyer with no ties to Kilderry or to the Church. What about this woman who got the information for us? You must have told her something to get her involved and her father knew Concannon. It was you who told us how good she is.'

'You mean Heather Ruddock?'

'Of course I mean Heather Ruddock. Can you get her now?'

***

Within 10 minutes, O'Donnell was talking to her.

'But Peter, I'm a corporate lawyer. I don't deal with real people. This will be very new to me.'

'This won't need too much law and, if you need advice, you know where to go. This job will need decisiveness and balls. That's what the bishop said when he asked me to get you.'

'Did he really say that?'

'They were his very words.'

'I like him already.'

There was no more hesitation.

'I'll have to talk to my partners but, since I bring in twice their income, there will be no objections. There might be a conflict of interest for me since my father represented Henry Alsop. But it was a long time ago and I think not. Yes, and it would be different. But ... do you think I'm the right person?'

'I'm certain of it. And one more thing. Your father would love you to do it. For him, Concannon was unfinished business.'

She was hooked.

47

....

Morgan Dannaher should have been happy. He was a player again, back centre-stage with a real role to play, no longer an irrelevant former ambassador.

But what role? That was the rub because he knew he had done it again. It was the same old weakness that had damaged his diplomatic career over and over. If there was a pot, he had to stir it; if there was a pudding, he was the man to over-egg it. He had shown once again what his colleagues had long known – he quite simply could not be trusted.

Peter O'Donnell and Tommy Newrie had brought him back from obscurity. They seemed to like him and they had trusted him, brought a little excitement in to his dull life and given him a new sense of purpose.

Why then had he rushed off to Valetti, so readily, almost gushingly given him information about Concannon and so crassly explained how he might find Paschal Robinson's missing papers? Was it to make himself more self-important, to be seen as a power broker? And more ominously, why had he steered Valetti in the direction of Joe Bradley or, more relevantly, his son Jeremy? Jeremy indeed – the man had been christened Jeremiah but had changed his name to Jeremy as soon as he got to Ampleforth. What pretensions!

He still shuddered when he remembered old Joe Bradley – a man about whom there were more murky questions than known facts. He knew Bradley was treated warily by those who had known him. And de Valera, who he had loudly supported, was the wariest of all.

But Bradley had been close to Concannon. Some would say Concannon was almost in awe of him. And Concannon was rarely in awe of anyone. In the back of his mind, Dannaher had a sense that, whatever happened to Concannon's mystery money, Bradley had a hand in it. Nothing else explained their friendship. What else could they have in common?

And then there was the debacle in 1945 with Archbishop Marcone and the Civil War in Croatia. In fact, Dannaher had been more involved in all that than he should have been – and certainly more involved that he had ever told his bosses. It would do his reputation no good if all that came out now. Why had he mentioned that to Valetti? He had sent the reports back from Rome that time –the ambassador was away – and had carefully played down the whole Croatian matter. What if all that surfaced now?

Why did he feel the compulsion to make unnecessary trouble for himself? And it hadn't ended there. He had confided to a judge friend in the University Club that there were financial issues in an unnamed diocese that would be highly embarrassing for the Church and could well end up in his lordship's court. He liked to be thought of as someone in the know but he, of all people, should have known that a rumour, once it reaches the Law Library, would inevitably sprout wings and grow.

He was sinking into one of his fits of depression. He could already see some of his old colleagues smirking to themselves – 'Old Morgan's done it again. No wonder he had to be put out to grass. And you know he was probably the cleverest of us all. Pity he had no judgement.'

He was awakened from his reverie by the phone – a rare enough occurrence these days. Would he take a call from Archbishop Valetti? He had no choice.

'Morgan, old friend. Just to say how helpful you have been. I found those papers exactly where you suggested. Lucky that dimwit of a monsignor had not shredded them. I glad to say they are helpful. Your friend Paschal sure kept good records, but I've still a bit to go.'

Dannaher said he was glad to have been of help.

'One more thing. You mentioned old Joe Bradley. His son was at the same reception as you. Suave guy, but when I mentioned his father and Concannon he just froze up. Any idea why? As it happens, I'm off to talk to someone who knows this town very well and he may be helpful, but I just thought you might have known old Joe.'

'I'm sorry Archbishop, I was out of Dublin in all of those years and never met Mr Bradley, or his son either for that matter, though his name keeps coming up in the newspapers with all his high-flying financial deals and his so-called philanthropy. But I will make some enquiries if that is helpful.'

Valetti thanked him and said they must meet again soon.

Dannaher put the phone down, feeling even more confirmed in his treachery. 'What a little shit I am,' he said aloud and, even though he never drank during the day, he poured himself a large Scotch, and then two more.

Eventually he dozed off and by the time he woke up he felt much better. He had made a decision.

It was never too late to do the right thing, he told himself. Tommy Newrie was a good and decent man and had shown a care and kindness towards him that he did not deserve. He had snapped him out of his loneliness and despair, and this was how he repaid him.

It would not be easy. It required a little humility on his part – a quality for which he had never been noted – and it would mean some painful delving in to his own past, maybe even resurrecting a ghost or two, but he knew he would never again have peace of mind if he did not.

He would do it.

48

....

May 27 1940

Colonel Dan Bryan was feeling the pressure. He knew how worried de Valera was and he shared Dev's concern. He had received two new messages from Daniel Woodman to the effect that the British were convinced Franco was just waiting for the right time to join the war on the side of the Axis powers. Woodman knew for a fact that the British embassy in Madrid was spending huge sums in bribes to Franco's generals just to keep Franco neutral, but it did not seem to be working. The Irish ambassador in Madrid had heard similar stories.

The specific problem for Ireland was that Churchill never believed the British should have vacated the Treaty ports in 1938 and that, day after day, British intelligence was attributing the loss of convoy ships on the North Atlantic to their absence from these ports. Bryan believed the reports to be wildly exaggerated but suited Churchill's purpose or, as Woodman had reported one British minister saying: 'We don't need much of an excuse – any excuse will do for us to seize the ports. And the sooner the better.'

Concannon's ill-judged intervention could be just such an excuse and could be used ruthlessly to seize the ports should it be thought necessary.

Bryan felt he now knew enough. It was time to be active. He had a meeting scheduled with de Valera for the following day – enough time to tidy up a few loose ends in preparation for that meeting. He had a feeling that de Valera was ready too.

He had in front of him a letter from Bishop Fogarty. The key part told him what he wanted to know.

At the last meeting of bishops, I used my senior position to raise the question of Irish neutrality. In truth Dan, and you may not believe it, we rarely discuss political matters. The Civil War divided us as much as anyone else.

There was some surprise when I raised the issue but I insisted that we needed to have a clear and unified view against the possibility of an invasion – from any side. I stressed we had a situation where all parties, most politicians and most of the people were united in support of neutrality in the dangerous situation now prevailing. I said it was important that we, as a country, do nothing to provoke an invasion which would impose untold hardship on our people and it was only right that we, as bishops, were careful that nothing we did, either by word or deed, would create mischief or damage this policy.

I could see some of my colleagues wondering what I was at, but it did provoke a discussion, most of it pointless blather until Kilderry intervened. He is always clear and speaks with confidence.

He agreed with me about not doing anything to endanger neutrality but then he said, and I quote his exact words: 'After this war we will be faced with a dramatic new situation and new challenges to our very existence. We are a universal Church and must look at new ways of proclaiming and sustaining the gospel. We should be open to new developments in the Church, especially movements that were now emerging in the Iberian Peninsula and we should not leave it too late to start preparing for an uncertain future.'

I believe what he said went over the heads of the others.

*But Concannon is not a man for idle words or vague rhet-
oric and, to tell the truth, he spoke with a sort of intensity
I had never seen before. It led me to believe something
may already be afoot. But, I can say categorically that no
other bishop is involved or even suspects anything. Nobody made mention of it at our lunch at any rate.*

*Bryan had already spoken to James Hogan, meeting him once
again in Larry Murphy's pub. As instructed by Bryan, he had
attended the latest meeting of Concannon's group. Some of the
other members were frosty, believing he had opted out. Hogan
said he could feel their hostility but Concannon, however, was
friendly and explained Hogan's absence had been due to urgent
university business.*

*As Hogan explained it to Bryan, the central point of what he
called 'the Crusade' (as Concannon had earlier described it) was
simple. According to Concannon, the Catholic Church had to prepare for survival in what will be a different, dangerous and hostile world. This would need new types of priest – warrior priests,
worker priests. It would mean an organisation built along military and conspiratorial lines. Members would be skilled and specialised and could act in secrecy, infiltrating other organisations
where necessary – just like Communist cells had been doing for
the past decade.*

*Concannon then explained that a model for such an organisa-
tion already existed. It was called Mysterium Fidei and was based in
Spain. Contact had been made with Mysterium Fidei through Señor
Sánchez at the Spanish embassy and Concannon had met a Spaniard in Dublin believed to be a senior figure in Mysterium Fidei.*

*Señor Oatizola, as the man was called, met Concannon in the
Stephen's Green Club and told him that, of course, they would be
pleased to help another Catholic country but it would require funds*

– they had nothing to spare from their work in Spain. A building was required as a matter of urgency where Irish volunteers – some of whom might already be ordained priests – would be trained, or as Concannon described it 'receive formation'. Señor Oatizola said it was essential that the money which Concannon said was available – or at least a sizeable chunk of it – was channelled to Spain as soon as possible. Concannon assured the assembled group that there was no time to waste in getting the money to Señor Sánchez without delay.

Concannon assured the meeting that sufficient funds were available and they must not arouse any suspicion by seeking funds elsewhere. No one asked him the source of these funds nor did he welcome any questions.

This, said Hogan, was the grand plan announced by Concannon. There would be three main players, apart from Concannon himself. Señor Sánchez would handle relations with Mysterium Fidei and any Spanish officials who might need to be bribed. Señor Sánchez assured them all was in place and already a large building near Salamanca was being considered. The second player would be Ted Nolan from the Munster & Leinster Bank, who handled the relevant account, and Joe Bradley, who had contacts – I cannot say more, he said – which would enable himself and Señor Sánchez to get the money through this Oatizola person to Mysterium Fidei.

The strictest secrecy was essential. He might need some help from Mortimer Buckley of the Department of Justice and FX Grace from External Affairs, but otherwise nobody needed to know the details.

Concannon assured the group that, in the fullness of time, each would have their own role to play. He specifically saw Hogan as being a major intellectual figure in explaining the new developments when the time came to do so.

Hogan told Bryan he thought the whole thing was crazy but, on Bryan's instructions, he had kept his mouth shut. It had not been easy, he said, when he saw Joe Bradley being put in charge of the money given what he – and Bryan – knew of Bradley's behaviour in the Civil War. He also had the height of contempt for most of the other conspirators.

Bryan asked Hogan for his estimate of Concannon.

'Very powerful, very certain in his own sense of being right. Highly intelligent but with no sense of people and no common touch. He thinks in concepts, a zealot maybe or even a holy fool.'

Bryan's immediate reaction to Hogan's report was to step up the surveillance he had already put in place on both Bradley and Señor Sánchez, and add Ted Nolan and Mortimer Buckley to the list.

The apparent key role Bradley seemed to be assuming came as no surprise to Bryan. He had not been surprised when Bradley had fled the country during the Civil War. And he knew it had nothing to do with political differences. The Irregulars were even more glad to be shot of him than the Free Staters. Bryan knew well of Bradley's penchant for settling personal differences in a very final way and dressing them up as political actions. He also knew of a number of bank robberies where Bradley was suspected of involvement and where there was never any trace of the stolen monies.

Bryan was surprised when Bradley returned to Ireland in late 1934 and was sceptical of Bradley's new persona as a self-made wealthy businessman. Bradley had money. Of that there was no doubt, but Bryan's enquiries through his FBI contacts had not yielded any evidence of specific businesses. The FBI's suspicions of his involvement in bootlegging were shared by some of the begrudgers who made up the Dublin social scene.

For once, thought Bryan, the begrudgers might be right. And he noted too that money, whatever its origins, opened doors. Not all doors, but enough.

Bryan had warned de Valera about having any involvement with Bradley, especially when Bradley loudly endorsed de Valera's economic war policies. Dev made sure never to be seen in public with Bradley or photographed with him. Lemass listened to some of Bradley's suggestions for industrial development, but never followed up on any of them. Bryan suspected the report Dev had asked him to make on Bradley had made up Lemass's mind. How typical of Dev, not to instruct Lemass but to make sure he got Bryan's report.

All of this made Bradley's friendship with Concannon all the more puzzling, but Bryan told himself this question would wait another day. He was waiting on some information he had requested from Leopold Kerney in the embassy in Spain. When he had that, he would be ready to act.

All he had to do now was to get de Valera's approval for his plan.

49

....

June 7 1940

Dan Bryan had outlined to de Valera his proposals for dealing with what they had both begun to call 'this Concannon business'. Dev had listened carefully before adding two 'suggestions' of his own. Dan Bryan knew that a suggestion from de Valera was much more than that and so he readily agreed that Dev would personally confront Concannon and brief the nuncio.

And now, as France was falling to the Germans, Bryan was sitting in the Taoiseach's office in Government Buildings as they reviewed the events of the previous days. Bryan would not say that Dev looked happy because he never looked happy, but he could see that he was very relieved as Bryan made his report.

'I decided from the outset that the key priority was to stop the whole thing in its tracks and to do so in a way that no word of any sort leaked out. That meant dealing with the three key people, disable them first and then tidy up the rest today.'

Bryan was anxious that de Valera's old enemy, James Hogan, should get full, if grudging, credit for his role. In his world, debts should be repaid in full.

'The three key players I had, and especially from the reports of Professor Hogan, were Concannon himself, Ted Nolan from the Munster & Leinster Bank and Joe Bradley. You said you would deal with Concannon so I will outline what I did and then you can fill in the rest.

'My first call was to Ted Nolan. He is a widower, living alone in his house in Rathgar. I called to his house at 7 in the morning. He was up but still in his pyjamas and I made sure he saw the army car parked in his drive. He was outraged and full of bluster. He quickly calmed down when I told him I was here on your specific instructions and we could talk in the house or I would take him into the Bridewell and might even tip off the press if I did. He invited me in.'

'And what happened?'

'I was rough with him. I told him we knew everything about the Spanish venture, about Concannon and Mysterium Fidei, and I could see how shaken he was. I told him we knew about the large sums of money and even hinted I knew its origin, which of course I don't – at least not yet – and told him we knew he was the conduit for the money. Of course, he denied everything but then I named his co-conspirators and told him he was being investigated under the Offences Against the State Act.

'That softened his cough and then I told him if he did not co-operate you would call in the Chairman of the Bank and he could say goodbye to his job, his pension, the lot. But I said, if he told us everything he knew, the matter need never go public.

'Taoiseach, it was not a pretty sight. The man is a bully, a nasty little one at that, but now he was blubbering like a child, all defiance gone, full of self-pity and saying he was only doing it for the Church and thought he had the full approval of the Church – as if that mattered.'

Bryan had Dev's full attention.

'Anyway, he told me Concannon had deposited a large amount of money on two occasions in late 1939. The first money had been transferred by a solicitor we both know, a man called Charlie Ruddock, a very decent man Taoiseach, acting on behalf of a very wealthy Englishman, a convert to Catholicism called Henry Alsop.'

Dev interjected.

'I know both of them. Mr Lemass told me about Alsop helping him get some industries going though nothing came of it. And I agree Mr Ruddock is a good man with a fine national record.'

In other words, thought Bryan, a good Fianna Fáil supporter. But he kept his thoughts to himself.

'In any event,' continued Bryan, 'the second sum of money – the money lodged a few weeks ago – was from the sale of some stocks and shares, which the original benefactor had given Concannon and which the bishop held in Kilderry. The sale of these shares was managed by Joe Bradley and the proceeds were briefly lodged in the bank before being used by Bradley to advance 'the project' as they had taken to calling it.'

'Follow the money and do it as clearly as you can, step by step,' instructed Dev.

Ever the schoolmaster thought Bryan.

'Yes Taoiseach.' Bryan would never call him 'chief'.

'Nolan said that after the sale of shares, the account amounted to £460,000.'

De Valera was visibly taken aback by the size of the funds.

'Nolan says there is now £60,000 left so Bradley spent £400,000 buying property in Spain and paying Mysterium Fidei to set up the college and other expenses. At least that is what Bradley and the Spaniard said, and they produced receipts to back this up. The only snag Taoiseach, is that all the receipts were in Spanish and on Spanish headed notepaper and, given the secrecy of the operation, Nolan was in no place to check their validity – even if he thought of doing so.'

'So as far as we know,' said de Valera, 'the money went to Spain.'

'As far as we know Taoiseach, as far as we know. But I have my doubts and I will be following up. But for the moment that has to be our working assumption.

'I asked Nolan for a full and detailed account and I told him that, in view of his helpfulness and the delicacy of the issues involved, I would ask you to be lenient. Though to tell you the truth Taoiseach, I have absolutely no sympathy.'

He did not expect de Valera to reply, nor did he.

'And Bradley?' Dev asked, moving things along.

'A different matter altogether. I had warned Nolan not to contact him and took the precaution of cutting the wire to his phone but, when I arrived at his mansion in Dalkey, Bradley did not seem surprised to see me. Actually, I felt he might even have been expecting me. He was utterly defiant, indeed insolent, but that won't surprise you Taoiseach. He denied everything except his friendship with Concannon. A dear family friend he called him and a true Church leader.

'Yes, they did have dinner together from time to time, sometimes at his residence, other times in the Stephen's Green Club. It was all very open and above board. What I was alleging was all fantasy, another of those malicious begrudging Dublin rumours put about – and I use his exact words 'by Free State bastards like myself'. He challenged me to arrest him and to charge him if I had evidence, but he knew I had none.'

Bryan paused, clearly angry.

'I could have arrested him Taoiseach, but I knew it would leak out and that is the last thing we want. I'm just going to have to keep digging and the most we can hope for just now is that, whatever it was intended to do, will not happen now.

'You did the right thing Dan. And keep at it until we get the full story. Now let me tell you about my encounter with the bishop.'

Suddenly it was a different de Valera. No circumlocutions or qualifying clauses. It was Dev being direct and simple and, moreover, pleased with the story he was about to tell.

'I called to the bishop's house in Kilderry at very short notice.

I was on my way to a by-election meeting in a neighbouring constituency so no one was aware of my visit to Kilderry. My office only phoned the bishop shortly before I was due to arrive. He met me at the hall door, clearly surprised but all smiles and civility. I wasted no time on formalities, no kissing of the ring and the barest of courtesies.

'He could see I was angry as I told him the game was up, that we had uncovered the plot and that any sensible person could see that what he was doing was a threat to our national security at a most dangerous time. It could even be seen as treason. I told him it had to end straight away.

'He was shocked and indignant. How could I speak to him like that? He began to talk about the supreme importance of the future of the Church, but I cut him short.

'I said in my coldest tone "It will end. This tomfoolery will end this very minute. It will end right now." And I told him not to think for one moment that I was bluffing. I said, "I will not hesitate to have you arrested, bishop or no bishop, unless you give me an answer right now. Right now. And if you don't, I will bring you before the courts. You had better believe me."'

Dev was clearly relishing the retelling of the encounter and Bryan reckoned that, apart from Frank Aiken, no one else would ever hear this story. The story would be as safe with Aiken as it would be with him.

'You know Dan, I stood up to the bishops before and I would not hesitate to throw one of them in jail if they gamble with the safety of the people.'

According to de Valera, Concannon was deflated. Nobody had ever spoken to him like that before. He almost physically caved in. 'I got him to give his word to bring it all to a speedy end or face a very unpleasant future. He agreed, but all he could say, over and over again, was something about all the money being spent. Almost in a mumble.'

Dev concluded: 'At this point I took my leave. He did not see me to the door. The only person I encountered was his driver, who had a warm welcome for me. If only he had known what transpired between myself and his boss.'

De Valera's smile was never more winterish.

'There is one more thing Taoiseach. I contacted Ambassador Kerney in Spain. He has good Church connections and I asked him to find any connections between Mysterium Fidei and Ireland. He came back very quickly. He knows their leaders and could say categorically they had no links with Ireland or with the Spanish embassy here at any time. They would hope at some later date to come here but, for the moment, they had more than enough to do helping Franco establish his Catholic state. Taoiseach, I believe Kerney and, if what he says is true, that raises some interesting questions as to what is really going on.'

Bryan was not quite finished.

'From what I can see, this fellow on Concannon's committee, what's his name, Sánchez, he does not seem to be of any real consequence. That at least is Kerney's view. He would not be in a position to buy property or the like in Spain. As soon as I get a chance, I will have a word with him.'

'Dan, what exactly is going on here? What is it we are really dealing with?'

'Taoiseach there is more here and less here than meets the eye. The conspiracy as we know it is no more and tomorrow I will talk to you about what to do with the others involved. The great thing is there was no publicity and nor will there be. The British will have no excuse to invade from that quarter, though I'm sure some other fools will try. But this one is over and that is the important point for you and for the country.'

Bryan was blinking at a rapid rate, as he did when he was thinking.

'But a great deal of money has disappeared and could come back to do damage. I sense you feel the same way?'

'Can we do anything?'

'Not just yet. And better not to stir anything up just now. We've other problems. I will try and sort out the other conspirators tomorrow and I will keep an eye on our friend.'

And with that he was dismissed.

Dev did not say thanks twice in the same day.

50

....

July 8 1940

Dan Bryan knew about the death of Gonzalo Sánchez Pena well before he read it in the Irish Independent, which reported it under the heading 'Sad Death of Spanish Diplomat' with the sub-heading 'Riding accident in County Wicklow'.

According to the newspaper, it was believed that Sánchez, an experienced rider who was riding alone, had been thrown from his horse close to a forest area in Wicklow at about 10 o'clock on Sunday morning. His body was discovered by the owner of the riding stables when Sánchez did not return at noon. Two hours later, Bryan knew of his death.

Bryan had issued instructions at the outbreak of the war that any incident involving a foreign diplomat, however minor it might seem, was to be reported to him as a matter of urgency. His immediate reaction was to phone the Commissioner of the Guards asking that, in addition to normal police enquiries, an experienced criminal investigator be assigned to conduct his own parallel investigation and to liaise directly with Bryan.

He now had Superintendent John Gantly's preliminary report in front of him, as well as the official Garda version of what happened.

The official report was succinct. Sánchez was an experienced horseman who knew that part of the countryside well. He rode regularly with the Bray Harriers on Saturdays and on Sundays would take his horse out for a long ride from the stables at Kilma-

That, according to the report, was the only safe inference to draw, though the stable owner said the rider would normally take such a ditch in his stride. The only suggestion the owner could make was the possibility that the horse had been frightened and reared up causing the fall, although she was doubtful that this was the case. However, in the absence of any witness or other evidence, the initial conclusion had to be accidental death.

The doctor who attended the scene, Dr Hennessey, said the head injuries were so severe that death was almost certainly instantaneous and did not feel a post-mortem was necessary.

The official report concluded that the death was almost certainly accidental and recommended the inquest not be delayed.

Such was the official report and Bryan's immediate reaction was that its authors wanted a quiet life. Diplomats in wartime were bad news and the fewer questions asked the better.

John Gantly's report told a different story, as Bryan thought it might. He had got to the scene almost as quickly as the official investigators and had a chat with Mrs Beechor, the stable owner. She was shocked but she was also puzzled. First of all, Sánchez was well off his normal course and there was no good reason why this was so. Secondly, she had examined the ditch and found no sign of any damage from the impact of the horse. Nor were there any marks on the horse's front legs from hitting the ditch. And thirdly, the horse had scampered away after the accident. This horse, she said, was deeply attached to Sánchez, who was a good horseman, and it seemed to her the horse would only run away if forced to do so through fear. She had no idea what might cause that fear.

Later that day, Gantly brought a young pathologist from UCD to examine the body in the morgue. Dr John Farrelly had no doubt that Sánchez had died from his head injuries, but was not at all sure they were consistent with a fall. The injuries suggested to him that the head had been bashed by a blunt instrument that did far more damage than would a fall.

Dr Farrelly took some samples from the injury area to have them analysed at the university, which would take a few days. He also examined the body and found heavy bruising in the lower back, which might have been caused by a fall, and some abrasions that might indicate the body had been dragged, possibly by the horse. However, Dr Farrelly thought it seemed more likely to be the result of a kicking.

Gantly told Bryan his investigations were continuing and would remain independent of the official investigation.

Bryan had Gantly's report with him when he arrived at de Valera's office. He knew it was a sensitive subject for de Valera – his own son Brian had lost his life in a riding accident in the Phoenix Park just four years earlier and it had affected him deeply.

He outlined his two police reports to de Valera who listened carefully – he could no longer read – but Bryan knew well that little escaped him.

'Taoiseach, I don't believe in coincidences. Nor I suspect do you. And this coincidence is far too convenient.'

'I agree Dan. I don't like it at all. But what should we do?'

'For the moment, I suggest we do very little. Accept the official version. Hold the inquest and bury the poor man. I presume he will have to be buried here. The last thing the country needs is speculation about a Spanish diplomat dying in mysterious circumstances – and especially if he is known to have friends in high places. The rumour factory would be working overtime and it would not escape the notice of the British.'

'I agree. It saddens me that we cannot bring his killers, if killed he was, to justice and maybe we eventually will, but the safety of the people and the State must come first.'

'The Spanish tomfoolery, as you called it, is over for the present at least, though not, I suspect, for good, and the death of this fellow Sánchez will probably ensure that,' Bryan added.

'It might be a good idea to keep an eye on the comings and goings at the embassy for a while longer but you know best about that sort of thing.'

'Meanwhile Taoiseach, I think there are one or two loose ends from the Concannon matter. Mortimer Buckley should not, in my view, be left in an important position in Justice. He has shown he cannot be trusted in a vital area of security. I'm sure Mr Boland can find some obscure posting for him. I don't think FX Grace of External Affairs meant any harm, but he is an idiot and he might be persuaded to take early retirement. However, that's your department and I am sure you will know what to do. Ted Nolan is in the business of the Munster & Leinster Bank, but a word with the chairman from Mr Lemass might not go astray.'

Bryan was not sure if he had overstepped the mark. You never knew with Dev.

'Yes Colonel, I will look after these matters in my own way and in my own time.'

Bryan was not giving up so easily. 'I don't doubt the next time you meet Professor Hogan you will give him a friendly nod.'

And hell will freeze over before that happens thought Bryan.

'Perhaps. I have a final question Colonel. What is the name of the bishop who was so helpful?'

As he looked up, Dev was smiling.

'Maybe, Taoiseach, I will leave that for another day.'

'Of course, Colonel. Oh by the way, I expect you enjoyed your visit to Ennis.'

I should have guessed, thought Bryan. The bugger has his spies everywhere. And he wants to make sure I know that.

As he left, Dev was still smiling. Bryan was not.

A few days later, Bryan attended the funeral of Gonzalo Sánchez Pena at University Church in Stephen's Green. It was a beautiful July morning with a blue sky and a new sense of life in the air but, inside the ornate and richly embellished Church, the mood was sombre. As Dean of the Diplomatic Corps, Paschal Robinson presided as a Spanish priest intoned an especially mournful Requiem concluding with a De Profundis that seemed to Bryan to go on forever.

Bryan noted with interest the absence of Bishop Concannon. Maybe he had another appointment or maybe he did not want to be associated with his one-time collaborator.

There were few people present, just the Spanish ambassador and his military attaché, a few diplomats from other embassies and a few of the Church's regular Mass-goers – and three news-paper reporters. Bryan was pleased to notice the discreet presence of two undercover policemen. Good. Gantly was doing his job.

And one other person. Taking centre stage and showing osten-tatious signs of grief and loss was Joe Bradley.

Bradley's presence – or non-presence – was the main reason for Bryan's attendance. He noted how Bradley made it his busi-ness to sympathise loudly with the ambassador and the nuncio, and made sure the reporters noted his presence. Sánchez was a good friend, he said loudly and more than once, and his 'accident' deeply upset him.

The only person Bradley made no attempt to speak to was Bry-an. But Bryan made sure to stand where Bradley could not ignore him any longer. When he felt they were out of earshot, he glared at Bryan.

'Well, he is safe from your lying calumnies now. He was a

good and decent man but no doubt you would have blackened his reputation just as you are doing now with mine. I know what you are saying but you know nothing and never will. I've bested better men than you, you little Free State lackey.'

Bryan could feel the venom and the barely suppressed violence. He smiled and said nothing. He was making his point and ensuring that Bradley knew he was a suspect.

A few days later he had a visit from Superintendent Gantly.

He had the pathologist's report prepared by Professor Farrelly. The injuries to the skull were too severe to have been caused by a fall. Fragments of wood had been found, suggesting a blow from a cudgel or hurley stick. The other body bruises suggested a beating rather than a fall and that the body had been moved some distance from where the incident took place. Professor Farrelly was in no doubt about the cause of death.

Gantly's own re-enactment indicated that the stable owner was correct; there was no evidence the horse had failed to jump a ditch.

And finally, a car had been seen in the area on the morning in question – an unusual occurrence on a Sunday morning where there were no car owners. It was this rarity that had prompted curiosity among people who liked to keep careful watch on the comings and goings of their neighbours.

Gantly also said they had a partial registration, ZD 5—. They were in the process of narrowing down the possibilities.

By the time the conversation ended, both Bryan and Gantly were sure they had a murder on their hands. Not an 'accident' as returned by the inquest.

Nor had Bryan or Gantly any doubt who was behind the murder. Gantly even felt he could guess the identities of the men Bradley had hired for the job. But for the moment, and they were in agreement, de Valera's dictum held sway.

But before parting, they agreed that this was one file that would remain open and active – even if they could not share it with their colleagues.

As Gantly said as they were parting, 'the mills of God and all that'.

But it was scant comfort to either of them.

Bryan made sure the record of his meeting with Gantly found its way to de Valera's desk.

51

....

Morgan Dannaher had been right. In a cellar that Archbishop Valetti did not even know existed –not because it had been hidden from him but because he had no good reason to see it being of any interest to him, at least until this moment – among various bits of bric-a-brac and coated in dust, he found an old wooden filing cabinet. In the second drawer were the missing papers of Paschal Robinson. They had not been hidden away – merely misplaced. So, there was no mystery there. Nobody was covering anything up.

When he asked the Peruvian monsignor, who had been at the embassy for over a decade, why the papers had not been properly archived, he got just a shrug of the shoulders and the news that his predecessor had no interest in archives and anything not archived when he arrived was simply dumped in the cellar.

'And some of it was shredded. He liked neatness. If that stuff you now have had not been in the drawers, it might have been dumped too.'

The Peruvian, who did not like Valetti, seeing him as brash and casually racist, made no attempt to apologise for what had happened.

Valetti had the papers dusted down and brought to his study. They were in good condition and seemed to be in some sort of chronological order. There was no indication that they had been touched since Robinson's death. So no cover-up and nobody else on the trail. Valetti's own instincts and his Roman training ensured he looked for conspiracies everywhere, and his life experience assured him he was often right.

He would get down to them tomorrow. Some college or other was having a centenary Mass and he had agreed to attend. Another boring evening.

And he had more than Robinson's papers on his mind. He had been puzzled by the reaction of Jeremy Bradley when he asked him about his father's past. Great charm at first, but when Valetti pressed for more detail the shutters had come down. He had clearly touched a very raw nerve. But what nerve? He doubted if Bradley's vague offer of a lunch sometime would be followed up.

Jeremy Bradley was hiding something. But what? Joe Bradley had been linked to Concannon. But how and why? From what he could see, they were very different people. He needed to know more or it would keep bugging him – and he knew the man who could help.

Nobody knew more about Dublin's hidden secrets than Sebastian Madden, his bookie. The Kilderry money, which finally arrived, had paid off a good part of his debt, although with few winners of late he was not yet out of trouble. But he was at least in a position to invite Sebastian for lunch –obviously not in the nunciature – and he would do that straight away.

The next morning, he began his perusal of the files after an early breakfast. He was careful and systematic in his approach. His training had been good.

One of his first finds confirmed what Dannaher told him and what he had noticed already in the earlier files. Robinson made careful notes of what he saw as significant conversations as much as of dinner party discussions.

The first note was dated 1940.

Met last night with junior official in Department of External Affairs. He had phoned to say he had information I might find useful. I believe him to be reliable but not yet convinced he is fully to be trusted. He had been present when de Valera had warned me of dangers to neutrality from within the hierarchy so knew my concern and my curiosity.

He tells me he has heard a rumour which emanated in the Department of Justice. He stressed the rumour was unsubstantiated and vague but that the department was concerned that Bishop Concannon of Kilderry was involved in unspecified activities which could be of danger to the State.

I have no way of verifying this rumour but if true will hugely surprise me. Concannon!! In my mind the most able and energetic member of the hierarchy and a possible successor to Armagh. Hard to make sense of it.

So Dannaher was telling the truth.

The next note was not long after.

Attended lecture at Royal Irish Academy by Professor Eoin MacNeill on the work of the Irish Manuscripts Commission. MacNeill is a scholar of the first rank but his reputation is tainted by his political misjudgement in 1916.

After the lecture, I met Professor James Hogan of University College Cork – also a medievalist. Hogan too is a fine scholar, at least as a medievalist, but somewhat eccentric as a political philosopher. An honourable and kind man.

I felt he was uneasy with me which has never before been the case. It was as if he felt there was something he should tell me but didn't quite know how.

We talked at length about the fragility of Ireland's neutrality and the danger of invasion by either belligerent. Finally he said, and I noted his words carefully: 'I know you are here as a diplomat and have no jurisdiction over the Irish bishops and are not privy to their thinking. You spoke about our neutrality, which you rightly say has the backing of the people. I have come in to some information which I am honour bound not to disclose but suggests to me one of our bishops is involved in a venture whose purpose is noble but whose consequences may well have serious implications for the safety of our neutrality. I am worried. I suspect I should not have raised the matter and I will say no more.'

I assured him of my silence but asked him one question.

'Has the bishop concerned shared a table with you in my residence?'

He did not answer, which confirmed to me that it was indeed Thomas Patrick Concannon. I remember that evening well and both Hogan and Concannon were present. Others present that evening were Professor Tierney, the TD James Dillon and another TD from Fianna Fáil, Patrick Ruttledge and that strange and very unwell Englishman Henry Alsop. I remember too that Concannon and Alsop spent much time talking after the meal.

The third piece of information was dated late June 1940.

Received a telephone call from Mr de Valera's office. He would like to speak with me but unofficially. Could we meet at Senator Robert Farnan's house in Merrion Square at noon the following day.

I know Senator Farnan. He is an eminent medical consultant, a very devout Catholic and one of de Valera's few close friends.

The meeting in Farnan's fine house was very cordial. Only de Valera and myself present. He stressed it was informal and off the record. He was very grave, strained and tense, and I saw that steeliness I had first seen when he had spoken to me at the President's residence at the start of the year.

He said Bishop Concannon had been very foolish. Apparently, he had financial backing from an as yet unknown source and had embarked on an illegal adventure involving some senior people here, a Spanish diplomat but not the ambassador, who knew nothing, and some religious group in Spain closely associated with General Franco. The problem was that if this became public it could be construed by our enemies as a breach of neutrality and used as an excuse to invade.

The British do not regard Spain as truly neutral and confidently expect them to give their support to Hitler shortly. This has made them very jittery and their Government is under strong pressure to seize the ports. Our enemies, de Valera said, were waiting for the slightest pretext and we could not afford to take the smallest risk.

He then told me his officials had acted speedily. The danger had been averted and I did not need to know the details, but he was happy that danger was over.

He told me he had visited Bishop Concannon in Kilderry the previous evening at very short notice. He had spoken firmly with him – and here he smiled thinly, remembering perhaps his own treatment at the hands of bishops in the Civil War. Anyway he told me with as near as makes no difference to a smile that he had warned Concannon that if 'this tomfoolery' did not stop instantly, he would not hesitate to arrest him and if necessary imprison him. 'And I would too,' he said looking at me through those near sightless eyes.

He concluded by telling me he did not expect any further trouble from that quarter.

I asked him why he had told me all this.

He said it was a necessary precaution. He saw no need for me to report this conversation to Rome. He said Concannon was a good man, if foolish, and he didn't want his career damaged. But should rumours emerge, or should either of the belligerents question our neutrality on the basis of this story, he wanted me to be in a position to assure the Holy See of our true position. It is a precaution and I hope one that will not ever be needed.

I assured him that he could depend on my confidentiality and understanding and he seemed reassured.

I then asked him if any of Concannon's fellow bishops were aware. He said he hoped not but 'with that crowd you never know. Some are a bit loose with their tongues and I suspect one of them may suspect something and that one is no great friend of mine. But they won't want to damage one of their own.'

It was my longest ever meeting with him and, as he left, he told me he was fortunate to have in me a 'man of tact and wisdom'. Mr de Valera does not often pay compliments.

I felt he is a worried man – not about Concannon anymore, but about the dangers facing his country.

All very interesting thought Valetti. But where's the money? Where did it come from? This fellow Henry Alsop?

Time to talk to Sebastian Madden.

52

....

Richard E Murdock could feel his situation getting even more desperate. The new Dublin solicitor who was now acting for Bishop Mullins had none of the orotundity or politeness of Archie Bowe. In fact, there was no politeness at all.

He was talking aloud to himself, as he seemed to do increasingly of late.

'She is telling me I have no case at all so fuck off and stop bothering us.'

And Murdock, for all his bluster and bravado, had realised that, unless he could come up with some evidence of his own, some vestige of proof as to the bishop's intentions, then this solicitor woman, what's her name, Heather Ruddock, was right.

He began to re-examine what he had.

With the help of Johnny Ryan, he had combed through the appointments books of the 1940s.

Three points struck him. The first was the great amount of time his uncle spent on his bishoply duties – parish visits, education committees, meetings in Maynooth, pilgrimages to Knock and after the war to Lourdes. In other words, most of his travelling was just doing his job.

Then there was the cluster of visits in 1939 and 1940 for which there were names and addresses but no stated purpose. Most of the names appeared more than once. He had noted them down and made some progress on some of them. Henry Alsop remained a mystery and Murdock suspected he may have been the source of the money. But who was he?

Then there was the solicitor Charlie Ruddock. Ruddock? Could he be a relation of the new Dublin solicitor? Probably not, but he'd better check it out. Ted Nolan, he knew, was the bank manager in the Munster & Leinster where his uncle held his money. Professor Hogan he had never heard of. He found Mortimer Buckley and FX Grace in old State directories, but could see no reason for their involvement. And none of them had ever even spoken to Johnny, so no help there.

And the Spaniard, Sánchez. Murdock had discovered from an old copy of Flynn's *Parliamentary Handbook* that he was First Secretary in the embassy from 1938 to 1940 but did not appear in subsequent publications. But here Johnny was of some help.

'We did not ever call to him at the embassy, although the bishop went there from time to time to meet the ambassador. No, this fellow lived in Northumberland Road and seemed to live alone. He was a tall, bald, surly fellow. Very arrogant and treated me as if I was dirt. Never recognised my existence. As far as he was concerned, I was a servant and beneath notice. The bishop noticed it and I don't think he liked it.'

Johnny had stopped as if searching for something.

'A few weeks after the last time we called to his house there was a report in the *Irish Press* that he had been killed in an accident – fell off his horse, it said, up in Wicklow. When I saw it in the paper – the bishop never mentioned it to me – I asked would we be going to the funeral. I thought we would because he was very scrupulous about funerals. He simply said no and said it in a way I knew not to push any further.'

And then there were the meetings with Joe Bradley.

Murdock had never met Joe Bradley but he knew the legend – the old IRA man who made his money in the States and then came back and cut a dash in Dublin society until his death in 1977. Everybody heard stories about Joe Bradley and not all of them were to his credit or kindly meant. There was a whiff of danger about him.

The third thing which struck Murdock was that, after about May 1940, Concannon never again visited any of the group. With the exception, that is, of Joe Bradley. He met Bradley two or three times a week in May 1940 and very frequently after that, including the baptism of his son Jeremiah in 1942. After that, the visits were about once-monthly until 1945, when there was a flurry of almost daily meetings. Then it all came to a sudden end. The bishop had been jumpy and agitated on the way to that last meeting and Johnny was certain there had been a falling out. He could put an exact day on it. It was the last time they ever met and Johnny knew the bishop well enough to know he was both angry and upset on the journey back to Kilderry.

Murdock had pushed Johnny for more information about the relationship. Johnny said that, yes, it was a strange friendship but, as long as it lasted, it was a strong one. No two men could have been more different – Bradley, loud, rough, full of himself; the bishop formal and proper – but they seemed at ease in each other's company. What struck Johnny most was that, while the bishop dominated most groups, he seemed to defer to Bradley and he always seemed at ease in Bradley's company. Concannon often said to Johnny that Bradley was a man of great judgement. It was almost as if he had a blind spot about him.

Murdock pressed him again on that last meeting and got the exact date.

'It was October 6 1945. It was in Bradley's house in Dalkey and the bishop had been even more silent than usual on his way up. He sat as always in the back seat and he seemed to be reading and re-reading some sort of report. He had a strange look – anger, but also, I thought, a sense of sadness.'

Johnny had a strange intensity as he relived the event.

'Normally when he visited Bradley it was for dinner and I would go to the kitchen. The cook would give me a decent plate of food – the same as they were having upstairs. This time, it was late morning, he told me there was no need for me to go in. It would be a short meeting and we were not expected. It was not that short as it happened and I was not pleased because, thinking I would get a feed, I had brought no grub with me.

'Eventually, the bishop came out on his own. There was no one to see him out. He never spoke a word the whole way home and I could see he was shaken. I didn't put too much heed on it at the time, but he rarely went to Dublin after that, except for a visit a few days later to see the nuncio in the Phoenix Park – and it was years since he had last been to see that gent. And he never saw him again either.'

Johnny paused as if to recollect more clearly.

'But when I think back on it, he was a changed man after that visit. Oh he was still the boss, still kept his eye on everything and continued to terrify his priests. I would even say there was a new edge of hardness to him, but somehow he didn't have the same jizz he used to have.'

So where does all this leave me, thought Murdock.

Murdock now had a strong sense that Joe Bradley was the key to the mystery of the bishop's money. He wondered if Bradley had been blackmailing the bishop. But about what? Or maybe he had robbed him? Or maybe there was just a row and they had fallen out.

Murdock was beginning to feel out of his depth. But he was desperate and had a brass neck.

Maybe a direct approach was the answer. He would continue his enquiries about Bradley but would switch his focus to Bradley's son. If there was a secret, he was probably the

– 315 –

only man who had the answer. He only knew Jeremy Bradley through the newspapers and he would find out as much as he could. And maybe then confront Bradley directly.

It wasn't much. But it was all he had.

53

....

Heather Ruddock had surprised herself by how speedily she had accepted Bishop Mullins' offer to act as legal adviser to the diocese, for what he called 'the duration'. It would not be a permanent relationship and would concern itself solely with sorting out 'the Concannon mess'.

She accepted, in part at least, because of her father. He had been a big part of her life and Concannon had been a significant – and irksome – part of his. So maybe she could deal with unfinished business.

But it was more than that. Most of her work was in corporate law. She was good at it and was one of Dublin's highest paid lawyers. But much of it was life-denying stuff and meant endless dealings with desiccated accountants, predatory lawyers, central bankers and EU officials. She was more than willing to be diverted to something different that promised a little excitement and, if she was fully honest, kept her close to Peter O'Donnell.

She had to admit to herself that she was starting to enjoy his company. What had begun for her as a challenge, and maybe even a little revenge on her friend Louise, had begun to grow into something stronger. And it wasn't just the sex – although that was good. He was good fun too and a great teller of political stories. Mustn't let it go too far, she told herself. Peter seemed upset when she told him there would be no commitment, but he seemed to be coming to terms with it and this made her a bit more relaxed.

And this work would be different. That was for sure. She would do it *pro bono*; she could be herself, which meant she would be in control. That was her agreement with the bishop.

And so, the very next day she had summoned the key people as she saw them – Mullins, O'Donnell and Newrie – to a breakfast meeting in her office. Not in Kilderry. She wanted the bishop out of his comfort zone and she was making a point by scheduling it for 7.30 am. She did not ask if it would be convenient and nobody, least of all the bishop who would have to leave home at an early hour, dared to complain.

From what O'Donnell had told her, she felt she would like Bishop Mullins. And she did. He was not a smooth man and certainly did not fit her stereotype – and since she had never actually met a bishop, she had to admit her preconception lacked any real substance. For someone whose job required her to make rapid character assessments, she decided at once that Mullins was somebody she could trust.

She had arranged to have coffee and croissants ready in the boardroom, which looked out on the Pepper Canister Church, and if it was not the bishop's normal breakfast of rashers and eggs then so be it.

She wasted no time in getting down to business.

'Bishop, we can start with you. You're the main man in all of this and, if we are going to have a clear strategy, and it is evident that you have no strategy of any sort, then we need to know what you want the end-game to be. We can work back from that.'

Mullins seemed relieved that the decisions would no longer solely depend on him.

'I want the whole thing sorted out and ended as quickly as possible. I don't want a scandal, but I don't want a cover-up either. A cover-up means one lie after another and, sooner or later, the whole thing unravels. In fact, what I want to do is find the truth and tell the story – but I know that may not be possible.'

'But what about the money? I thought this was all about money.'

'So did I in the beginning. To tell the truth, I became obsessed, telling myself all the good things I could do. I could see myself as a modern-day Robin Hood.'

'And?'

'I don't feel that way at all now. I asked myself two questions: why did I become a priest in the first place and what was the money intended for?'

'And your answer to those two questions – or have you reached that point yet?'

'I'll answer the second question first. It is now certain the money was given by this man Henry Alsop to Bishop Concannon for a purpose. Straight away we can draw a number of conclusions. The first is that the money was never intended for Kilderry – if it was, Concannon would have used it and used it spectacularly. Nor was it meant for Concannon's worthless family and I hope we have sorted that one out. It certainly was not intended for the papal nuncio who, in my view, is a naked opportunist. We have heard nothing from *Mysterium Fidei* and, if those boys thought they had a claim, we would have heard from their high-powered lawyers by now.'

He paused to drink his by-now cold coffee. He would have preferred hot sweet tea but this was Dublin 2.

'Maybe when Archie Bowe opens that last letter from Concannon, which he seems to be guarding like the Third Secret of Fatima, we will get some clarity about it all and get Concannon's version of what it was all about. But I doubt if he will tell us very much. I think all we will get is some self-justifying whinge. His pride won't let him do anything else.

– 319 –

'So, in the absence of any clarity on the original purpose of the money – and knowing that circumstances will have changed out of recognition since 1940 – and when we have a clear valuation of the shares that remain, I want to set up a trust – you might even chair it,' he said looking at Heather, 'to allocate money to good causes. That is where it should go. I want it as simple as that. That is what you can call my end-game.'

This was the first O'Donnell had heard of this and he couldn't help contrasting the Bishop Mullins he had first met, so impatient to get his hands on the loot and spend it on his version of good causes, with the chastened Bishop Mullins of today, who couldn't wait to get shot of the money. He wondered what had brought about this sudden change. Before he could ask Mullins what had made him change his mind, Heather Ruddock cut in.

'And that first question you asked yourself. Your reasons for becoming a priest. What is the relevance of that?'

Mullins seemed almost eager to answer. 'I think I've always had a fairly simple view of life. I became a priest not because of any great sense of faith but because I wanted to help people. And when I was ordained I loved the work I was doing, working in the parish, working with ordinary people, consoling and helping them. I was one of them, I never talked down to them, I gave simple sermons. I was never hungry, I slept well and I was never lonely.'

'And then?'

'And then I became a bishop. I've no idea why I was chosen, though I suspect Concannon had pissed everyone off so much that, out of sheer spite, they picked someone he would hate – and he did.'

Mullins stopped and reflected. 'But that's not the point. I hate being a bishop. I hate being in charge of my fellow priests and I'm not good at it. I hate the bishop's meetings in Maynooth and all the half-truths and lawyerly cover-ups. I hate having to read letters from Rome that have no relevance to the lives of our people – or have anything to do with Jesus Christ for that matter.'

'Is there anything about it you like?'

'Yes, I like my number two – Monsignor Nestor – a good man who should have been bishop and who has been more than loyal to me. And the only other thing I like – and I think it keeps me sane – is when I put on my civvies and go to work with Nurse Martha Keane in her hostel in Brannocksbridge. Some of those down and outs are the victims of our own child abuse. She is a great woman. That's the only work that really fulfils me.'

'Nurse Martha Keane. Is that the Browngrove Centre?'

'Yes, do you know it?'

'I do and I admire the work it does. I even send the occasional subscription. But let's get back to the question of strategy. I think the bishop has given us a clear way forward. Is there anything else we need to know before we move in that direction?'

Tommy Newrie had a report to make.

He told them of his meeting the day before with a very distraught and repentant Morgan Dannaher.

Newrie told them his first reaction was one of anger and he was convinced they should have nothing more to do with him. But on reflection, he felt Dannaher had done no real damage and, what he had done, could be turned to their advantage.

'The rumours Dannaher feels he may be responsible for are relatively harmless and pretty vague. If they are published in the media they will be no big deal, and they may oblige Archie Bowe to reveal what's in Concannon's last letter, which is what we want – although I don't think there will be an awful lot in it. In my experience, people who spend their lives justifying their own behaviour to themselves have usually forgotten what the truth ever was – and I am certain that will apply to Concannon in spades.'

Dannaher had told him of his meeting with the nuncio and again Newrie saw no real danger coming from that.

'If the nuncio discovers evidence relating to the purpose of the money, then that solves our first problem – but I doubt he will. And Dannaher is right when he says the fact that Concannon left 20 thousand to the nuncio indicates the rest of the money was not for them. Otherwise why leave them a pittance in the will if they were entitled to the lot.'

Newrie then turned his attention to Morgan Dannaher.

'The old boy says he genuinely wants to help us. I believe him but, more importantly, I believe he can be of help.'

'How? And can we trust him?' asked Heather somewhat sharply.

'He told me that a man called Joe Bradley was a key associate of Concannon. In fact, Dannaher had pointed the nuncio in the direction of Bradley's son Jeremy at the reception. From what he observed, the encounter was not overly friendly. According to Dannaher, 1945 was the key year in the Bradley–Concannon relationship and he believes he can find out what exactly happened – that is if we are willing to forgive what he called his indiscretion.'

Newrie was clearly well-pleased with his contribution. He should have been angry with Dannaher but his job had told him life was full of little betrayals and he had come to like the man. And, as he said, it was worth a try. Whatever damage he had done was done, so they had nothing to lose by giving him another chance.

Heather Ruddock was gathering her papers. It was 8.30 and a day of fee-paying meetings beckoned. She finished up with a salvo of instructions, telling O'Donnell and Newrie to meet up with Dannaher as quickly as possible and instructing Mullins to stay on friendly terms with Archie Bowe – 'we might need him yet'. She said they would meet again in a day or two.

Meanwhile she would devise a new strategy.

54

It was said no man paid more attention to his public image or paid more to his PR advisers than Jeremy Bradley. It mattered to him that people would think well of him, respect his undoubted integrity and appreciate his very generous support to a variety of philanthropic ventures.

Some people wondered why he bothered. He was clearly very wealthy, controlling a string of well-run companies in finance and property, though these were mainly based overseas, and spent his time between his main home (an estate in county Carlow), and his houses in Epsom and Bermuda. When those close to him asked about his great loyalty to Ireland he would smile and say: 'My father, who was a great Irishman, always said to me never to forget you are Irish and that Ireland matters. And it does indeed matter a great deal to me.'

Those few who knew him well would say that his father was the central defining force in his life, right up to his death at the age of 80 in 1977. There were Joseph Bradley scholarships and chairs in all the universities, a community centre in the small town in Armagh where he was born was named after him, and he was a donor to many of the country's cultural institutions. And it was whispered – mainly it has to be said by his PR people – that there were many acts of personal charity that he wanted kept private.

But, and this was not known, the memory of his father haunted him. He knew things about his father he swore nobody else would ever know and he promised himself to be as different to his father as lay in his power.

In some strange ways, his father encouraged him in this. A rough Armagh man, a gunman with a shadowy past in Ireland and in the US, a man who had not been accepted by the top echelons of society in the new Ireland, determined his son would be different and would be fully accepted at the top levels. At an early age, he sent Jeremiah, as he was then called, to school at Ampleforth, where his name became Jeremy, and thence to Oxford, where he very quickly adopted the accent and manners of his English contemporaries. Jeremy's few friends all dated from that period and he was far more at ease in that society than he ever was in Ireland.

After Oxford, there had been an MBA at Princeton before coming back to run his father's collection of small, well-funded businesses, mainly in property and construction. He wasted no time in establishing some of these businesses in the UK, where they thrived in the various building booms.

Jeremy had flair and energy, and benefitted from his Oxford contacts in the boardrooms. Before too long he began to feature on the business pages and became a major donor to the Conservative party. He was offered a peerage, but turned it down because of his loyalty to Ireland. It was said – again by his PR people – that he was 'basically a simple Republican at heart'.

Joe Bradley was very proud of his only son and, from an early age, always referred to him as 'Junior'. It was a name Jeremy hated but it stuck and, in spite of the best efforts of his PR people, it was the name by which he was most widely known.

Jeremy's problem with his father was quite simply that he knew too much about him and his past, and hated what he knew. Or, more to the point, he feared that, should it become public, it would do him and his carefully crafted image great harm.

Over the years and especially after a few drinks, his father had told him stories of his days in the War of Independence and Civil War, of fellows he had to 'bump off', of the burning of the houses of the Anglo-Irish, of dealing with 'informers', of his hatred for the 'Free State bastards' and how 'that ungrateful bastard de Valera' had never appreciated him and had soured Lemass against him.

He told, too, of his adventures in the US, how he made and lost money, how he came back with just enough to impress people and to persuade them he was far wealthier than he actually was. He hinted at the source of his fortune, but it was the one area he was reluctant to say much on. Jeremy, who hated these sessions, never pushed him. It was enough for Jeremy to know, as his father never tired of telling him, that one day all this would be his.

Why his father insisted on telling him these stories, Jeremy never knew. It was always late at night when much whiskey had been taken and Jeremy could only surmise that, even though he was now at Oxford, his father was telling him he should never forget his roots. Jeremy was always in awe of his father and never had the courage to tell him how repulsive he found the stories or even to warn him, if these stories leaked out, how much it would damage Jeremy in the eyes of the only people who really mattered to him – his English friends. These feelings and fears he kept to himself.

Old Joe Bradley died in 1977. He had been ill for some time and when Jeremy last spoke with him, just two days before his death, his father held his hand and asked for one last favour.

'Tell Concannon I'm sorry. Tell him I had no choice. I had to do what I did and his plans would never have worked in any event.'

Jeremy knew who Concannon was. He had baptised him and he vaguely remembered the bishop visiting the house in his early years. But he had no idea what his father was talking about. The late-night stories had never touched on his relationship with the bishop. So Jeremy had done nothing. But it puzzled him and he had not forgotten it. He had read of Concannon's death and had briefly contemplated attending the funeral, but did not.

Jeremy had worked hard at sanitising and honouring his father's memory, but worked even harder at obscuring any examination of the details of his life. Press releases always referred to 'a public-spirited man, a great benefactor' and stopped at that.

When a few MA students had written to meet him in the hope of doing their theses on Joe Bradley, they were told there were no surviving papers or relevant documents and so there was no basis for them to proceed. And when an occasional journalist wanted to do a feature on his father, a word with the owner of the paper was enough.

The truth was Joe Bradley was a vague but largely forgotten figure, whose name lived on only in the buildings and university professorships which carried it.

And that was the way Jeremy Bradley wanted it.

But now, in the space of a few days, he had two enquiries about his father and Bishop Concannon. First there had been an incoherent letter from a nephew of the bishop talking about a mysterious bequest in the 1940s and his father's role in this. Then the nuncio had asked him about his father and Concannon, and something about missing money in Kilderry.

He was worried. He knew how his father would have dealt with all this and shuddered at what might have happened to

Concannon's nephew. The nuncio, though, would be a tougher matter. He remembered with distaste his father once boasting of still being in contact with some old comrades from the Civil War, including one particularly repulsive fellow who went on to become a TD and who boasted of having 'his own private graveyard'.

His father hinted these contacts had come in handy from time to time and you never knew when you might need them again. It was a conversation that Jeremy remembered particularly well because his father's obvious pleasure in recounting these stories had almost made him physically sick. He never said a word but resolved that would not be his way.

No. His way was different. He picked up the phone to Cornelius Lyster, his media adviser. It would not be the first time Lyster had got such a request – quite simply to dig up the dirt on people who got in the way of Jeremy Bradley.

He gave the two names and, if Lyster was surprised to be asked to do a job on the papal nuncio, he did not say so. The matter was urgent and he need spare no expense.

55

....

'You mentioned 1945 as a key year when you talked to me yesterday. What happened that year?'

Tommy Newrie was having a drink with Morgan Dannaher in the University Club. A very relieved Morgan Dannaher, who thanked Newrie profusely for having overlooked his 'little indiscretion' and telling him he believed he could still be very helpful. Newrie was sceptical but saw no harm in hearing him out.

'Yes. Late 1945. I was still in Rome and the war had ended, but there was no return to normality. The Communists were seizing power all over Eastern Europe and further afield. Both France and Italy seemed in danger of falling, with the Communists having strong political parties and their own paramilitaries in each country. This was a huge worry for the Vatican and the word went out to support new Catholic parties everywhere and help them to power. The story I'm going to tell revolved around Concannon's old and close friend Marcone.'

'Who the hell is Marcone?'

'Ah yes, I'm going too fast. Ramiro Marcone was Concannon's great friend and protector in Rome. They were both professors, Marcone in San Anselmo. Philosophy, I think, and for some reason they became very close friends. He was very much an "insider", highly regarded in papal circles. He was a Benedictine and it was unusual to have a Benedictine moving in such elevated circles. But Marcone was an unusual Benedictine in my view – ambitious and a bit of a fanatic, not the usual laid-back, laconic type you find in that order.'

Since Newrie knew little and cared less about religious orders, he was keen to move the story on.

'In any event, in 1945 Marcone, now an archbishop, had been made papal nuncio to Croatia, which was in a very nasty Civil War. It was a really brutal war with terrible atrocities on both sides. The word got around fairly quickly that Marcone was out of his depth and had no political judgement. But that was not the view apparently of the Pope, who was said to hold him in high esteem. But then Pius was never a great judge of people.'

'I knew Marcone; the Vatican in those days was really a village, but he had somewhat frozen me out when I asked him about Concannon's Spanish adventure. So I was more than surprised to get a call from him in 1945 asking to meet just before he set off to return to Zagreb in June. I can't say I liked him. He was very full of himself and the more he talked the more I wondered how he could have been chosen for such a dangerous mission. He seemed to know nothing about international politics and saw himself as a leader in some moral crusade for Christ rather than as a mere diplomat facing in to a very complicated and murderous cauldron.

'He behaved as if our previous conversation had never taken place – perhaps he had forgotten it. In any event, he wanted me to make contact for him with Concannon. He said Concannon had told him a few years ago of a wealthy Catholic who offered to help Concannon 'reshape the Church in the dangerous post-war years'. He told me Concannon was very excited about the prospect but he had heard that it had been postponed. I felt he knew all about it but he was vague about any details and, of course, he had not met "Tomazzo" since the outbreak of war.

'It seemed to me Marcone was the only person who did not accept that his time in Croatia had been a disaster. His enormous self-certainty led him to believe there could be a new Catholic resistance there. He also saw the Christian Democrats in Italy as being of vital importance for the Church. He was full of that naïve optimism and self-delusion that only a truly stupid person can have. He clearly felt this sort of "crusade" to save the post-war Church would appeal to Concannon.

'It soon became clear to me that this was about money. He wanted to get his hands on some of Concannon's loot. The future of God's Church, he told me, could depend on the outcome in Croatia and he added that this was the Pope's view also.'

Dannaher now had Newrie's full attention.

'I should have walked away from him there and then. As a diplomat in the government of a neutral country I could have no part – however remote – in helping supply arms to another country, however Catholic it might be. But of course I did not – my old failing.

'In fact, all he wanted from me was to get a letter securely delivered to Concannon. He was a suspicious sort who did not trust the postal service – Communist unions he said – and would not use the Vatican's own diplomatic channels because he did not trust Paschal Robinson in Dublin. So he wanted me to send the letter in our diplomatic pouch.

'That is what I should have done, but of course I could not resist the temptation to get involved. My first leave since coming to Rome was coming up and I agreed to bring the letter back with me. When I got to Dublin, I phoned Concannon and told him I had a letter for him from Marcone who had asked me to deliver it personally.'

Dannaher was now totally absorbed in his narrative. 'I met Concannon for lunch in the Stephen's Green Club – not a club I much like but Concannon seemed very much at home there. It was my first time to meet Concannon and he was courteous and attentive. I filled him in on all the Roman gossip – I was always good at that – and I had an appreciative audience.

'He wanted to know in particular about his friend Ramiro. He was quite open about how much he admired him and about how helpful he had been to his early career. I told him that Archbishop Marcone was said to be one of the few people with a direct line to the Pope and this seemed to please him greatly. He then told me that Armagh would be vacant shortly and he had high hopes of being offered it. He certainly seemed to think he was the best qualified candidate.

'I gave him Marcone's letter and he excused himself to go to the library to read it – apparently it was not done to produce any sort of document in the dining room. The reason he did this was in case he needed to give me a reply. I did not tell him that I was already aware of the contents of the letter.'

Dannaher paused again. He clearly liked to drag the full drama from a story.

'When he came back he seemed almost elated. I remember his exact words, though it was almost as if he was talking to himself. "It was so good to hear from Ramiro. A good man. A man of vision. I believe I can help him and I know just the man who can make it happen. Praised be to God." With that he thanked me profusely, but it was clear his mind was already on the next step.'

Dannaher had not finished. 'Later in my break, I went up to see Paschal Robinson in the Phoenix Park and, being the little shit I was, I asked him about the Concannon incident five years earlier. Since I was the person who had tipped him off in the first place, he had no problem answering.

'He was very American in his openness and always very direct. He said he was still puzzled by the whole affair. He couldn't figure out why Concannon was organising direct links with *Mysterium Fidei* and apparently spending large sums of money. He knew de Valera had taken it seriously and saw it as putting the country's neutrality in danger and that de Valera had spoken directly with Concannon and not in a friendly way.

'The strange thing, he said, was that the whole thing was over almost before it started. Not a word ever appeared in print and he never heard a whisper about it from any of the other bishops – and if they had known anything, he would have been told.

'He said Concannon had been a bit subdued for a while afterwards but he was a conscientious bishop, more able than most of the others, and he felt he might yet get a major promotion.'

Dannaher hesitated, almost as if he wondered if he should go ahead. He did.

'I couldn't resist stirring the pot. I told him that I had heard talk in Rome about Concannon being very helpful to Archbishop Marcone on his Croatian mission, although I was careful to add this was only a rumour. Robinson was most startled to hear this. He was well informed on the Croatian war and, being a Franciscan, probably did not relish what he was hearing about the murderous behaviour of some of his confrères. He told me Marcone, in his view, was not the right man for that job, but then he more or less shut up. I am certain he made his own enquiries afterwards.'

Tommy Newrie was silent when Dannaher finished. He found the story interesting, but how was it going to help their enquiries?

There was one possibility. Concannon had been prepared to spend Alsop's money on the Spanish venture. Did he then spend even more on Croatia? Would they ever find out?

He would ask Dannaher to dig a little deeper.

56

....

October 28 1945

The war was over and the policy of neutrality had survived. De Valera had got the credit for that. However, if Colonel Dan Bryan could read the public mood – and he could – de Valera was getting very little thanks from a public that was cold and hungry, and fed up with shortages, low wages, too much officialdom, too few jobs, and a country too broke to invest in anything. They were fed up with a government that had grown stale and complacent. But Bryan, like most other people, saw little alternative to Dev or Fianna Fáil emerging from the squabble of opposition parties. For many people, that was the hardest fact of all to swallow.

Bryan was in a reflective mood as he prepared his weekly report for de Valera. He knew that he himself had had a good war. De Valera had thanked him warmly – well as warmly as Dev ever could. However, he knew this gratitude would never extend to de Valera giving him the one job he really wanted, and believed he deserved, Chief of Staff of the Defence forces. Dev's magnanimity to those who had been on the 'wrong' side in the Civil War would never extend that far.

These thoughts were prompted by two files he had on his desk. They both concerned Bishop Thomas Patrick Concannon, who Bryan's clerical sources told him was being spoken of as a possible Archbishop of Armagh. Cardinal MacRory was not expected to last much longer, it was said.

The truth about neutrality in Bryan's mind was that it suc-

ceeded, but they had been dammed lucky. Lucky that Hitler had invaded Russia and that America had come in to the war. The invasion of Russia meant the main theatre of war had moved inexorably eastwards and, thus, an invasion of Ireland was no longer vital to Britain's survival.

But they had no way of knowing that in 1940 and, in Bryan's view, there was a very real and immediate danger that year. As far as he was concerned, the most dangerous moment of all could have been precipitated by what Dev had called Concannon's 'tomfoolery'. Bryan had a stronger word for it.

The British government believed there was a real danger and there were strong voices, including Churchill's, who wanted to invade. Bryan's reports from his London spy, Daniel Woodman, made that clear. All they needed was a half-credible excuse. Any excuse and their propaganda machine would dress it up. So if 'neutral' Ireland was seen, to use Churchill's own words, to be 'frolicking' with Franco's Spain at the very moment their own intelligence told them – and Bryan knew this – that Franco was under intense pressure to join the Axis (and indeed seemed likely to do so), the stage would have been set for an invasion.

It was a close-run thing, Bryan reflected. For endangering this, Bryan, the soldier and patriot, could never forgive the arrogance of Concannon that had put his country in such peril. And all for what? His own vanity and self-importance. No more than de Valera, Bryan did not do forgiveness easily.

But that was not his direct concern this morning. He had a new and puzzling piece of news in front of him. This time there was no threat to neutrality and no threat to public safety, but it could have serious implications for what Bryan called 'the national interest' as Ireland sought to rebuild its relations with Britain and the US, neither of which were in the mood to help any rebuilding of the Irish economy.

'More fucking mischief' was Bryan's reaction when he got a report from the Department of External Affairs. There were rumours from the Holy See of some activity involving the Vatican's envoy to Croatia, Archbishop Marcone, and Bishop Concannon, with suspicion of some involvement in that country's Civil War. The rumours were vague, but experience told Bryan the Holy See mission had a good nose for these things. He always took them seriously.

De Valera had seen the report and he too was concerned. He felt he was getting no great help from his own department and especially from its rabidly pro-Vatican Secretary Joe Walshe. Dev was getting tired of Walshe and would soon move him on, but he had insisted on ensuring that Bryan was given the files. Walshe had objected but was brusquely overruled. That was five days ago.

The report was vague but Bryan had immediately done two things. If Concannon was implicated, so too was Joe Bradley. He directed that Bradley be put under immediate surveillance and asked his contacts in the Central Bank and in the Munster & Leinster Bank to be on the lookout for any unusual movements of large sums of money.

He had already made some progress. His sources in the Stephen's Green Club confirmed that Bradley and Concannon had met on three occasions recently for lunch and the passport authorities reported Bradley had made three recent visits to London. But neither the Central Bank nor the Munster & Leinster reported any unusual financial movements. Early days yet, he thought.

In a conversation that would never be minuted, he would ask de Valera for permission to tap the phones of both Concannon and Bradley. He had been in touch with his contacts in London, Cecil Liddell and Jo Stephenson. On the basis of favours owed and, more importantly, because of their trust in Bryan, they had agreed to have Bradley tailed in London and, in particular, to follow up on any bank accounts or transactions by him in financial circles.

Bryan would report all this to de Valera and would be interested in Dev's reaction. Would he be as angry as Bryan was beginning to feel? His own sense of injustice had been sharpened by the second file on his desk, which confirmed to him that, lurking deep in all of this, was an undetected and unpunished murder – that of Sánchez, the Spanish diplomat.

The second file was an update from Superintendent Gantly.

Superintendent Gantly, an old-fashioned, conscientious policeman, was as convinced as Bryan that it had been murder. When they took in to account the report of pathologist Professor Farrelly, the evidence and suspicions of the stable owner, and the fact that Gantly was certain a strange car had been spotted in the locality at about the same time as the 'accident', and given what both Gantly and Bryan knew of Joe Bradley's past activities, their suspicions had hardened into a certainty. They were both stubborn and determined men, but the inquest verdict faced them with a blank wall.

He would tell Dev of his suspicions. He would tell him Bradley was behind it all and would ask permission to bring him in and maybe even rough him up a bit, but he knew Dev would refuse. He knew Dev believed him but would put 'the best interest of the State' first and, on reflection, he was probably right. Bradley was as tough as they came, he could afford the best lawyers and Bryan would not succeed. But he still hoped something would turn up.

Maybe that would now happen. Both he and Gantly had kept a close eye on Bradley since 1940. They were aware of the rumours in banking and business circles that Bradley had been in financial trouble before the war. There was talk of unpaid bills and loans that had run into trouble. He was being refused credit by all the banks and had become a figure of suspicion.

But that all changed in early 1941. Old debts had been paid off and he had been buying up property and land – quietly and without recourse to bank borrowing. According to Bryan's sources, the lands would be of value only to someone who could afford to wait. And Bradley clearly appeared to be someone who could now afford to do just that.

As Bryan left his offices in Parkgate Street to make the short journey to Government Buildings, he contemplated asking de Valera to call Concannon in again and confront him with all the facts at their disposal. He wanted to ask him directly what he knew of Bradley's activities. Was the bishop a knave or a fool? He would put this question directly to Dev.

And if Dev was not willing to do so then, later maybe and at the right time, he might have to do it himself. He was conscious of the danger of such an approach, but it might be the only way he could put his mind at rest.

De Valera was waiting for him in the austere and cheerless room he worked from. Bryan noted with approval that the two prime ministers he had worked with – Cosgrave and de Valera – remained men of simple tastes. No socialising, no ostentation, none of the extravagances or fripperies he had read about with other heads of government. Bryan liked it that way; it simple and modest.

The only one of them who had ever lost the run of himself in that regard was O'Duffy and the Commissioner's uniform he had specially made for himself in Italy. He never got to wear it, though. When he heard that his associates were calling him 'Napoleon', he quickly dropped the idea. Bryan had begun to wonder where that uniform was now when he realised de Valera was waiting for him to speak.

'Sorry, Taoiseach. I got a bit distracted.' Then he launched in to the two reports.

As he expected, de Valera shared his suspicions of Bradley. 'I spoke to Mr Aiken about him. He was part of his Brigade in the

*early days. He tells me he was more than glad to see the back of
him and was worried when Mr Lemass was talking to him about
economic development. He may even have had a word with him
to dissuade him. But we cannot reopen the Sánchez case now – or
probably ever. Sometimes we really have no choice. But if he steps
out of line again, show no mercy.'*

Bryan knew he was clutching at straws and de Valera knew
that too.

On the question of Dev calling in Concannon, the answer was
even more adamant. 'From what I know of Concannon, he is the
sort of cleric who sees the Church as superior to the State. He has
an innate contempt for all politicians, myself included. Maybe
especially myself. But he is tough and able and, unless we have
strong evidence – which we do not have – he could be a difficult and dangerous enemy. When it comes to politics Colonel, we
are mere amateurs compared to this crowd. They have their own
ways and means, as I well know.

'I will do nothing for the moment, but I do want you to keep
up your enquiries and tell Superintendent Gantly to do likewise.
If you feel you must listen to phones, do it solely on your own
authority – and make sure to keep me up to date.'

A typical Dev solution, thought Bryan sourly as he drove back
to Parkgate Street. The best of both worlds – all the information
but no responsibility. But in fact, Bryan agreed with de Valera.
He above all had to be protected and Bryan knew it was his job
to do so.

But his sense of injustice still burned. If Dev would not confront Concannon, then he would. It would have to be discreetly
done and in such a way that Concannon would have no easy
comeback. But do it he would and he would work out a way. Of
that he was determined.

57

....

Archbishop Valetti was certain he had finally hit the jackpot. After all the dross he had to wade through, he felt his instinct had been right and he had now struck gold. And all thanks to that fussy little man Dannaher, who had pointed him in the direction of the missing files.

But the examination of the files was taking longer than he expected and it was only on his third trawl he found a file headed 'Kilderry' with a handwritten note in the top right-hand corner. It simply said 'not dispatched'. In other words, something had happened to make Robinson change his mind about sending them to Rome. But if he had changed his mind, why had he kept the original?

As he brushed away the dust and opened the ribbon binding the pages together, he saw there were three separate documents in the file.

The first was headed Advice to the Holy See on appointment of Bishop to Armagh.

The introductory paragraph noted that Archbishop MacRory was unwell and it would soon be necessary to appoint a co-adjutor bishop with the right of succession. Robinson had been asked to supply the names of three properly qualified possible successors in the order of his preference.

Right at the top of the list was Bishop Concannon of Kilderry followed by two other names – Bishop John d'Alton of Meath and Professor James Duff of Maynooth.

There followed biographical details on all three, with observations on each from Robinson. To Valetti's trained eye, Robinson clearly favoured Concannon. One sentence in particular stood out.

A scholar who nevertheless speaks simply and clearly and who in public debate defends the Church's position persuasively and without causing needless offence.

Of d'Alton he wrote: 'A fine scholar and a good priest – perhaps a little diffident.'

James Duff, a Professor of Classics at Maynooth was simply described as 'an outstanding scholar with no proven aptitude for pastoral work'.

Had this document been sent to Rome, Valetti was certain Concannon would have been the chosen one and no doubt, in the fullness of time, become a cardinal. So what happened to make Robinson change his mind?

The second document was dated October 1945. It was a short note written in the form of an *aide-mémoire*.

Reliable source in the Department of External Affairs called last evening and, in the course of conversation, mentioned a rumour he had heard linking Bishop Concannon to assisting Archbishop Marcone's mission to Croatia. He suggested possible difficulties with Irish Government should this be so because of possible infringement of policy of neutrality.

This source was reliable in 1940 about a proposed, if vague, venture by Bishop Concannon which involved Spain. That issue greatly perturbed Mr de Valera, who intervened and, in the event, nothing materialised.

The third document was a record of a meeting Robinson had with Bishop Concannon at the latter's request in November 1945.

Bishop Concannon was clearly upset and had none of his composure or self-confidence. He explained the urgency of his request for a meeting because some matters he was involved in could be misinterpreted and damaging to the Church. He wanted me to be aware of the true position.

I calmed him down and he began by reminding me of the dinner I hosted in the nunciature six years ago, in 1939, where Henry Alsop had also been a guest. Arising out of a conversation at that dinner about the dangers likely to face a post-war Church, he had several further meetings with Alsop. The net result was that Alsop had made a very large donation to him personally to fund a project upon which they had agreed. He said Alsop had been clear that Concannon should have full discretionary control over the funds and had full freedom to use them as he thought fit in pursuit of their goal. I asked about the sums involved but, even when pressed, he was vague about the amount. All he would say was its value varied because it was in stocks and shares. They had been affected by the uncertainty of war but the amount was significant.

I asked him how these funds related to the diocese. He replied almost angrily that there was no overlap or conflict. The finances of the diocese were impeccable and would stand up to scrutiny. The two issues were strictly separate.

I began to question him about the nature of his 'project' and found him reluctant to elaborate. All he would say was that it was legitimate and dictated solely by the best interest of the Church.

I cut in at this stage to ask if his proposed intervention in Spain in 1940 was part of the 'project'. He was clearly taken aback, asking me almost aggressively how I knew about that.

I answered very clearly: 'Mr de Valera told me. He feared it could do irreparable damage to his policy of neutrality and lead to an invasion of the country.'

He was by now visibly angry and I made a clear note of his exact words.

'That was all nonsense. De Valera was listening to the wrong people. We were entirely concerned with religion. There was nothing political about it.'

I asked him to explain the elements of this non-political project.

It was very simple he said. Irish Catholics, priests and lay people were to be trained by *Mysterium Fidei* in Spain in a seminary they would buy. When properly 'formed', they would come back to Ireland as hard-edged crusaders, as real soldiers of Christ, as soon as the war ended.

'Show me the politics in that,' he said angrily. 'We had made our plans. We had strong contacts with *Mysterium Fidei* through a man we unfortunately trusted in the Spanish embassy. Through him we had bought a disused seminary in Salamanca to train our people and were already embarked on a discreet recruiting mission in Ireland. It was all nonsense for de Valera to say it could damage our neutrality. Spain was a neutral country too, but he even threatened to put me in jail if I did not drop everything immediately. It was an intolerable intrusion in to the affairs of the Church.'

His grievance still loomed large so I decided to press him a little further on the 'project'.

'So you lost all your money?'

'No. Maybe about a third of it.'

'How much?'

'Close to half a million pounds.'

He was clearly uncomfortable but I persisted. Now at least I could clear up one mystery.

'But if you never got to Spain, how could you lose so much?'

'It may have been bad luck or it may have been treachery. I really don't want to talk about it.'

'I think you had better do so. If I am to help, I need to know everything.'

He was still reluctant but felt trapped.

'The person who was looking after the money and who was investing in Spain on our behalf and had paid monies to *Mysterium Fidei* was killed in an unfortunate riding accident shortly after de Valera's intervention. He left no records, there was no trace of the money and we had no way of recovering any of it.'

'You mean this one man had control over all the money?'

'Well it was wartime. He was answerable to a man I trusted implicitly who had only recently transferred the monies to the man who died. When we could find no trace of the money, we could not make a fuss about it and could not run the risk of scandal. We were robbed, but we were stymied as well.'

I told him I remembered that man. He was a second secretary at the Spanish embassy and, as Dean of the Diplomatic Corps, I presided at his funeral in University Church.

'Are you sure his death was accidental?' I asked.

'What else could it have been?'

Bishop Concannon had clearly not been expecting to be cross-examined on the Spanish 'project', so I allowed him proceed to the purpose of his visit.

'I'm here for another reason. You probably know Archbishop Ramiro Marcone is an old friend of mine.'

I did not say I had known this only a month or two and through Morgan Dannaher.

'As you know, Ramiro has been papal nuncio in Croatia, where he has been entrusted with an important mission by the Holy Father – saving the Church from the Communists. I had told him in vague terms of Alsop's endowment. A few months ago, he wrote to me asking if some of the funds entrusted to me could be used to help the Catholic cause in Croatia. I thought very hard about it and, after much prayer, decided that the funds entrusted to me by Henry Alsop were meant for just such a purpose, to help the Catholic crusade in that country.'

At this point I thought, but did not say, that the Ustaše did not fit my idea of Crusaders. Instead I said that if this was what he had done, why was he telling me about it now. It was not any of my business, I was nuncio to Ireland, not Croatia – though I had to admit I was genuinely curious.

'Well that is just the point. You may well hear from Rome that large sums were promised but never arrived. Not a single pound. You may hear of bad faith on my part but, I can tell you categorically, I released a large number of bonds, had them traded and handed over a sum of close to half a million pounds to the man who was acting as intermediary. Now this man, who I trusted implicitly, claims that when he got to Italy his arrival was anticipated by some criminals. He was held hostage until he had told them how to get the money and was lucky to escape with his life.'

I asked him to tell me the identity of this man.

He hesitated. Clearly very embarrassed.

'Mr Joseph Bradley – you know him.'

I asked if he had been the man dealing with the Spanish embassy person.

'Yes, he was.'

'Might there be a coincidence in all this? Is it possible you were robbed, that you have fallen victim to a confidence trickster not once but twice?'

He was an abject figure as he said almost in a whisper, 'I'm afraid that is the only conclusion I can draw. I trusted this man, loved him almost as a brother. I confronted him yesterday but all he could say was I misjudged him, that he had told the truth. I asked him about the death of the Spaniard and he was adamant it had been an accident and this was what the inquest had determined. But I have to say, I am at the stage where I can believe nothing he tells me. And to think he had my total trust.'

I assured Bishop Concannon that I regarded his actions as misguided and potentially damaging, but I believed he was a man of integrity and had broken neither civil nor canon law. I asked him what funds still remained of the original bequest and if he had any further plans to disburse it. He said no, but he did feel an obligation to Alsop to do as he had promised. He said that, if I had any suggestions, he would like to hear them. I said perhaps he should let matters rest for the moment.

That was the end of Robinson's account of the meeting with Concannon, but attached to the account he had written was a short note:

Bishop Concannon was foolish, conceited and showed extreme bad judgement but no crime committed and no scandal likely to ensue. No action needed.

Withdraw name of Bishop Concannon from Armagh list. Recommend that Bishop John d'Alton be appointed.

Valetti was elated. This was it. The 'smoking gun'. Whatever about getting his hands on the Kilderry money, Jeremy Bradley would be prepared to pay dearly for his silence. His entire family fortunes were based on money stolen from the Church by his father. In spite of himself, Valetti had to admire the sheer effrontery of it all.

Well, let's see some of that money coming back where it belonged, or where Valetti deemed it to belong – with himself.

He was going to enjoy this, but he had to think how he might best go about it.

58

....

Jeremy Bradley had chosen well when he appointed Cornelius Lyster as his public affairs consultant. Lyster was a one-man operation – no staff, no office, no computer – but he had a bulging contact list, another list of favours to call in and a mind overflowing with information – especially about things others would like to forget.

Lyster was a man of style and a man of mystery. He had flair and wit; nobody told a story better and he was a wicked mimic. He bought his suits in Jermyn Street and was to be found in the best restaurants and most fashionable pubs. He always had a great welcome for himself and a smile that could disarm all but his harshest critics.

It was an image he carefully cultivated, but he could just as easily get down and dirty. Some of the sleaziest journalists and dodgiest policemen were close friends and it was said with awe that there was no area of Irish life – be it business, politics or even the Catholic Church – where he did not have his sources.

Lyster did not come cheaply and was careful that those for whom he worked could pay top dollar. He knew he had enemies who called him a hatchet-man, without principle. He knew some journalists were sceptical or even suspicious of his activities. He knew the top gardaí would dearly love to find his sources within the force and would have been surprised to learn just how high up his best sources were. It was said he was prepared to pay for his information and that he was also prepared to threaten blackmail or intimidation should the need arise.

But Lyster's greatest assets were his personal warmth and charm. He could tell great stories, he knew how to do favours and he knew there were few who could resist a free lunch in Patrick Guilbaud's or l'Ecrivain. And probably his greatest asset was to make it look as if he was the giver and not the receiver.

Bradley had summoned him to a breakfast meeting at his country house in Carlow. He had been to Ballywilliamroe just outside Bagenalstown before and admired Bradley's understated good taste. Nothing was flash, everything pointed to 'old' money.

He knew too – because he handled much of it – that Bradley had built up warm but somewhat distant relations with his local neighbours, sponsoring St Andrew's football team and Myshall hurling team (not that it did either much good), and a range of local charities and good works. He had even become a trustee of Borris Golf Club, to which he would bring his English house guests. In other words, he played the role of local squire, but in a way that seemed natural and caused no offence.

Lyster, who was a sharp judge, believed Bradley to be one of the coldest men he knew but a man of extraordinary style. He liked both qualities in him.

As he drove down to Carlow, Lyster reflected on some of the jobs he had already done for Jeremy Bradley. Bradley's oldest son Joseph was a bully. He had been involved in a brawl in a nightclub, which led to another young man spending a week in hospital. It was just one, but the most public, of a number of such incidents involving Joseph. It had not been easy, but Lyster had 'squared' the guards and 'persuaded' the tabloid editors that the story was not newsworthy. Only *Phoenix* carried the story and none of Bradley's friends read *Phoenix*. Joseph Bradley was now spending a year interning in Australia.

And then there was the problem with Jeremy's wife. Lyster

had met and liked Marguerite Bradley, but he knew Jeremy had outgrown her and had a long-term partner in London. Marguerite probably knew this too and was quite happy to spend most of her time in Ballywilliamroe. But she had been involved in a night-time car crash and was well over the limit – and there was a small question of the identity of the man travelling with her. Lyster had not just kept that story out of the papers, but out of the courts as well.

So as he drove down the avenue to Ballywilliamroe House, he wondered what it would be this time.

He was met by a sombre and strangely subdued Jeremy Bradley. As soon as they sat down to an insubstantial breakfast of coffee and croissants, Bradley got to the point.

'This is the most serious problem to come my way in years. It has the potential to do real damage. Let me give you the basic facts as I know them.'

Lyster knew his employer well enough to know their working relationship depended on each being utterly truthful with the other. Lies were for other people.

Bradley put it simply. The problem was one of blackmail. Information had surfaced about his father's role during the Second World War, which was very damaging to his father's reputation. He had not seen the records, but he knew enough about his father to believe they were credible. He had always feared something like this might happen and Lyster knew he had been paranoid about warding off any digging in to his father's past. Up to now, it had been successful.

Lyster being the professional he was had wondered about this and made it his business to find out. It helped him now that he knew quite a lot already about Joe Bradley's darker side and would be well prepared.

Jeremy had always feared something would surface, but of late he had begun to relax, feeling that bit more secure as time passed with no questions being raised. Now, suddenly and out of the blue, he had been struck with two differing threats. He had put off dealing with either while he prepared his own strategy, which was why Lyster had been summoned so abruptly from Dublin.

'First, I got a letter from this country solicitor who claimed to be a nephew of old Bishop Concannon, who was a close friend of my father during the war. He claims my father illegally got hold of a great deal of the bishop's money, which is now rightfully his. It was a hysterical sort of letter and I'm sure has no legal basis whatsoever, but I want it killed before it even begins to go public. His name is Richard E Murdock. I want you to get every bit of information about him before we devise a strategy to deal with him.'

Lyster had heard vaguely of Murdock and knew where to start on this quest. It would not be too difficult.

'The second case is trickier. The papal nuncio, an Archbishop Valetti, spoke to me at a reception lately, quizzing me about my father and Concannon. I don't believe in coincidences, and this followed the day after I got Murdock's letter, nor do I trust this fellow. He is a bumptious, vulgar sort and spoke to me in a way that suggested he had information I would not like. I put him off, but he insisted we meet – almost threateningly I might say.

'I told him the first free date I had was two weeks from now. I want to be prepared for that meeting. You have that time to get me information. My intention is to squash these two fellows – yes, squash them so they can never again be a threat. I know what my father would have done but his ways are not my ways. But the end result will be the same. I want them dead in the water.'

Lyster was in no doubt as to what Bradley meant and wanted. And he knew exactly where he would start. It was a while since he had a challenge like this and he knew he was going to enjoy it.

59

....

Within hours of leaving Ballywilliamroe, Lyster was making progress. This was the sort of work he enjoyed and the fee Bradley had promised him was a further source of happiness.

He set to work methodically, starting with Archbishop Frank Valetti. He established straight away that the archbishop had been born and brought up in Toronto of Sicilian parents.

A Sicilian connection could always come in handy. What sort of family were they? Had they any record of misbehaviour or connections to shady groups? It didn't matter how flimsy these connections might be because, however flimsy, Lyster would find ways of making something of it.

His first contact was an Irish journalist working with the *Toronto Star*. He called, got his man and made his request. He had worked with Ged Casey in the past and they both understood each other. They were both mercenaries and never pretended – at least to each other – to be otherwise. Lyster wanted anything Casey could find about the family of Archbishop Valetti and he was not looking for a laudable report. If there was dirt, or anything that could be made look dirty, he wanted it. And there would be double the normal fee.

He noted Valetti had spent much of his formative years in Roman seminaries and later working in the Vatican. Lyster rubbed his hands. He had what he called a gold card contact working there. Monsignor Percy Phillips was from his home town. They went to the same national school before Phillips went to boarding school and from there to Maynooth.

Lyster was one of the few people who knew that Phillips was gay. He knew this because Phillips had come to him in despair when he was being blackmailed by a former classmate on the eve of his ordination. Lyster was the only person he could talk to and, for Lyster, it had been easy work to frighten off the blackmailer. It had been crude but effective – he organised a few thugs to give him a good beating, followed by a threat of more to come if he did not desist. He disappeared from Phillips' life and Lyster had acquired another debt, which was now being called in.

He felt, in fact, Phillips was enjoying paying his debt. He had met Valetti and found him arrogant and, without asking why Lyster wanted the information, said he would love to help. Lyster knew Phillips was a natural gossip and a skilful ferreter of information.

Phillips was somewhat puzzled by Lyster's afterthought – what would it take to buy Valetti off should other means of persuasion not prevail – not that Lyster thought it would ever come to that. And Lyster's last words to him were, 'Percy, I want the dirt, the whole dirt and nothing but the dirt'. That was clear enough and, if there was dirt to be found, he would find it.

Lyster noted with interest Valetti's short spell in Cyprus. It was usual, he thought, for nuncios to be left in place for longer periods, unless they had in some way misbehaved or fallen foul of local politics. Valetti had been in Cyprus for less than two years. Why? What had he done?

This gave Lyster a problem. Cyprus was off the beaten track. He had no contacts there. Who might have contacts? It didn't take him long to remember the gardaí had worked closely with the Cypriot police on a number of banking and fraud cases. A quick phone call to an assistant commissioner assured him that there were indeed good working relations between the two forces. The assistant commissioner had been there recently and, if he wanted a good contact, he had the very man and just mention his name. No questions about the nature of Lyster's business, just a willingness to be of help.

A few more routine calls were followed by his last major call as far as Valetti was concerned. Once again to An Garda Síochána. This time to his very close friend high in the ranks of Special Branch. He knew the gardaí paid a great deal of attention to what they called 'protecting the diplomatic corps'. He knew this was genuine, but he knew too that it often provided cover for a little spying as well.

Not all diplomats were honest – some were in to smuggling, others exploited their Filipino staff and some were just careless about observing laws they thought should not apply to them. The guards liked to nip these cases before they became public and were seen as an embarrassment by the Department of Foreign Affairs. Even the nuncio might come under surveillance from time to time. He would soon know.

While these lines of enquiry were getting under way, he turned his attention to Richard E Murdock. The approach would be much the same.

His first call was to the district judge in Murdock's home area. Again, an old friend who enjoyed his company and hospitality, and was always willing to be helpful. Henrietta Scott, or Henny as she was known, had once had a relationship with Lyster when she was a young solicitor. Not very serious – at least on his part – and they had remained good friends. This was especially so since Henny always believed it was Lyster's intervention with the Minister for Justice that led to her appointment as a judge. What Lyster did not tell Henny was that the Minister was going to appoint her anyway, since he thought she was the best candidate, and actually resented Lyster's intervention. That part of the story he had not told her.

They would meet the following evening for dinner in the Shelbourne.

Next on his list was a senior figure in the Law Society – the very same Law Society that had been threatening Murdock of late. Iggy Stuart-Henry was a lowlife in Lyster's view – pompous, snobbish and stupid, but cunning and mean-minded in to the bargain. 'Just the sort of person I need,' thought Lyster, 'and I don't even have to be civil to him. He knows what I know about him and that I would not hesitate to use it.' In fact, Lyster had no intention of ever using the demeaning information he had, but Stuart-Henry would never know that. Whatever the Law Society had on Murdock would soon be his.

Then finally to the editor of *The Brannocksbridge Observer*, a journalist well known to Lyster. Joey Martin and Lyster knew each other of old, so there was no need for preliminaries. They were both in the business of trading information and Martin expressed no surprise at the request. He filled Lyster in on what he knew of Murdock and the various rumours he had heard, mainly of his drinking, his boorishness and his womanizing, 'though if what I hear is true, the wife has the upper hand there now'.

Lyster then asked him what he knew of Concannon.

'He was gone before my time. The fellow who followed him, John Mullins, is a very decent man, but Concannon had few fans. Most people thought he died years ago. There is one fellow who could help you. Old Johnny Ryan lives here in town He drove the old bishop for years and he knows Murdock as well. You'll find him in Hickson's pub any afternoon watching the racing and having a few pints. Maybe a few fivers will get him talking. He's my best bet for whatever it is you want – and I doubt if it is good things you want.'

Martin paused and Lyster knew what was coming. 'If there is any bit of a story in all this, you might give me first option.'

Lyster assured him and, with full sincerity, he hoped there would be no story. However, if there was, Joey Martin would be the first to hear.

Lyster felt he had enough to go on. But he was intrigued about what it was in his father's past that Jeremy Bradley so feared. It was important not to be ambushed. As Hamlet said, or as he remembered it from his school days: 'The readiness is all.'

With that in mind, he decided to drop in to Grogan's pub the following afternoon where an old friend of his, an expert on modern Irish history, might be able to enlighten him on the exploits of Joseph Bradley in the murky days of the War of Independence and Civil War.

Professor Andrew Cass, as usual, did not disappoint.

60

....

October 30 1945

Dan Bryan was uneasy and was blinking even more than usual. He believed major crimes – murder, fraud and maybe even national sabotage – were not being pursued for 'reasons of State'. He was not so naïve as to think there were not times when even a civilized state had to turn a blind eye 'in the national interest'. He had been party to such decisions himself, indeed may even have advocated such a policy.

This time he was angry with his own conscience. He believed Concannon and Bradley had recklessly endangered the very independence and well-being of the State, Concannon believing himself to be above the law and answerable only to some higher calling, and Bradley (about whose past he knew all too much) was almost certainly guilty of murder and theft on a massive scale.

He found it hard to accept that they should get away with it as easily and as completely as they were, and there was apparently nothing he could do about it.

He knew he had often had to tolerate unpalatable facts in the past but this time, if only to ease his own conscience, he had to do something. He knew he was circumscribed by de Valera's decision but there were two things he would do, de Valera or no de Valera.

He would meet Concannon and confront him with the full story. He would make it clear that, if the opportunity arose, he would make use of what he knew. That, at least, should make life uneasy for Concannon. He might even hint that others knew the story too, which was true since de Valera had been fully briefed.

And secondly, in the fullness of time, he would prepare a com-prehensive dossier on Concannon and Bradley, outlining all he knew and including the reports from his spies and informers and the file prepared by Superintendent Gantly. It was something he was good at doing and he would enjoy compiling it – he might even discover new evidence. But he knew this had to be done se-cretly. If his superiors got wind of it, his career could be over – probably would be over – because he knew that he had a few enemies who would pounce on an opportunity like this.

And then there was the question of where he should keep it. Certainly not in the Intelligence archives, but he would work on that. What he didn't want was its discovery while he was still serving but he wanted to place it somewhere it could eventually be discovered and made public.

Bryan was a keen historian. This would be his record and it might take 50 years or more before some archivist came across it. Things might be different and less secretive then and, weak as this gesture was, it was all he felt he could do. He had to put whatever faith he had in some future archivist who might or might not stumble across his file.

He turned his mind to the meeting with Concannon. He persuad-ed himself that what he had from de Valera was a request not an order. He knew he had certain flexibility and argued to himself that Dev was as angry as he was. As long as Dev could deny any involve-ment, he would not mind too much. He knew Dev well enough to know that this sort of Jesuitical thinking would appeal to him. And Bryan felt that, should word leak out, none of the opposition parties would want to pursue the matter for fear of offending the Church. So he felt secure enough to go ahead.

Before doing so, however, there was one man he had to get advice from. Which is why he was now sitting in the lobby of Mrs Lawlor's Hotel in Naas. He had phoned Bishop Michael Fogarty

*a few days earlier and had been pleased by the warmth of Fog-
arty's response – very different from the frosty tone of their last
meeting.*

*'Well Dan, you want to meet me again. No more spying work
I hope.'*

*Bryan assured him it was a serious matter and all he asked for
was advice – nothing more.*

*'Would it be about the same gentleman we spoke about the last
time we met?'*

*'I'm afraid so and this time it is even more serious. I wouldn't
bother you if it were not.'*

*'I know you wouldn't Dan. By chance, I have a meeting in May-
nooth on Thursday. It wouldn't do to meet you there. Too many
old women around that place. Mrs Lawlor in Naas has a nice
discreet hotel. They know me there and we will not be disturbed.'*

*From his quiet corner in the lobby he saw Fogarty come in,
with Mrs Lawlor clucking around him like a mother hen. He was
a vigorous, ramrod straight man who looked a decade younger
than his 85 years. Fogarty had that stern look that rarely seemed
to leave him – silver-haired, bespectacled and scholarly.*

*Bryan reminded himself that Fogarty had been a bishop now
for 43 years and, in spite of his stern appearance, he had always
found him fair-minded and principled. He remembered that Fogarty had been the only bishop to condemn the sectarian attacks of
the War of Independence.*

*When they were seated in a private room, Bryan told the story as
he knew it. Fogarty listened intently, asking the occasional question
but showing no reaction. When Bryan finished, Fogarty asked who
else knew the full story – or even suspected it.*

'Two people, de Valera and Superintendent John Gantly.'

'And why are you telling me?'

'Because I trust you and need your advice.'

'Fair enough and I am glad you told me. So what do you propose to do?'

'Well, Dev told me to do nothing. He is as angry as I am, but wants it all kept quiet.'

'As we all do,' said Fogarty sharply. 'As I'm sure you do too, or do you?'

'Yes. Reluctantly but I agree. Too much scandal as you would say. But I hate like hell to see them get away with it. Bradley does not surprise me. As you well know, he is bad to the core. But Concannon has been reckless, arrogant and I would say treacherous. That he can get away scot-free, I find unacceptable.'

'What do you want to do?'

'I want to meet him face to face, to confront him with the consequences of his actions. I want him to know that I have the full details of all he has done and, should it be necessary, I am willing to use it.'

'You mean blackmail him?'

'Yes. Not for money. But to make sure he never attempts anything like this ever again. If you can excuse the language, my Lord, I want to frighten the shite out of him.'

Fogarty nodded. 'And what's holding you up?'

'Dev advised me not to – but in this case, I won't tell him and I doubt if Concannon will either.'

'And why are you asking me? You said you wanted my advice but you seem to have your mind made up.'

'I want to know everything I can about the man before I confront him.'

Suddenly Fogarty's stern face broke in to a smile.

'You're a wise old owl Dan and, even though you work for the Long Fella, I admire you. You were right to come to me when this all started. To tell the truth, I have been worried about Tom Concannon for a very long time. I watched him carefully after the

Spanish thing and for a while he was somewhat deflated. Of late, though, he has been back to his old self – even more so maybe.'

Fogarty paused. 'Dan, before I tell you my story I think we could do with something stronger than tea.'

He pressed a bell Bryan had not even noticed. Within a minute, Mrs Lawlor was back with two discreet but generous tumblers of whiskey. After a few appreciative sips of Power's Gold Label, Fogarty began.

'Tom Concannon is a dangerous man. When I was a younger bishop one of my jobs was to keep an eye on the students in Maynooth, especially the brighter ones, with a view as to which ones we would send for further study – our potential officer corps you might call them. Concannon came to Maynooth in the early 1920s and was the outstanding student of his time, but both the then President of Maynooth and myself had some reservations about his character.

'There was something of the fanatic, the zealot about him. He was so certain of his own rightness on every issue and maybe even a sense of his own moral and intellectual superiority. He discussed things, not to learn but to win, and he did not like being crossed or rebuked. The sin of Lucifer we used call it – intellectual and moral pride. He looked down on his fellow students, and indeed on the staff, as second-raters and had no friends. He saw himself as utterly self-sufficient.'

Fogarty was now absorbed in his memories.

'We sent him to Rome after ordination. As a scholar, we knew he would do well there and that would in turn reflect well on us. I would have been very happy for him to stay in Rome and climb the ladder there and, when I asked him, he said that was his hope as well. He made no secret about his ambitions and they did not include coming back here. But, life can be funny Dan.

'He did so well at his studies that he caught the eye of this

fellow Ramiro Marcone you have mentioned. In fact, he was seen as a protégé of Marcone, who was very close to Cardinal Pacelli, as he was at the time. He told us all this in his reports – boastful reports if I may say so. We had no problems with that – a good contact in Rome is always helpful.'

'But then things went wrong – at least from our point of view. Pacelli felt the Irish Church was too independent and a bit lax and needed new leadership that would be more amenable to Rome. It was known that my good friend Ned Byrne, the Archbishop of Dublin, was not well even though he was only in his sixties. He was not expected to last too long and that would mean a vacancy right at the top.

'That, Dan, was the background to the sudden appointment of Concannon to Kilderry in 1937 – to have him in place to succeed Ned Byrne in Dublin.

'I remember well the day we were told of his appointment. It was at a bishop's meeting in Maynooth and the nuncio had asked to be present for part of the meeting. That was unusual and usually meant some message or other from Rome, so we did not pay too much heed. But what he had to say surprised us all. The last thing we expected was that he would name a new Bishop of Kilderry on the specific instructions of Cardinal Pacelli.

'I knew Tom Concannon, but most of the other bishops had never heard of him. To tell you the truth Dan, we resented it and especially the status that the Vatican was conferring on him.

'When we discussed it at lunch the only explanation we could find was that Pacelli did not expect Pius XI to last much longer and was putting his own men in place. He had appointed six new bishops elsewhere at the same time. That was our suspicion and it was confirmed early on when Concannon began to throw his weight around, reminding us of his special links to Pacelli and the Vatican.

'But he didn't get Dublin. When Ned Byrne died in February 1940, it was believed the contest would be between Monsignor Boylan, who the priests wanted, and this unknown bishop from Kilderry. But as you know Dan, God works in mysterious ways and your friend de Valera had different ideas. He owed Fr Mc-Quaid a favour and he saw Blackrock College as his second home so he swung it for McQuaid.

'I don't know which would be worse, but I'm not telling you a secret Dan, when I say the cardinal in Armagh is not well and Concannon is seen by some as the favourite. He has made no se-cret he wants it and expects to get it. His only real rival is John d'Alton over in Meath. And I'm reliably told that Paschal Rob-inson is backing Tom Concannon and his view will probably be decisive. But what you have told me today will ensure that does not happen.'

Fogarty rubbed his hands and pressed the bell for a replenishment.

'You may think this is all clerical intrigue and I suppose it is. But my point is simple. Concannon is dangerous. Dangerous morally and temperamentally. He has unlimited self-belief and no judgement. You know that as well as I do.

'So, what I am saying to you is this. You must confront him with all you know. Be brutal and direct. That is the only language he understands. Show him you have a file and let him know you have spoken with me. He has to be spancelled so he can do no more harm.'

Bryan was taken aback at the intensity of Fogarty's words. Clearly he had been waiting a long time for this moment and he would not waste it.

Bryan told him he would take his advice and be happy to do so.

The bishop suggested one for the road and Bryan was happy to accept. He was clear now what he had to do.

61

....

October 30 1945

When Dan Bryan returned to McKee Barracks after his meeting with Bishop Fogarty, his mind was made up. He would waste no more time. This was a boil he had to lance. It was coming between him and his peace of mind.

He had never met Concannon and doubted if the bishop even knew of his existence. He was certain Joe Bradley never mentioned him. It would not be in his interest to raise issues that could be embarrassing. So he would have the benefit of surprise.

He knew the bishop was in the habit of saying 8 o'clock Mass in the cathedral and then returning to the palace for breakfast. It was the one time he would be certain to be in his residence.

Bryan left Dublin at 7am in full military uniform and with an army driver. He arranged that an officer at headquarters would phone Kilderry at 8.45 to say that Colonel Bryan would be calling to see Bishop Concannon at 9am on a matter of considerable urgency. No details, no questions.

When Bryan arrived on the stroke of 9 o'clock, he was met by a flustered young cleric who, sweating profusely, told him that the bishop had other engagements and it was not convenient to meet at this time. Perhaps the Colonel could ring later to make a mutually convenient arrangement.

Bryan had expected this.

'Tell his Lordship it will be a short meeting but it is of national importance. Tell him I would not be here otherwise and I will not *leave until I have my meeting. If it helps him make up his mind, tell him it concerns his friend Joe Bradley.'*

The by now even more flustered cleric withdrew. After an interval of five minutes he returned and, with a bad grace, Bryan was led to Concannon's study.

Concannon did not shake hands or extend any greeting. He simply ushered Bryan to a chair while he remained standing. Was this how he greeted errant priests, Bryan wondered – a striking and powerful figure against the backdrop of his intimidating study.

'This is an outrageous and ill-mannered intrusion. I have phoned my solicitor. He tells me I have no obligation to meet you and that I should report the matter to your superiors. And I may well do. But out of a misguided sense of courtesy, I will give you 10 minutes.'

Bryan was relaxed. The blinking had stopped. He might even enjoy the encounter.

'My Lord, you had better sit down. I'm here to speak to you and you had better listen carefully to what I have to say.'

Concannon reluctantly sat down behind his desk.

'As you already know, the Taoiseach knows every detail of your Spanish venture. He wanted to arrest you and have you face trial but decided that, on balance, it was not in the national interest to do so at this very vulnerable time.'

Concannon was quiet. If de Valera told this man, who else had he told?

'I am here to tell you that, in addition to being potentially traitorous, there were aspects of your so-called venture that were deeply criminal... no, don't interrupt and don't try to end the meeting.'

Concannon was red in the face but, for the first time, Bryan could sense an element of fear.

Bryan continued: 'Criminal, yes. Let me explain. The death of Señor Sánchez was not an accident. He was murdered and probably on the instructions of your collaborator, Mr Joe Bradley. The investigation in to his death continues.'

Concannon's red face had now drained of colour.

'Secondly, may I tell you that we have investigated your so-called links to Mysterium Fidei. We know for a fact that Mysterium Fidei never heard of you or of your intermediary, Señor Sánchez. There was a conspiracy between Bradley and Sánchez. It was about the money – and before I leave I want to know just how much – and it was because of the money Señor Sánchez was killed. Now I can also tell you that, from sources in London, we know at that time Mr Bradley opened several bank accounts in London with a series of heavy deposits. But I suppose you know all this.'

Concannon remained silent.

'And yet you remained close to Bradley. His best friend, some would say. And now you are involved in new adventures with him – financing and arranging the purchase of guns for the Catholic side in Croatia and meddling in Italian politics.'

There was no reply.

'How much have you given Bradley for that cause? I can tell you here and now that not a penny of it will be used to buy a single gun or save a single soul, which I suppose is what the guns were for in the first place.'

Still no response.

Bryan opened his satchel and took out a file.

'Maybe a quiet read of this will refresh your memory.'

Concannon made no attempt to accept the proffered file. Suddenly Bryan could see him deflating. When he spoke, his voice was barely more than a whisper.

'I don't need to read it. I know already. I was betrayed by a man I trusted. God forgive me. I allowed myself be misled.'

Bryan noted the first reaction with interest. Shifting the blame to a man he 'trusted'. Not a word that what he was doing was wrong. He was 'betrayed', 'misled'. But of course, no guilt or responsibility attached to him.

'Well I'm glad you know that now. But it does not lessen your own culpability. Through arrogance and vanity, you were prepared to endanger the lives of every man, woman and child in this State. You thought yourself above the law, you knew better than the elected politicians. Oh yes, all that and worse, and I don't see a sign of remorse. Do you ever think of Señor Sánchez in his cold grave, battered to death in the Dublin mountains? Have you ever said a Mass, even a prayer for him? I doubt it very much.'

Suddenly Concannon was sitting upright. Bryan could see he had regained some of his composure.

Concannon looked Bryan straight in the face and in a cold calm voice asked him: 'What do you want. Is it revenge? Is it money? Is it blackmail?'

'I want you to know that you are complicit in all that happened and how you deal with that is a matter for your own conscience. I couldn't care less about the money so long as it is not used against the State. The murder I will leave to the guards, who have no intention of doing anything at the moment – but that might change. No, I have a simple proposition for you. Answer the questions I ask you and to my satisfaction and, as far as I am concerned, that will almost be the end of the matter.'

'What do you mean almost?'

'If I ever see you interfering again against the public interest or hear of any new crusades, I will pass this file to the nuncio, to the Taoiseach, whoever he may be, or even to the newspapers. Am I understood?'

An hour later an abject and crumpled Concannon had finished answering Bryan's questions. Bryan was coming to the conclu-

sion that he was more a fool than a knave. He was a bad judge of character, as is often the case with self-obsessed people, and he had been fooled by Bradley. Bryan was not altogether surprised. He had seen how charming Bradley could be. The charm of the psychopath, he mused.

Bryan was happy that he now had all the information he needed to complete his dossier. There was no point in talking to Bradley. He would laugh contemptuously, guessing correctly Bryan could never go public with what he knew. He knew de Valera would never allow it happen. No, he thought and with a real sense of bitterness, Joe Bradley will walk away rich and unscathed and the others were only bit players.

Concannon had not offered tea or coffee and was clearly impatient to see Bryan go. But Bryan had one last surprise.

'You didn't ask me who else knows about your role in all this?'

'Surely nobody else does, apart from de Valera that is.'

'You don't have to worry so long as you behave yourself but yes, there is one other person who knows the full story. It is one of your brother bishops. I won't say who.'

'Who? This is treachery on your part. I thought our conversation was confidential. Outrageous behaviour.'

'Calm down. You can probably guess, a man who has long suspected and distrusted you, but he has no more interest than you in causing a scandal that would damage the Church. But he was helpful to me and I thought it a wise precaution, should you lose the run of yourself again, to have someone to nudge you back to reality.'

Bryan showed himself out and headed to the Brannocksbridge Arms for an early lunch.

62

....

Archbishop Valetti should have been on top of the world. He was within sight of solving his immediate financial problems and maybe even of opening some new options – maybe a real chance to get out of this god-forsaken country. God, how he hated being here.

He should have felt good but, to his surprise, he had an uneasy feeling. His run of good luck with the bookies had come to an abrupt end and his stock exchange gambles were faring no better. The Kilderry bequest, of which he had mentioned nothing to the Vatican, had given him a false burst of confidence. The realist in him told him that the patterns of behaviour that had led to his Cypriot troubles were recurring.

It was only a short matter of time before the bookies lost their patience so it was all the more important that he be properly prepared for his meeting with Jeremy Bradley. And this feeling of anxiety was heightened by a call he had just had from Rome.

The call had come from a friend, not a close friend since Valetti didn't do close friendships, more a gossip and trouble maker, who clearly had unpalatable news to impart. His diplomatic colleague told Valetti that somebody was asking questions about him and especially about his time in Cyprus. The 'friend' was sure Valetti had nothing to worry about – hadn't he been cleared by the inquiry – but thought it better to tell him. Valetti was curt in his response but was concerned. He had hoped to keep everything under the radar.

And his headaches were back – a sure sign of the tension that always presaged a bout of depression.

It was vital he concluded his business with Jeremy Bradley quickly and positively.

When he thought of the ammunition he had to use against Bradley, he did feel positive. The material he had from the Robinson papers should be conclusive. If necessary, historians would be found to attest to Robinson's unimpeachable probity and veracity. On Robinson's evidence, Joe Bradley was guilty of treason, theft on a major scale and possible – probable – murder. It was all here in black and white.

Jeremy Bradley could not afford the risk of this information going public. It would destroy his carefully crafted reputation, it would lead to questions in parliament, maybe even calls to reopen the murder case, and provoke a media frenzy. In Valetti's mind, he had the trump card and Bradley could not afford not to buy his silence.

How much should he demand? He did not know how much money was involved in the original bequest, but JJ Gilmartin had assured him that Concannon had left millions. So Bradley must have stolen multiples of that.

Valetti was a poker player – not a great one his companions would say – and he knew he should not make impossible demands. Give Bradley room to manoeuvre and let him save face. Don't force him to dig his heels in. Valetti did not want the process to drag on, nor did he want to run the risk of publicity. So it was important to set the right tone, no heavy stuff, and to appear reasonable. Maybe he should start at a half million and be prepared to settle for £400,000.

Out of nowhere, his debt to JJ Gilmartin sprung to mind. He would have to do something for him. Yes, he would make him a monsignor before he left Ireland. He quickly dismissed Gilmartin from his thoughts.

He had to concentrate on the matter in hand. He must not

underestimate Bradley. He would be no pushover so Valetti, who fancied himself as a negotiator, determined his key objective would be to persuade Bradley it was in his best interests to accept Valetti's terms. Bradley was a man of the world who valued his reputation. If faced with a reasonable demand from Valetti, he might not like it but would quickly see where his own interests lay. Or so Valetti told himself.

Valetti's good spirits were rising. He poured himself a generous grappa to have with his coffee. He prided himself on being meticulous, so he looked for possible flaws in his plans but could find none. The thought of the money filled him with a sense of giddiness. Happy days indeed. He would leave this awful city and his drab residence, he would find a sinecure in Rome, buy a small house in Tuscany, be financially independent and, yes, emphatically he would give up gambling.

He still had not heard from Bradley, but that did not worry him. He would phone Bradley's office and leave a message asking for a meeting.

For the first time, he thought about a possible venue for the meeting. It had to be utterly private with no possibility of being seen. Not his own residence. Too many snoopers about and he did not trust that little Peruvian. Perhaps he should give the first small victory to Bradley and let him say where suited him. Let him think I am an amateur. I will invite him here and when he refuses I will offer to go to his place. Preferably his place in the country. That might lull him in to a false sense of security.

It doesn't really matter where we meet, he thought. I have the paper. The original was secure in his safe and he had a high-quality copy for Bradley. When the deal was done and the money transferred, he would hand over the original with a note from himself declaring it to be a forgery. That should satisfy Bradley.

He poured another grappa and decided that maybe his luck was turning again. He phoned his stockbroker to buy some more shares in Atlantic Resources. He had got a tip from a good source that they were on the brink of a major oil find.

***

Down in Ballywilliamroe Jeremy Bradley was not surprised to hear about Valetti's call. He had deliberately left the first call to him. Let him feel he is in control. Bradley needed time to let Lyster do his work.

He now felt confident. Lyster had done his work thoroughly. Every aspect of Valetti's career had been scrutinised, from his family's Sicilian background to his growing up in Toronto, his career at the Vatican and, most of all, his time in Cyprus, not forgetting his Dublin activities. He now had a fat file in front of him.

But fat as it was, it might not be enough. Lyster's Vatican friend, who was earning a good fee for his efforts, had done his work thoroughly, but had said to Lyster that Valetti's case would probably rely heavily on material he may have dug up from the 1940s and of which they would be unaware. They talked about where such material could have come from. If it was in any of the major Irish archives, historians would have spotted it ages ago and, if it were sensitive, it would have been withheld. It could only come from within the Church itself and maybe even the nuncio's own archive.

Lyster's friend was clear that there was only one possible source, especially given Valetti's own position, and that was the files of a predecessor. In other words, from the files of a man whose name was, up to now, unknown to either Bradley or Lyster – a man called Paschal Robinson, who was nuncio during these years.

Lyster had his friend in Rome and another friend in May-nooth search about for some information that could be used against Robinson, or in Lyster's words smear, defame, vilify him – the whole works, should Valetti's case depend on his record.

They had not found this an easy task. Lyster could find no historian to say a bad word about Robinson. Saintly, austere, honest, scholar and humble were the only words they heard. The worst they could come up with were the words of the President of the Irish College in 1928 when he warned the Irish bishops that their new nuncio 'was a man on the make and not to be trusted'. But Lyster's source said the problem here was that Monsignor O'Hagan bad-mouthed most people and could be easily enough discounted. He had already found a historian who would swear to that.

However, Jeremy Bradley had no doubt Lyster would find a way.

He might need some more time so Bradley would phone Valetti and invite him to Ballywilliamroe a week from today.

Besides, before meeting Valetti he wanted to get Richard E Murdock sorted out. He had no fears on this score. Lyster had done a very thorough job. The bishop's old driver; that was a bit of genius and that was why Lyster was so good. He would let Lyster handle Murdock in his own way.

63

....

Murdock was in his usual place in the bar of the Lazerian Hotel just after opening time. But instead of his usual starter of gin and tonic, he faced a lonely cup of coffee. He had got a phone call to his office just an hour earlier from Jeremy Bradley's office. An icily polite lady told him that Mr Bradley's personal representative would meet him at 10.30 'in his usual place in the Lazerian Hotel'. With that abrupt and unexpected message, the call ended.

He was bemused and apprehensive. This did not auger well. How could Bradley, whom he had never met, know so much about his daily routine? Was he being spied upon? What else did they know? And why was he not meeting Bradley himself rather than this personal representative?

There were two ways of looking at it, he mused, looking disdainfully at the cooling coffee. The better one was that Bradley saw the strength of Murdock's claim but was too proud to admit this in person and was sending his personal representative to discuss terms. The fact that the meeting was on Murdock's own turf was possibly a gesture of conciliation.

Somehow Murdock was not persuaded by this explanation. The alternative was that the time and venue and the sending of a mere messenger was a gesture of contempt, a not-so-veiled message that he was being spied on and an indication that he was not being taken seriously. But how could Bradley know much about him? They had never met and Bradley had never heard of him until a few weeks ago.

'God how I'd love a gin and tonic,' he said almost to himself, but no, it would not be the right image to project. Better not be seen drinking so early in the day.

He was so absorbed in his thoughts that it took him a few seconds to realise there was someone sitting beside him at the bar.

'Two gin and tonics please. Cork and Schweppes.'

Murdock looked up startled. Sitting beside him was an elegant, relaxed man with an outstretched hand and a disarming smile.

'Hello, I'm Cornelius Lyster. You're Mr Murdock. I wouldn't like you to break the habit of a lifetime, so let's start the day the way we both like,' he said, pointing to the gin and tonics.

Murdock's relief at seeing the gin and tonic was ruined by the realisation he had been wrong-footed by this smooth operator. Whatever initiative he might have had was lost.

Lyster got to the point straight away.

'Mr Bradley was not available himself but felt it would be best if we could settle this matter in a civilized and friendly way. Maybe we could move to that table in the corner?'

As soon as they had settled in, Murdock noticed for the first time the very large briefcase Lyster had with him. Not a good sign. If he was going to settle, a smaller case would have been sufficient.

'As I understand it, you feel Mr Bradley has some money that is rightfully yours. Now I have to tell you at the outset, Mr Bradley is very scrupulous about such matters. He feels very strongly that his integrity is his most valued asset and if there is some injury to your family – about which he knows nothing – he would want to have it righted.

'Normally a letter such as yours, with no supporting evidence, would have gone straight to the bin or maybe to the police but, coming as it did from a reputable country law firm and from a solicitor of your standing, we felt it had to be treated seriously and with respect. A man such as you would not write this type of letter casually. So perhaps we can start by you telling me your story.'

Murdock could not decide whether this was the prelude to a capitulation or whether he was being toyed with by this smoothie with his look of concerned benevolence. But this might be his only chance so he launched in to his prepared speech.

Like many lawyers, he had never mastered the art of being concise. He began with a rambling account of his widowed mother and how 'Uncle Thomas' had more or less adopted the family, paying school and university fees and very much more. He spoke of Thomas's affection for the family and how he made it clear they would be looked after in his will.

As he rambled on – and he spoke for nearly 30 minutes – Lyster noted there was not one verifiable fact that could be seen as an entitlement. He began to wonder where Joe Bradley came in to the story – the only part relevant to him.

Murdock finally came to Joe. He said his uncle had been given a huge bequest by an unknown benefactor. He had entrusted much of this money in to the care of Joe Bradley for some unspecified, but almost certainly philanthropic, purpose. In 1945 Joe Bradley had robbed this money and, in the process, deprived Richard E of what should have been his rightful inheritance.

Lyster's reaction was that this was threadbare stuff, but he wanted to see if there were any aspects that might go public and cause problems. He thought not, but he had not built up his reputation by taking chances.

'So that's it. That's your story. And what is it you want from Mr Bradley?'

Murdock could not believe his ears. Was this a capitulation?

'Well the first thing is, I don't want any unpleasantness or publicity. I don't want to embarrass anyone. Let's just say adequate compensation, the amount to be negotiated.'

'And could you give me an approximate figure?'

'Around the half million mark, with a full confidentiality clause of course.'

Lyster was silent, apart from ordering two more gins. He let the silence drag on for three or four minutes, during which time Murdock began to feel more and more confident. The negotiations had started already. Lyster's next step would be to try and beat down the price. This suited Murdock. When it came to negotiating, Murdock rather fancied himself – 30 years' experience behind him. Everyone said he was a sharp negotiator.

Lyster was still smiling when he began to speak quietly. 'And suppose we tell you to fuck off? But before I do, what sort of evidence or proof do you have to make your case stand up?'

Murdock was expecting this. He was surprised it had not come earlier.

'First-hand evidence from the man who was at my uncle's side throughout these years, a man who drove my uncle and kept a record of every meeting he ever had and who has given me that record. He will aver to regular meetings between my uncle and Bradley during these years, he will tell of the final meeting, which ended in a row and my uncle saying to him "I have been robbed".'

Murdock stopped to see the impression his words were making. He was pleased to see Lyster's smile was gone. Good.

'So you see, I have a strong case. And if you refuse to accept it, I will go to the newspapers and they will have fun with it. No matter what happens, Mr Bradley's name will be tainted, his reputation in ruins. It will be the beginning of a media persecution of the family. I know from my own research that old Joe Bradley has a dirty past. This will open the floodgates, mark my words.'

Murdock stopped abruptly. Had he overplayed his hand?

'But of course, my preference is an agreed solution. It's always the best thing to do and I am wide open to discuss your offer.'

Better calm things down and that should do it.

Lyster remained silent while he beckoned the barman for two more drinks.

When he spoke, it was a different Lyster. Any pretence of bonhomie or charm was gone, replaced by a quiet sense of menace.

'I have listened very carefully. Everything you say conveys one thing to me. Blackmail. Crude, ugly blackmail. Now at least we know what we are talking about.'

This was not what Murdock had expected.

'The basic truth is you have fuck-all evidence that would survive five minutes' scrutiny in a district court. You're a small-town solicitor and not a very good one. You are totally out of your league. Your crude attempt at blackmail could see you in Mountjoy. Pathetic.'

Lyster had not raised his voice. His tone was icy calm. He reached for his briefcase.

'In ascending order of seriousness, let me tell you what we will answer you with.'

He pulled a file out of the bag.

'This file is based on information from the Law Society. And before you start bleating about privacy or breach of rights, we didn't get these papers from the Law Society and it doesn't matter how we got them. We have them and that is all that matters, and you will see they are genuine. It is the evidence of the society's own investigator, which you know all about since you are trying desperately to suppress it at present. It does not make pretty reading and I will have no difficulty in sharing it with your unsuspecting clients – and maybe even give snippets to your rivals. You can imagine the consequences.'

He took out a second file.

'This is the report commissioned from a private detective by your wife and is at the heart of your current unhappy relations. We did not get it from your wife. She doesn't know we have this report and we have no intention of dragging her in to this, especially since we know how she is enjoying her new freedom. But if we are pushed...'

Lyster left the sentence unfinished. Murdock felt he had been kicked in the stomach. This was dirtier than he ever could have imagined. That bloody bitch. He didn't believe she had not given it to Lyster. She would do anything to get rid of him. Treachery and disloyalty of the first order.

Lyster was talking again.

'One more file should be enough, though I have half a dozen others. You don't command much loyalty Mr Murdock and, having met you, I'm not surprised. You really are a bit of a sleazebag as the Americans would call it, but let's continue.'

Murdock could feel the contempt radiating from Lyster. He readied himself for what Lyster clearly saw as his knockout punch.

Lyster produced a slim file with a single sheet of paper and an old-fashioned school copy book.

'This,' he said holding the single sheet, 'is a sworn statement from a man I believe you know, a Mr John Ryan, or Johnny Flowerpot as he is locally known. In simple terms, he states he was Bishop Concannon's driver for most of his time as bishop, he describes many visits to the home of Mr Joseph Bradley, which continued on a regular basis until Mr Bradley's death in 1977, and declares emphatically that their relationship was cordial and warm right to the end.

'He is not aware of any row or cooling of relations between the pair and states that, while the bishop did not attend Mr Bradley's funeral because of a meeting in Maynooth, he did visit the house to convey his condolences. He is prepared to stand over this statement in court.'

Holding up the copybook, he continued.

'This copybook, which you can see is a 1940s school exercise book, was used by Mr Ryan to record all visits before transferring them to the bishop's official register, which you say is in your possession. Mr Ryan will swear that, after 1945, the bishop preferred that record to contain only official not social visits, hence the omissions from the official record. You can check for yourself if you wish.'

Murdock could feel the ground going from under him. Yes, he knew the copybook had to be a forgery and he knew that Johnny Ryan, the man he thought was a friend, was betraying him and perjuring himself in the process. But what could he do? All his aces had turned to deuces. He was angry, bewildered and helpless.

'That dirty little fucker, that treacherous little bastard. He's lying and you know it. He's done all this for money.'

'I agree, he is a dirty little fucker. And an expensive one too. But he is our dirty little fucker and that's all that matters.'

Lyster allowed Murdock brood while he ordered more drinks. Murdock brushed his aside.

'I take it we will be hearing no more of your claims. I have a document here that says you renounce any claims against Mr Bradley. You will need to sign it.'

Murdock took the proffered sheet while Lyster continued.

'You said at the outset that you hoped we could settle this whole matter in an amicable way. That too is our position. We believe any publicity would be distasteful. In return for signing this document, we will make a one-off payment of 10 thousand to cover your expenses and will hand in to your custody copies of all the files I brought today, even the ones I have not shown you. They'll make interesting reading for you. I know it's only a gesture, but then life is about gestures – even meaningless ones.'

He handed over the files to an utterly deflated Murdock.

'Now sign up, drink up your gin and tonic, and fuck off out of our lives forever. I mean it, fuck off forever. We were gentle with you today. We don't always do gentle.'

With that, he left the Lazerian Hotel hoping he would never have to darken its doors again.

64

············

Archbishop Valetti was enjoying the early morning sun as he drove his Mercedes down to Carlow. He hadn't travelled much since coming to Ireland, nor had he received many invitations. In fact, Dominic Irwin was the only bishop who had ever invited him.

This had not bothered him one bit. He found most of them boring and, as he drove through Naas, Kilcullen and Castledermot, he did not think he had missed out on too much on the scenery either. The countryside was too neat, with its prosperous well-tended farms and studs and unexceptional towns and villages. He would have preferred something more raw and a bit elemental, more like Calgary or Calabria.

He had some difficulty finding Ballywilliamroe on the back roads outside Bagenalstown, but he arrived just before noon. Bradley had suggested they have their meeting and then Valetti would stay for lunch. Valetti had agreed but could not decide if Bradley was overcautious, simply seeing the meeting as a formality, or if it was just old-fashioned courtesy. Perhaps a bit of each.

Valetti was surprised at how relaxed he felt. He put this down to what he called his gambler's gene. He felt he had chosen his cards well and the playing was as important to him as the outcome. He told himself he had much to win and nothing to lose. But as always with his gambles, he did not think he would lose.

He was surprised by the modest dimensions of Ballywilliamroe House – basically a large nineteenth-century farm-house with discreet extensions to each side and what looked like a gym standing on its own to the left of the house. A well-surfaced drive led past a walled orchard, through a large smooth lawn with a towering oak tree and well-kept gardens. The whole effect was of restrained good taste, an avoidance of ostentation, solid old money that didn't have to show itself off.

Valetti was surprised. He had expected to see a flaunting of wealth with all its extravagances. Clearly Jeremy Bradley was confident enough not to need these trappings.

Valetti's earlier encounters with Bradley, brief as they were, had confused him. What he saw was almost an archetypal English toff, hair that bit too long, the languid world-weary air and lazy drawl, the courteous superiority. He had met many such men in Cyprus and Rome, but never an Irishman like this.

How did all this square with being the son not just of a rebel republican but a ruthless killer and robber, if what his bookie friend told him was true, which it undoubtedly was? Then he remembered some of the men he knew from Sicily, refined and cultured and understated, yet the sons of gangsters and often far more ruthless and cruel than their fathers had been. Or godfathers. He shuddered at the thought.

In fact, as Valetti reminded himself, it was a persona he admired. He himself was always well dressed, as he was today in his expensive Rome-tailored suit and shining brogues. He told himself he could be just as aloof as Bradley, should that be needed.

It wasn't. The Bradley who greeted him at the door was warm and respectful.

'Excellency, you honour us by coming to this quiet place right in the heart of the hidden Ireland. You may not believe it but Carlow, especially south Carlow, has some of the best scenery in the country. But we like to keep it to ourselves. Maybe I can bring you down to Borris after lunch but let me offer you a coffee. You had a pleasant journey I hope.'

Valetti was on his guard, but Bradley had set the tone and he would follow suit. Unless of course a change was warranted.

They went straight to Bradley's study, a bright spacious room with one all-glass wall looking out on Mount Leinster and on the other walls a small collection of paintings.

'All by Stephen McKenna – the only top painter to capture the real quality of this county.'

There was a small table where a jug of coffee, biscuits and some cups were laid out. Bradley beckoned Valetti to one of the armchairs at either end of the table. There were some neatly stacked files on the table.

Bradley began. 'Archbishop you will of course stay for lunch but, as we are both men of business – yours spiritual, mine temporal, but business nonetheless – why don't we get to the heart of the matter, resolve what can be resolved and then go and drink some of the very special Italian wines I have awaiting your attention.'

Valetti realised he had not spoken a word so far. Bradley had done all the talking but, before he could intervene, Bradley cut in.

'Archbishop, why don't you tell me what this is all about. Be as brutal and as frank as you wish, but perhaps you might let me summarise what I think it is you want. Or would you care to do that yourself?'

Valetti was beginning to feel isolated and decided to take what he hoped would be the initiative.

'I'll talk,' he said perhaps more peremptorily than he might have wished. He felt he was being soft-soaped in to some form of acquiescence.

'The matter is very simple and I will be as brutal and as frank as you have invited me to be. I think it is better we have no misunderstandings.'

'Of course, please go ahead.'

'The story is very simple and not so very pleasant. So please forgive me. This is not personal. It's business, no more, no less. I'm sure you can understand that.'

'Of course. It's the way I like to do things.'

'Good. The story is simple. Your father was a close friend of Bishop Thomas Concannon of Kilderry. You probably knew Concannon, so you know who I am talking about.'

'Yes of course. I have some very fond memories of the bishop. A fine man.'

'Good. Well the bishop got a major bequest in the early 1940s to be used for unspecified projects on behalf of the Church. He devised a scheme, something allegedly to do with the Spanish Church and, in the operating of this scheme, your father was the chief manager, the fixer, the man of business. The government found out and didn't like it and the scheme collapsed.

'In fact the scheme, unknown to the bishop, was a hoax from the start orchestrated by your father and a Spanish diplomat. The Spaniard died in mysterious circumstances very shortly afterwards. The money disappeared. It was stolen by your father. Am I clear?'

'Perfectly. I am listening carefully.'

'The bishop was unaware of your father's duplicity, and in 1945 Concannon and your father got involved in a scheme to supply arms to Catholics in the Croatian Civil War. Arms for the Ustaše, no less. The Irish government got wind of it and the plan was aborted, but not before the money disappeared and once again ended up with your father. This time, however,

Concannon discovered the truth but could not get the money back – in all about a million at wartime values.'

'And?'

'And that's the money your fortune was built on. Money that rightly belongs to the Catholic Church, for whom I and I alone as nuncio act.'

'That's indeed very serious and shocking. But I fear you must have been misled. Can you prove any of this? Do you realise the embarrassment, indeed the scandal, this would visit on the Church which you say you represent?'

'Not just for the Church. The Church can handle these matters. The embarrassment and the shame will be entirely yours. I'm sure you realise that,' Valetti replied.

'Indeed. It could be most unpleasant. But before we go any further, could you tell me what sort of evidence you have to stand up these extraordinary allegations.'

This was the moment Valetti had been waiting for. A moment he had rehearsed over and over again.

With slow gravity he took an envelope from his breast pocket and even more slowly opened it. He extracted a single sheet of paper. Bradley could see it was a photocopy.

'This is a note written in late 1945 by my predecessor Archbishop Paschal Robinson, a saintly man of unimpeachable integrity. He was the first papal nuncio to Ireland and it was to him that Concannon confessed the full story. You will see here in black and white that Concannon says he was betrayed and robbed by your father on two occasions, 1940 and 1945, and that after the 1940 incident, there was an accidental death of a Spanish diplomat, which may have been a murder. He also confirmed to Robinson the total amount involved.'

Valetti handed over the sheet, which Bradley read slowly and carefully. Lyster had indeed warned him that something like this would probably happen and he had happily made his own preparations. He spent some time examining the paper.

'And tell me, how did this paper suddenly appear. Where has it been all these years?'

Valetti visibly relaxed. It had worked. Bradley had been caught off guard. He could be a little forthcoming.

'I discovered it myself in Robinson's archive. I got a tip-off from a former diplomat, but nobody apart from myself is aware of its existence.'

That was the information Bradley needed. Nobody else knew. That made things a bit easier.

'I have to say I'm devastated. I had no idea about any of this – and my father told me most things. But certainly not this. I am dumbfounded.'

There was a long silence, finally broken by Bradley.

'What do you want me to do?'

Valetti felt he could move in to generous mode.

'Well, no more than yourself, I don't want publicity. It would not be good for the Church or for any of us. I want you to make some restitution to the Church, through me, to be used at my discretion for the type of purpose intended by the original benefactor.'

'And you will be the sole judge of these good works?'

'Precisely. I'm sure it's what the benefactor would have wished and it avoids the risk of unhelpful leaks or speculation.'

In spite of himself, Bradley had to admire the sheer nerve of Valetti. The man was brazen and transparent.

'You are probably right. And tell me, what sort of sum do you have in mind as a fair restitution as you call it?'

'Half a million dollars, paid in to a bank nominated by me. I think that's a fair sum, but I can be flexible.'

'I don't doubt that. Well, let me think about it. I don't want to delay our lunch, but perhaps there are a few things I need to say and a few documents you might see before we adjourn.'

Valetti began to get an uneasy feeling. This had all been too smooth. He sat back as Bradley began.

'You had some very hard things to say about my father, which I resent very deeply, but as you made clear, this is not personal, just business. So forgive me if I continue in that spirit.'

With that he lifted the first file on the desk.

'This is a bit of research I commissioned on your family in Sicily and Toronto. It is detailed and specific and may come as a surprise to you, but I doubt it. Your Sicilian family could be described as well-established but, perhaps, well established in the wrong places. One uncle will die in jail – kidnapping and extortion I believe – and your brother in Toronto could be described as being well known to the police. The details are all here, but of course we cannot be held responsible for the sins of our families – as you might even say in my case. Sadly the media might not be so understanding, as indeed you have already suggested.'

Valetti remained silent as Bradley picked up the second file. His appetite had all but disappeared.

'This one concerns your time in Cyprus. A rather short posting. Apparently all did not go well. I need not go in to details, but the papers here are a record of the enquiry held in Rome after your return, which established beyond doubt that you were laundering money – and large sums – for the benefit of your Sicilian friends. And it is backed up by a report from the Cypriot police that recommends you be prosecuted or deported.

'All very unfortunate, but I must say I admire the way you have kept it covered up so far. And indeed how you so quickly got back on the nuncio train. You are indeed a survivor and I admire survivors. It would be a shame should all this surface now.'

Valetti could contain himself no longer. He could feel himself engulfed in anger.

'This is blackmail, pure and simple. I'm telling you now it won't work. I've still got the incontrovertible evidence, the testimony of Paschal Robinson. This is one piece of evidence that speaks for itself. I've got you there.'

Valetti realised he was close to shouting. He took a deep breath, forcing himself to calm down.

'Yes that is impressive, very impressive – except for one very sad fact. You probably don't know that the unfortunate Dr Robinson suffered a severe nervous breakdown in late 1945 and was for a while a patient in St Patrick's Institution. The breakdown was sudden, brought on, it was said, by stress, but one of the symptoms was a tendency to the delusional. He did make a complete recovery and, as you can understand, these things were kept quiet in those days. Happy times you might say?'

'That's all lies. It never happened. This is an outrage.'

Bradley was smiling.

'Of course it didn't happen, but that's just between you and me.'

He took the third file from the table. 'This is the report dated November 1945 from Professor Henry Belcott, a leading psychiatrist of the time. As you can see, it's on St Patrick's Hospital notepaper and gives full and persuasive details of Dr Robinson's condition and notes his delusional tendencies. Dr Belcott sadly is no longer with us, and medical ethics prohibit us from revealing our sources, but I can tell you it will stand up to the closest scrutiny.'

Valetti was now shouting. 'This is a forgery. Dr Robinson never had a breakdown in his life.'

'Of course it's a forgery,' Bradley smirked. 'But we tested its authenticity on a leading medical archivist and he solemnly confirmed it. He is prepared to swear it was typed on 1940s notepaper and is consistent with other records left by Dr Belcott in the hospital archives. Now sit down and compose yourself.'

Valetti felt his world spinning. Bradley was now talking in a calm soft voice.

'My dear archbishop, you didn't think we would lie down in front of your assault. I know enough about you to know that this is about money and, specifically, money for you. The Church will never see a penny of the money you are demanding. You know that and so do I. So let's stop fooling each other. Nor is there any way you will go into court to challenge the veracity of Dr Belcott's note. Your superiors would not let you for one moment. And if you did, we would squash you.'

Bradley looked at his watch.

'It's time for lunch. Let me say just one more thing. You said hard things about my father. They are all true. But you forget one thing. I may speak differently, behave differently but at heart I am my father's son. We just do the same things differently. He would probably deal with you as he did with that Spanish diplomat, so thank your lucky stars it's me you are dealing with.'

Valetti was feeling helpless. His world had turned upside down in a matter of minutes.

'So now, let's go to lunch. We have good wine to drink and we have many matters to discuss so we can end this whole affair as friends. I would rather have you as a friend than an enemy. Let's go but, before we do, let me tell you a little more about Stephen McKenna and these paintings – all of which I specially commissioned.'

65

....

Archie Bowe did not like being out in the cold. Being the trusted adviser to the Bishop of Kilderry was a very important part of his life and to some extent – at least in his own eyes – defined his status in the community.

But for over five weeks now he had not had one call from the bishop and, more importantly, he had been excluded from all discussions about the fate of Bishop Concannon's money. It irked him greatly that a matter that was rightly his to resolve was being handled by a stranger, a Dublin solicitor who knew nothing of Kilderry or its history.

This blow had been softened – but only slightly – by the courteous call he had from Heather Ruddock telling him she would not be intruding on any of his usual work. She would be dealing exclusively with the Concannon business. She finished her call by telling him how much her grandfather, Charlie Ruddock, had respected Archie Bowe's late father and how much her father respected the Bowe legal practice. But there was no invitation to participate and no indication as to when the project would be finished.

Archie was stubborn, but he was also a realist. Hard facts were his business and he knew it was his refusal, his dogged refusal, to open Concannon's last message that had persuaded Bishop Mullins to act as he did. Yes, it was a question of principle, but it was also a question of stupidity. Events had gone beyond anything Concannon had foreseen and, if his letter could help towards finding a resolution to the remaining issues, it was his duty to bring forward the letter.

He had not come to this decision easily. He would need to find a formula that would save his face and give him an honourable way out of an impasse he had helped create. Eventually, and after much agonising, he had come to the conclusion there was no easy way out. He knew there were rumours in some clerical and legal circles of his estrangement from the bishop and, if not nipped in the bud, these rumours would worsen. His vanity was hurt; his reputation was at stake.

Reluctantly he phoned Mullins. He did not say he was sorry or that he was wrong. Solicitors rarely do. He did say he believed circumstances had changed and he in turn, after serious reflection, believed it was now right to open Concannon's letter. He would be happy to do so in the presence of the bishop.

He was surprised by the warmth and friendliness of Mullins, who was delighted to accept the offer.

'We are having a meeting here tomorrow with Ms Ruddock and a few helpers to try to finalise some matters about this trust we are setting up to handle the money. We've made a lot of progress over the past month or so and I'm sure your presence will be helpful. Here, at 11.30 tomorrow. Good. Come and bring the letter. It may put us out of our misery, but my own view is that the old bugger will be as unhelpful at the end as he was in the beginning. Anyway, one way or other we will see.'

Archie was pleased with the welcome and with Mullins' readiness to accept him 'back' – but what was this 'trust' he was talking about and who were these unnamed 'helpers' he had so casually mentioned?

***

Bishop Mullins had indeed been working hard. He and Heather Ruddock had not just established a good working relationship but had become genuinely fond of each other.

Ruddock was enjoying her work in a way she had not done since her days apprenticed to her father when every sort of legal work came her way. In those days, her work was about people, usually people in trouble, and she had enjoyed the variety and the little dramas involved. But then she specialised in corporate law since her father told her that was where the big money was going to be. He was right and she had become very rich, but there was little enough drama and no excitement, and she found dealing with many of the corporate players a bloodless substitute for real life. She had no intention of giving it up. She was far too fond of money for that, but Kilderry was a welcome diversion.

In addition, and she was honest enough to admit this, she now had much more time with Peter O'Donnell and was enjoying it. 'Her Peter', as she had taken to calling him, seemed as infatuated as he had been that first day in her office. It was an easy, undemanding relationship, with enough physical activity to keep them both happy, all of which seemed – for the moment at least – to suit them both. The best of both worlds she thought, though in her experience that rarely lasts and, in any event, she had no intention of leaving her rose-growing and very amiable husband. But there was a lot to be said for *carpe diem.*

They had been making real progress in sorting out the Kilderry mess. O'Donnell and Tommy Newrie had gone through all of Concannon's papers. This time nothing was off limits. They had three main objectives. How much money did Henry Alsop give Concannon in 1939? How was the money spent and what were the remaining shares worth?

Their first breakthrough was finding the Munster & Leinster bank statements of the two accounts set up by Alsop and mentioned in Concannon's journal. Curiously, these statements were not among the papers taken from Concannon's house,

but were in a dust-covered box in the safe that had been overlooked by Mullins and later by O'Donnell himself. It clearly did
not seem to be of any interest at the time.

Both accounts were in the name of Thomas Patrick Concannon. The first account of £10,000 was a current account; the
second, with a lodgement of £100,000, was an interest-earning
deposit account that required just three weeks' notice to effect
a withdrawal. And in certain circumstances, with the permission of the manager and the named holder of the account, notice need only be three working days.

They quickly established a pattern. As soon as the current
account dropped below £5,000, it was topped up to its original
£10,000 from the interest-earning account. This was generally
done on an annual basis and they quickly established that this
was what Mullins had originally referred to as Concannon's
'slush' fund – the money he had used to fund his own personal
projects and presumably his family's. The account was totally
separate from all diocesan accounts and unknown to all except
the bishop and the bank.

The first movement of money, presumably from the sale of
shares, came in late 1940 when £400,000 was added to the deposit account. It only rested there briefly before it was transferred to the current account.

Over the coming months, this money was withdrawn in
four separate bank drafts all payable to 'Mr Joseph Bradley'.
There was nothing to suggest the fate of this money.

For the next four years there was little or no subsequent activity, apart from the annual topping up of the current account. The
deposit account at this stage depleted somewhat. By 1945, when
the next phase of activity began, it stood at just over £75,000.

Then in 1945 a further £400,000 was placed in the deposit account. More shares being sold, O'Donnell reckoned. The same

pattern followed. This time the money was moved within weeks to the current account and once again withdrawn using bank drafts – only two in this case to the same 'Mr Joseph Bradley'. Again there was no indication of the fate of this money.

From this point on, through the 1950s, '60s and '70s, the deposit account remained virtually dormant – apart from the accruing interest. The 'topping up' of the bishop's own account continued with greater frequency. Just before Concannon was finally 'retired' in the early 1980s, the account stood at just over £75,000. That was when Concannon finally closed the account, withdrawing its total remaining sum, which eventually made up the bulk of his estate and was dispersed in his will.

At this point, just weeks before Concannon left Kilderry, the record ended.

Tracing the money had been an exhausting process but, by the time Newrie and O'Donnell had finished, they had a clearer picture of what had happened. Concannon had undertaken two major enterprises with the money, the first in 1940, the second in 1945. Morgan Dannaher would no doubt fill them in on the nature of the enterprises later. There was nothing after 1945. There was no evidence of any further shares being sold, though Concannon may have offloaded some for his own benefit. They thought it unlikely, however, since he had a ready stream of income from the deposit account. But Newrie advised them to keep an open mind.

The other hard fact they had was that this man 'Joseph Bradley' was the money man. The money went through him. That was clear. But went where? There was no clue in the financial records. They needed to know a lot more about Bradley, and again Dannaher could be helpful. O'Donnell was glad they had taken Newrie's advice and kept him on the team.

Bishop Mullins could at least rest at ease on one score. Concannon apparently had not used diocesan money for his adventures or, it would seem, for his family, although there was no way of being certain about that – but no way of proving he did either. Mullins could feel sure there would be no 'Kilderry scandal' – and for a bishop, that was something that really did matter.

O'Donnell and Newrie also examined the other area that had been off limits – the personal files Concannon kept on his priests and, indeed, on others.

'J Edgar Hoover could have learned from this fellow,' said Newrie after an hour's reading of the 'spy' files kept by Concannon. 'He had his spies everywhere. Curates spying on parish priests, parish priests spying on other parish priests, seminarians on their professors and of course the creepy legion of pious lay people. Not a nice world.'

'No wonder Mullins called it a reign of terror,' O'Donnell remarked.

'Yeah, but there's fuck-all here for us. One thing I have learned though, a lot of priests are not very nice people and, do you know, they don't seem to like one another very much either.'

'I blame it on celibacy – and having too little to do.'

And with that they passed on to the other parts of their investigation.

They attempted to learn more about the original donor, Henry Alsop, in the hope that it might influence how the money might be used. Apart from an old *Who's Who* entry, they learned little. Dannaher was asked to dig around further but, in the absence of any surviving family and with a life lived mainly in Africa and the US, there was little likelihood of much emerging.

They were more successful in quantifying the market value

of the remaining shares. There were three tranches of the original shares remaining -- DuPont, bought in 1936; Standard Oil of New Jersey, now Esso, bought in 1930; and Goodyear Tyres, bought in 1930.

O'Donnell felt no need this time to make the mistake of consulting Sigerson Keane. Instead, he gave the details to a smart post-graduate student and, as an exercise, asked him to compute their current value. The student concluded the shares were now worth between 50 and eighty times their original value – so his estimate of current value was a reassuring £6.5 million. The new trust would start in a healthy fashion.

And Heather Ruddock had been more than talking about the new trust. She was on the way to finalise its setting up. It was a complicated legal process, but easy enough for somebody from a firm that specialised in setting up all sorts of trusts. She had a young, would-be partner do all the donkey work, which was done in record time and to her own satisfaction.

The trust had really been the idea of Bishop Mullins. He was adamant the money should not belong to the diocese of Kilderry. He argued that, if the diocese claimed it, they would run the risk of a raft of rival claimants – the nuncio, the Vatican, Murdock or even *Mysterium Fidei*. But more than that, it was a moral issue for Mullins.

Kilderry had no entitlement. The money was meant for 'God's work' and, in this case, it would be Mullins and the trust who would define what 'God's work' meant and who would do it. For Mullins, it meant helping the poor and disabled in ways that were sustainable, enlightened and compassionate. No more, no less.

But who would be the members of this trust? Ruddock had no doubt it should be made up of 'persons of known integrity, judgement and achievement, unencumbered by any conflict of interest'. And she said these people were to hand. She would be the first Chair, the Bishop of Kilderry would be an *ex officio* member and the other members would be from the academic, medical and diplomatic worlds – in other words O'Donnell, Newrie and Dannaher. She would find a competent and tough woman to act as administrator.

She said very simply: 'This makes sense. We know the background, we know how we got here and we trust the bishop to steer us in the right direction. I'm sure that once we have it on firm foundations, the trust will develop a life of its own. We have a robust constitution and we work within that. Otherwise it could be months and months before we get anything going.'

There was no disagreement and they decided the new trust would be known as the 'Alsop Concannon Foundation' in memory of the benefactors who had (unknowingly) made it possible.

Newrie had one last suggestion. They should be open to doing some fundraising of their own once the foundation was established. If his hunch about Joseph Bradley was right, then Jeremy Bradley might be a good starting point.

In all of these activities, Mullins had played a major role. He had shed years and showed the sort of energy that must have impressed those who had first appointed him to be a bishop. And he had his own secret, which he confided only to Ruddock and which would stay secret until the foundation was securely established.

None of this activity leaked out. Archie Bowe and those who talked to JJ Gilmartin knew something was happening. But even with so much coming and going, the revitalised Mullins and the Protestant solicitor so much in evidence, all they could do was surmise – with no facts, they did not get very far.

And now it was time for Bowe to come in from the cold.

66

....

When the post arrived, JJ Gilmartin was in his silk dressing gown, enjoying a leisurely read of *The Irish Times* over an even more leisurely breakfast. It was the part of his daily routine he most liked. The curate would say the early Mass and, unless he was heading to Dublin or had a funeral, JJ rarely made a public appearance before noon. He had worked hard enough as a curate to a succession of crusty parish priests and now it was his turn to take it easy. And it was something he felt he had earned the right to.

Gilmartin lived in some comfort and not a little style in Ballinbo. The inheritance from his parents ensured his home was warm, comfortable and well equipped with high quality television and music centres, not to mention the most up-to-date coffee-maker the market could offer. And of course, there was the upmarket housekeeper who came in each afternoon to ensure that whatever he needed for breakfast was to hand and that the house reflected a level of sophistication not usually found in a remote parish.

He was concerned that he had not heard from his friend the nuncio for more than six weeks and had begun to wonder if he had fallen out of favour. He hoped not, especially since he had so much that was new to tell him about developments in Kilderry. His problem was that all his information was second hand and some of it obviously built on surmise. That would not have stopped him in the past – nor would it now.

He would tell the nuncio that there had been big changes at

the bishop's house in Kilderry. There were rumours that Archie Bowe had been sidelined and replaced by a bossy woman solicitor from Dublin, and not just a woman but a Protestant as well. Apparently Monsignor Nestor's nephew, the fellow from Trinity College, had been a frequent visitor as well. Something was clearly afoot and, in Gilmartin's mind, it could only be about the missing money. He felt Archbishop Valetti would appreciate knowing this.

He had also heard from Bishop Irwin that Bishop Mullins seemed like a different man – energised, buzzing around the diocese like a man who had a lot to do and not much time to do it. Irwin also felt that Mullins was behaving like a man who had a big load lifted from his shoulders and seemed very much at ease with himself. It made a pleasant change from the hitherto overwrought and nervy Mullins he had been accustomed to meeting. Did that mean the money issue had been resolved and to Mullins benefit? That should be of interest to the nuncio.

Yes, he would phone the nuncio and invite him to lunch. Not to the club. He knew Valetti found it stuffy. He would bring him to a good Italian restaurant – Nico's probably.

But first he opened his post. Most of it was routine stuff, but one letter stood out. It had a Vatican postmark. This had never happened before. He opened it with anxiety (was he in trouble?) and apprehension (was he being offered something?).

It was a short letter from the Congregation of the Clergy, written in Latin, which was no problem for Gilmartin. It said that the Holy Father, on the advice of the papal nuncio to Ireland, was pleased to elevate him to the rank of monsignor. A *Domestic Prelate* it was called. He would be a bishop in all but name, but of course with no power. But his title from now on would be *Right Reverend* and he would be able to wear purple – purple piping on his soutane, a purple cummerbund, a purple

tassel on his biretta and, yes, purple socks. He would have to
buy them in Rome.

He read the letter over and over, bathed in excitement. Wait
until his Maynooth classmates heard. That would show them.
As he reflected, he began to notice the involuntary emerging
of an erection. Just as had happened and so discomfited him in
the Stephen's Green Club. Now however, he was home and on
his own. This time it would not be wasted.

Soon after, he phoned Valetti to offer profuse thanks.

Valetti sounded excited on the phone. 'Yes. I told you I would
make you a monsignor but have you not heard my news? Well
if you haven't then nobody has and that's good as far as I am
concerned. I'm leaving, two weeks from now. Health reasons,
although to tell the truth I've seldom felt better. I will be getting a good rest and I don't know what happens after that, but
I hope to stay in Rome. Yes indeed, the Lord works in mysterious ways and all that... Yes, of course I accept your invitation
to lunch... Nico's? Good. So long as it's not that stuffy club of
yours. And yes, feel free to tell people my news.'

Gilmartin had never heard Valetti in such good form. He
didn't pause to wonder how all this had happened so suddenly
and how it had remained secret until now. That speculation
might come later, but for now he had two pieces of news to
impart and no better man to impart it.

***

Back in the nunciature in Cabra, Valetti was still chuckling
about his conversation with *Monsignor* JJ Gilmartin. For all of
JJ's pomp, Valetti decided he liked him and could imagine the
visit to Rome to get the full monsignorial regalia – that should
put him back a few bob – and could see him on the phone this
very minute eagerly spreading his two bits of good news to all

and sundry, including diplomats, professors and priests. That suited Valetti too – and saved him the bother of putting out an official statement. God, and wasn't JJ easily pleased – a mere monsignor, a consolation prize for losers who didn't become bishops. Oh well.

Valetti was enjoying his own special coffee with the help of a grappa and his fragrant Toscanello Bianco. The strong coffee smell blended with the grappa and the whiff of the Toscanello, wrapping him in a fug of pleasure. He was tidying up his papers and reviewing the events of the past six weeks. My God. What a whirlwind it had all been, beginning with that lunch at Ballywilliamroe House.

Valetti had to admit to himself that he was a broken man after his morning meeting with Jeremy Bradley. Why he didn't just walk out and drive as far away from Ballywilliamroe as he could, he had no idea. He was in such a stupor that he didn't realise there was another guest in Bradley's dining room. A tall, smartly dressed, smiling man who shook his hand warmly: 'So pleased to meet you – though I feel I know you already. I'm Cornelius Lyster. Jeremy may have mentioned me to you.'

Valetti was still in such a daze that he barely registered Lyster or what he said. Bradley's dining room faced the Blackstairs mountains and Bradley was talking about the beauty to be found in this calm county and especially around the village of St Mullins. Valetti barely registered his surroundings or noticed the wines and dishes that awaited on the sideboard.

'I think we know one another well enough to dispense with formality. May I call you Frank? Good,' Bradley said as they sat down to plates of smoked salmon and crunchy brown bread.

He turned to Lyster. 'Frank and I have had a good and honest meeting and I think we have resolved the main issue between us. But there are a few odds and ends we need to tidy up and I am sure we can do that over lunch.'

He poured a glass of the white wine – a Gavi di Gavi, 'a good Northern dry' – sniffed and nodded approvingly, and poured out a glass each for Valetti and Lyster. 'Good vintage, 1993. One of the best I have drunk,' Bradley said as he took a sip.

'Frank, I said to you earlier that you are a survivor, and that you most certainly are. I like survivors and I like to think I am one myself. I would not be one of the wealthiest men in Ireland today if I were not. So let's start on that basis. We both talk the same language. We understand each other.'

Valetti, still somewhat shocked by the turn of events, just nodded – although he had recovered sufficiently to admire the excellence of the wine.

'Let me tell you Frank why we had to take you so seriously and perhaps why we had to be that little bit rough with you, and I apologise for that. My father and his reputation are two of the most important things in my life. It's not just a matter of sentiment, more importantly it's a matter of survival.'

Valetti was now paying full attention. 'Let me tell you about my father Joe Bradley. He was a powerful man. He dominated me while he lived and haunts me since he died. In many ways he shaped me, making me what I am today. It's his legacy that made possible the wealth and influence I now have.

'But this is far more complex than the usual father-son stuff and, believe me, I have read widely on that subject. I loved my father and I hated my father. I admired him and I despised him. I loved his sheer energy, his imagination, his generosity, his fearlessness, his sense of fun. I hated his brutality, his vicious-ness, his crudeness at times. I hated the way he wanted to own and direct my life; to live his unfulfilled ambitions through me, to see my successes as his revenge on an establishment he hated because it rejected him, men who would never give him recognition and never spoke well of him. And in some ways that is what I am – his revenge on the establishment, not that anyone much cares anymore.

'Until the day he died, I lived under his shadow. It was not always easy, believe me. And I would be back under that shadow, and darkly under it, if you had succeeded.'

Bradley paused to eat some food and drink some wine. Valetti noticed for the first time that they were alone – no serving staff to wait on them. Lyster removed the plates and put a platter of slices of rare roast beef and a large salad bowl on the table.

Bradley poured three glasses of Barbaresco – 'dark and brooding,' he said, 'my favourite Italian red'.

Valetti was at least beginning to enjoy the food, even if he had no idea where all this was leading.

'All fathers embarrass their sons, but what I hated most in my father was his crude, amoral approach to matters and to people. I know about some of the awful things he did during the Troubles and Civil War. I know Michael Collins wanted him out of the country and so did de Valera. And I know some of the thugs – one of whom became a TD – he kept up with on his return from America. I know how he made his money – and lost much of it – in America.

'It is not a pretty story. He was a gangster and, when he came back to Ireland, he remained a gangster – both in heart and in fact. As I said, I knew he kept in touch with some of the very worst types from the Civil War. I know all of this and I know it because he told me – night after night when he was drinking. I never had the guts to tell him what I thought, and he never asked me. He just assumed I would approve.'

A by now totally absorbed Valetti was at least beginning to appreciate the quality of his roast beef. 'So you may begin to understand why I am so protective of his past, why I spend so much time and money on perpetuating a view of him as a swashbuckling benefactor, on setting up chairs and charities in his name, and why I try to nip in the bud any historians or journalists who become too nosey.'

Bradley paused and ate some beef. 'It can't go on forever, I know that. Some day the Civil War archives will be opened and some of the story will come out. Rest assured I will use every bit of influence I have to keep this from happening and, happily for me, none of the politicians have any interest in history. Cornelius here keeps a sharp eye on that and he assures me it won't happen.

'But of course some day it will, maybe 20 or 30 years down the road, but by then it will be seen as history not as current affairs. Not like today when it would be an explosive story and, with many of those with scores to settle still around, God only knows what else might emerge. It's too dangerous to look too deeply in to that particular past and it is something I will do my best to prevent.'

He looked Valetti straight in the face. 'So Frank, perhaps now you can understand why the approach from you and your insinuation that you had something on my father caused me such consternation. You were not some pimply post-graduate student or gormless hack; you are a man of power who understands power and you knew what you were doing.

'You knew enough to know you had me over a barrel and that I would pay out; that I could not afford to take a chance. You're a gambler Frank and you had a very good hand of cards and you played them well. But not well enough for *el diabolo* at my left here. It was Cornelius who thwarted you with his very good research and even better forgery.'

Lyster was happy to accept the accolade.

'We had to do this Frank because, as I said, you were a formidable foe. But more important, once I succumb to the first blackmail, there's no going back. That is why we had to crush you and we were prepared to be as ruthless as we had to be.'

'You sure were,' mumbled a confused Valetti. Where was all this going?

'So you see where we're coming from. But now it's time to move on.'

'What do you mean move on? On to where?'

'Well I said earlier I don't like loose ends and, as things stand, you are a loose end. Relax. This is 1997. In my father's day you might have ended up on the side of a road in Wicklow like that poor man, Señor Sánchez. But times have changed.'

In spite of himself, Valetti was relieved, but only a little.

'Is that a threat?'

'No, of course not. My father's way is not my way. I prefer to believe the best solution is where both sides leave the table feeling happy. That is what I am saying.'

'I don't understand.'

'Okay. Let me make a few suggestions'.

Valetti had not expected this turn of events.

'You can't stay in Ireland. That would be uncomfortable for me. Your temperament is a bit unreliable; you will always be a gambler and need money, and you might be tempted to be indiscreet. Who knows?'

For the first time Valetti was angry. 'I hate this fucking place. I'd leave in the morning if I could. But I'm not a free agent. If I just decide to get up and go, where the fuck do I go? And what do I do? What do I live on? You must know that.'

'Of course we do. Cornelius, tell Frank what we can do. I've hardly had a chance to touch my food.'

Lyster leaned behind him and took a file from the sideboard.

'This is a letter signed by one of Dublin's leading medical consultants. A genuine letter this time – a little outstanding favour or, more accurately, a debt being honoured. The letter is about you and describes the dangerous levels of stress and hypertension that currently afflict you. It says you need a prolonged rest and should be relieved of your responsibilities. It suggests a full recovery is possible and you should be fit to return to work in a less stressful area in six months.'

'It's true. I do feel stressed,' said Valetti, who saw what was coming and was not too unhappy.

'And that letter you will send with your resignation tomorrow. We have ensured that there is an awareness in Rome of your health problems so it will not come as a surprise.'

Lyster proceeded to pull out a few more sheets of paper. 'You will have to excuse our intrusions in to your privacy, but it's all in your own interest. First, this is a list of your gambling debts and stock exchange debts as of yesterday evening. Hefty sums in each case, which you are in no position to pay off. I have two bank drafts here for the precise amount of each debt. You will settle these debts tomorrow and under no circumstances open any new account.'

Valetti was now open mouthed. 'Why are you doing this?'

Bradley cut in. 'Because we don't like loose ends.'

Lyster continued. 'We will ensure you leave with your honour and integrity intact. Two of the national newspapers will write warm accounts of your time here, a number of prominent Catholics, including at least one minister, will write equally warm letters of sadness at your departure to the Holy See. Cornelius has them written already. They only await the signatures, but we are certain of our people and there will be no hitches. You can be assured of that and it will help you to get a decent new job, if that is what you want.'

It most certainly was what Valetti wanted, though his head was still spinning at how completely he had been outmanoeuvred.

'And of course, we are aware you will have significant relocation costs. We will help you in that regard and we will do so generously.'

Bradley had put a cheese platter on the table and was pouring three glasses of grappa. 'Try some of this Wexford Cheddar. It's a secret we keep to ourselves.'

'So that's it,' said Valetti. 'You want me out of here. You're threatening me and at the same time you're buying me off.'

He paused and, for the first time that day, smiled – a broad, almost happy, smile of relief. 'I can live with that. And that's it?'

'Not quite. One other loose end. We want the original of the Robinson file. And we would be obliged if Cornelius could look through any other Robinson papers that might be relevant.'

Valetti had already taken the precaution of photo copying all of the files. 'No problem,' he said almost too quickly.

'And any photocopies you might have. Cornelius will travel back with you and you can satisfy him on this score.'

Valetti was now glowering. 'You're saying you don't take my word?'

'Not at all. But as you said, business is business. As soon as Cornelius is happy – as I'm sure he will be, the cheques you carry back with you will all be cleared.'

Valetti was surprised he had even thought for a moment he could have pulled that one off. Old habits die hard, he told himself.

By this stage, the archbishop agreed with Bradley that the Wexford cheddar was indeed good and they finished the meal with a couple of grappas. Bradley told Valetti to leave his car at Ballywilliamroe and a driver would have it back to Cabra by early morning. Meanwhile, the same driver would bring Lyster and himself to Dublin, where the official business would be formally concluded.

That night back in Cabra after Lyster had left, Valetti sat back and took stock. It had been a very bruising encounter with Jeremy Bradley and that reptile Lyster. But against that, he was getting out of this goddamned country with his reputation enhanced, no debts and a nice sum in his back pocket. Yes, he could live with that. And to think it all started with that phone call from JJ Gilmartin. Sorry, he corrected himself, *Monsignor* JJ Gilmartin.

67

....

Archie Bowe put a lot of thought into preparing for his meeting with Bishop Mullins. It was important that he reassert his authority as the rightful solicitor to the diocese of Kilderry and he must do this in a firm way. He would not be arrogant but neither would he be a supplicant. He would not admit to being wrong, but he would be tactful. He knew he had a solid reputation, built up over the years in court as an effective advocate. And, as he never tired of telling his colleagues, you can never be too well prepared.

As it turned out his preparations, careful as they were, were not necessary. He arrived just before 11.30 expecting to meet the bishop straight away. However, Mullins' secretary informed him that the bishop's 'group' was still meeting, but would be ready to see him in ten minutes.

He was taken aback – what 'group'? He had expected to meet the bishop alone.

When he was shown into the bishop's shabby meeting room, he found five people already present – the bishop, a somewhat severe-looking middle-aged and expensively groomed woman who he assumed was Heather Ruddock, the nephew of Monsignor Nestor and two complete strangers who were introduced as Dr Newrie and Ambassador Dannaher.

'Come in Archie. You're very welcome. Have you brought that Third Secret of Fatima with you?'

Was there a hint of mockery in Mullins tone? He wasn't sure, but wondered if he had walked into some sort of ambush?

'Seriously Archie, you are very welcome and we are delighted you are here. As I've already told you, this group, led by Ms Ruddock, has been examining every aspect of this whole business – I think we have been making real progress and I hope that what you have with you may bring matters to a happy end.'

Bowe was somewhat reassured by Mullins' friendly tone, but he was still somewhat uneasy. Should he stand on his dignity and demand to speak to the bishop alone – after all, this was strictly diocesan business and of no concern to these outsiders. Why was Monsignor Nestor not present? As he was weighing his options, Mullins cut in.

'Archie, this business is bigger than Kilderry and, if it goes wrong, it has the capacity to do serious damage to the diocese – a diocese you and your family have served loyally for over a hundred years. So I am going to ask you to listen to what we know. It is, to the best of our knowledge, based on hard evidence. Then you can open that letter and we will see what the late bishop has to say. I expect there will be serious discrepancies.'

'But surely you should listen to what the late bishop has said first,' Bowe argued. 'After all he was there. He is really our only first-hand witness.'

'Maybe he is but, as much as it saddens me to say so, he was not always a credible witness. My predecessor could be economical with the truth and had a capacity, I believe, to persuade himself of the rightness of what he did and the purity of his motives. Archie, if you think hard – and you are a hard thinker – you will know I am right.'

And in his heart Bowe knew Bishop Mullins was right. It was something he had long felt but, for some reason, had always excused, perhaps even hoping he was wrong.

'So what are you suggesting we do?'

'Ms Ruddock here – Heather – will sum up what we know. Some of it you will know already, more of it will be new to you and may even shock you. It certainly shocked me. There may be things you know that we don't, so ask any questions you like, and then we will hear what his late lordship had to say from beyond the grave.'

Heather Ruddock looked every inch the high-powered lawyer as she marshalled the closely typed pages in front of her. What she had written was based on their combined research and would form the nucleus of the report they would write at the end of their work.

She began with the finding of the papers after Concannon's death and what they had learned from the fragments of the early journal, of Henry Alsop and his bequest of shares and cash, of the transfer of the monies to the Munster & Leinster Bank and the opening of the personal (and permanently topped-up) account in the bishop's name, which explained his spending power over the years.

All of this was new to Bowe and deepened his sense of betrayal. Much of this had happened in his father's time, his revered father who, like Archie himself, had just assumed bishops had other sources of income and had been totally unaware of what was going on.

'Are you sure of this? Can you prove it?'

Ruddock handed over the Munster & Leinster statements. There was no response. She then went on to describe the two ventures in Spain and Croatia. Morgan Dannaher had written detailed reports, including his own certain knowledge that Concannon had twice clashed with the government, incurring de Valera's anger.

Again in my father's time, Bowe thought with real bitterness, and even he knew nothing about it.

Clearly Concannon was living two lives – one in Kilderry and one very much away from it. The Bowes, who should have been at the centre of things, were totally excluded from this other life. How much else had his father not been told? Whatever residual loyalty Bowe had to the old bishop was fast running out. At least he would not feel guilty now about opening that letter.

Ruddock then moved on to the question of the monies and, in particular, the two black holes – the disappearance of £400,000 not once but twice – at the time of first the Spanish and then the Croatia ventures and the subsequent cover-up by Concannon.

At this point, Ruddock introduced the name of the mysterious Joe Bradley, a name Bowe knew of, but only vaguely and generally disapprovingly. But it was a name neither he nor his father had ever heard from Concannon.

'It became very clear to us that Joe Bradley stole that money, not once but twice.' Turning to Dannaher, Ruddock added: 'Morgan here will tell you what we now know about Joe Bradley.'

Dannaher proceeded in clear, emotion-free civil service language to outline Bradley's record and reputation up to his death in 1977 and the fact that the Bradley family fortune – now a very significant fortune – was almost certainly built on this money.

Bowe felt affirmed in his low view of Joe Bradley, who had never impinged directly on his life, but was totally shocked by the details he was now hearing. He wondered how a bishop, whom he always believed to be a pillar of rectitude, could have been so close to this rogue. What sort of madness had gripped him?

Ruddock then told Bowe that Peter O'Donnell had established that, after 1945, no more shares had been sold. Concannon had continued to use his personal fund, which in the year before his death stood at £75,000 when the account was closed and the funds moved to the bishop's other personal account. This was the money that had appeared in the bishop's will. No wonder he had gone to another solicitor to draw up that will, reflected Bowe.

For the first time that day, Bowe felt Bishop Mullins had been right to give him this information before he read Concannon's deathbed letter. The fact that Concannon was on the way to 'meet his Maker' was no guarantee he would tell the truth. Was he even capable of recognising the truth or was he utterly delusional?

Ruddock now moved to the question of the remaining shares. O'Donnell, she said, put an estimate of well over £6 million on the value of them. She said it was clear to her as a lawyer that the diocese had no automatic or even strong legal right to this money, nor did the Vatican, the Irish Church or Concannon's family. The only way it could be safely handled would be through the setting up of an independent and legally registered trust to disperse the funds in a way appropriate to the wishes of Henry Alsop. It would be up to the trust to determine what these wishes might mean in contemporary Ireland.

Before Bowe could object, Mullins intervened. 'Archie, I hope you will be a member of this trust. A trustee of the new foundation. We need your integrity and experience.'

This was the first the others heard that Bowe would be joining them and they recognised it as an impulsive sop made on the spur of the moment by Mullins. Bowe, to their surprise, was happy to accept. It would ensure an end to any further rumours of his being out in the cold.

He now moved to open the last letter from Bishop Concannon but the sense of drama he had anticipated had long dissipated. He extracted a single handwritten letter. O'Donnell could see that the writing was firm if a little spidery. He noted too that it was written on the headed notepaper Concannon had been using when he was bishop.

Bowe, in his dry and precise way, read the letter.

My Dear Archie,

I am preparing for that time when I must meet my Maker and I know that time cannot be far off. I believe I have left my affairs in order, but one matter troubles me. As you will see, this is a matter of the utmost delicacy and secrecy and, for reasons which were not of my making, I have not been able to resolve it.

It involves a significant sum of money in cash and in shares bequeathed me in 1939 by a benefactor who need not be named. His instruction was that I use the funds over which I had sole discretion to help the Church fight the new battles of a new age. It was a duty I undertook with great humility, seeing it as a sacred trust.

I attempted on two occasions to aid the universal Church. The details are not now relevant and for that reason I felt it prudent to destroy my remaining records rather than risk their being misinterpreted and do damage to our Church.

Sadly, on each occasion my attempts to aid the universal Church came to nought, not through any fault of mine but because of the hostility of de Valera and the treachery of the man I most trusted. I regret to say that man defrauded me of a great deal of money.

I want you as my loyal solicitor to know of these facts and to accept that I acted at all times in the best interest of the Church we both love and revere.

The bequest now consists only of the remaining shares, which I have kept safely since 1945, while dispensing the remaining monies on various charitable causes. I do not know the current value of the shares but it is my wish that they be used solely for the good of the Church as it fights the new battles of today.

Archie, I ask you to remember me in your prayers.

Yours in Christ Jesus Our Lord.

† Thomas Patrick

There was silence, but not for long. Mullins was the first to speak.

'The crooked bugger, it is just as you said Tommy – arrogant, self-serving and in denial to the very end. And destroying the journals in to the bargain lest they be misinterpreted. Lest he be found out he means. And not even an apology to you Archie for keeping you and your father in the dark all these years.'

'Agreed – and worse than that, he's a liar,' raged O'Donnell. 'There were no charitable bequests. But let's stick to the main point. What about the money? Does this mean he is instructing Archie to give it to some Church body or other, that we can't set up our trust?'

'No fucking way,' said Mullins to the shocked horror of Archie Bowe, who had never heard a profanity from a bishop before. 'He can fuck off. The Church today and since the Second Vatican Council means "the people of God" and the money will be used for the people of God. Full stop. End of story.'

Bowe began to splutter. 'This letter is a legal instrument. I am obliged to obey it.'

'Obey it my arse. It's not a legal instrument; it's the delusions of an old man.'

Then more quietly: 'Archie, I don't think you want to see

this case going public. Can you see the headlines "The solicitors who never saw what happened", "Gullible solicitors sat on gold mine". Archie, you can hear the sniggers already. You and, worse still, your father would be laughing stocks.'

Bowe had already regretted his intrusion. He saw clearly the threat to what he valued most – the good name of the Bowe family. He didn't much like Vatican Two but, like a good lawyer, it would serve to resolve the current problem. In the unlikely event of this ever going public, he reckoned Mullins would produce a few theologians to back up his case.

Mullins was now much calmer.

'Look, Archie. That letter was self-serving and he was delusional to the end. The fault was always someone else's. It was de Valera's fault, Bradley's treachery, but never Concannon's own judgement or arrogance. But at least it confirms what we thought about Old Joe Bradley. The Bradley family will have to be dealt with, but we have time to think about that.

'Archie, that money will do God's work through the new trust and you, as a trustee, will be there to see it is all done properly.'

68

....

It was a week after the reading of Concannon's letter and Bishop Mullins had never been busier. He had caught up on his backlog of diocesan work, making new appointments to parishes and committees. He wondered what had possessed the nuncio, on the very eve of his sudden and mysterious departure, to nominate that lazy, self-indulgent little prick JJ Gilmartin to be a monsignor.

Gilmartin had of course called personally to tell Mullins of the great honour bestowed on him. His chins wobbled over his clerical collar as he recounted the messages of congratulation that had been flowing in from embassies and universities, but which he felt were, of course, really not for him but for the diocese as a whole. Oh, what a load of shit thought Mullins, but he forced himself to be courteous even if Gilmartin found his reaction distant and underwhelming.

More important, he had asked Peter O'Donnell to write a full account of the entire Concannon episode and to place it, along with the bank statements and any other material he felt to be relevant, in a box that would be sealed and put in a secure place. It might be useful or even necessary for some future bishop to revisit the Concannon era and they should at least be aware of its existence. Not that he foresaw this ever having to be made public.

And, with the agreement of his advisers, he asked Morgan Dannaher to prepare a short paper on the role of Joe Bradley in the whole affair. Unlike the nuncio, he had no desire to go after Jeremy Bradley in any vindictive way. However, he argued to himself, he owed it to the memory of Concannon that the Bradley family be aware of the part played by old Joe Bradley. The farmer's son in Mullins whispered in his ear that, if there was a financial spin-off – and he thought there should be – that would be another good outcome.

He had already decided that Dannaher was the right man to deal with Jeremy Bradley. He was a smooth and unthreatening operator. He had a rare talent for understatement, an ability to leave things unsaid while making their meaning very clear. There would never be raised voices, but there would be no ambiguity either. He would meet Bradley, give him the document, assure him the diocese had no intention of pursuing him and had absolutely no intention of going public. The whole affair reflected no great credit on Concannon and any publicity would be as unwelcome to the diocese as it would be to Bradley.

But he would also let Bradley know of the establishment of the Alsop Concannon Foundation to fund worthy ventures as was intended by Henry Alsop – but this time within the law. If Bradley was so minded, they would welcome him as a trustee. 'Get the bugger inside the tent' was how Mullins had described it, but Dannaher preferred to see it as squaring this particular circle.

According to Dannaher, the meeting with Bradley had gone very well – an entirely civil affair was how he described it. Bradley read the document, made a few notes and told Dannaher he had been expecting something of the sort. He very much appreciated the sensible approach being adopted by the diocese and was touched by the invitation to become a trustee of the new Alsop Concannon Foundation. He described the offer as 'a stylish gesture', but did not think this was quite the right moment for him to accept. However, his own trust would look in a very positive way as to how it might be of assistance.

Mullins had come to appreciate the silky skills of Dannaher

and, with the Bradley angle covered, all the preparatory work on setting up the foundation was in place. Heather Ruddock had taken charge of the shares. She was arranging for a stock-broker to sell them over a period of time and transfer the funds to the Alsop Concannon Foundation.

They could now start looking for the right person to act as administrator and, in a few days, would announce the setting up of the foundation. There would be no fanfare and no public relations, just a short announcement in the *Brannocksbridge Observer*. There would be no mention of money, just a vaguely respectful note about Henry Alsop and Bishop Concannon. 'Keep it boring,' was O'Donnell's advice.

It was to put the final touches to all this that Mullins asked Ruddock to call a meeting of the group – or trustees as they now were – including Archie Bowe, who seemed very relieved to be on the inside once again.

***

For John Mullins, the moment of truth had come. He had never been happier than in the past few weeks, working closely with Heather Ruddock to sort out the Concannon business. He was working with people he had come to like and trust; they had sorted out the problem and had got a result. The Alsop Concannon Foundation would really make a difference to the lives of those he most cared about and who needed his help. Now they would get it.

That was all very fine, but now he had to get back to business as usual, dealing with the everyday problems of administration, attending meetings in Maynooth, endless committees, appointing parish priests, moving curates about, dealing with the Department of Education – but it all bored him and, in his own words, gave him no sense of fulfilment.

This was not why he had become a priest. He thought back to his parents, decent people whose second nature was helping neighbours. They were part of a living community where people liked and cared for each other. He saw the priesthood as a continuation of that role – the preaching of the gospel, while important, was second only to the care of the weak and vulnerable.

He knew his views were not theologically sound, but his parishioners had no problems with that. His 15 years as a curate and parish priest had passed in happy obscurity until it all changed when he became a bishop. Now it was all about administration and episcopal politics. How he hated it all. His only source of fulfilment in recent years had been his work with Nurse Martha Keane in her hostel.

He had been disgusted by what he had learned of his predecessor Concannon – the greed and arrogance, the sense of being above the law, not to mention the pomp and pretension and self-indulgence, and the craving for power and place.

He knew it was unfair to blame the whole Church for Concannon. He knew good bishops – Dominic Irwin was one – who were holy men and who did their best not to be ground down by the system, which was the fate he feared lay in store for himself. How much longer could he persist as an outsider, distrusted by the archbishops and some of his colleagues. Or more to the point, how much longer did he want it to persist. What age was he now? 56. 19 more years before he retired as a bishop, 19 more years of futility, tedium and self-hate. He couldn't face that. And he wouldn't. That was that.

And so, when Heather Ruddock and the other trustees met for their first meeting that afternoon, they found him nervous and somewhat subdued.

It was O'Donnell who noticed the bishop had taken more

care than usual to prepare for the meeting. Beside the tea and coffee was a bottle of whiskey and some tumblers on the sideboard. Mullins had never been known to offer a drink – as O'Donnell could testify.

They got through the details of the meeting quickly – the financial arrangements, governance issues, the public announcement of the establishment of the foundation and the appointment of auditors. Ruddock's brisk style of chairing and her eagle eye for detail ensured the business was despatched speedily.

This was Mullins' moment.

'I want to thank you all for what you have done and I want you to be the first to hear my news.'

He had their full attention.

'I have decided to resign as Bishop of Kilderry. After this meeting, I will tell my great friend Monsignor Nestor and I have already posted my letter of resignation to the nuncio.'

He allowed a moment for the shock to register although, to O'Donnell, it seemed the logical thing for him to do.

'My mind is made up. My decision is absolute. But I will remain a priest. As far as I am concerned I am a priest forever as I vowed on my ordination day, and also because that is what I want to be. It's what I always wanted to be and, as soon as I am finished here, and that will be very soon – I will work full time with Nurse Martha Keane in her ministry and I will work in harmony with whoever my successor as bishop is.

'I had thought perhaps I might work in something similar overseas, and I am sure that is what the four archbishops would like me to do, but I like this country, I like the people and I am too old to start a completely new life somewhere foreign. I will move away from Brannocksbridge and I can promise I will not interfere. My successor can be assured of that.'

He paused and looked around the table.

'Don't try to dissuade me. I am at ease with myself for the first time in years.'

Nobody made any attempt to dissuade him. Not even Archie Bowe, who was shocked to his core by what he was hearing. What would his late father have made of this?

There was one last thing. He would not be a trustee of the foundation and asked to be replaced by Monsignor Nestor. This was agreed.

Then to break the tension, he reached for the whiskey bottle and, without asking if people liked whiskey or not, poured six large tumblers. It reminded O'Donnell of the late-night sessions he had endured during many a by-election campaign in his political days. Now they all drank to John Mullins and his future.

69

············

May 8 1998

The new Bishop of Kilderry stood on the steps of the bishop's house to welcome the members of the Alsop Concannon Foundation. This was to be their third meeting, six months to the day since the foundation's formal establishment. Peter O'Donnell noted with approval the formal well-cut soutane, with its discreet purple piping and plain wooden pectoral cross of the new bishop. Standing there, tall, grey haired and scholarly, his uncle looked every part the bishop. A welcome change, the occasionally fastidious O'Donnell thought, to the scruffy, shambling cut of his predecessor.

The new bishop was delighted to see his nephew, but he noted with a slight twinge of unease that he had arrived once again with Heather Ruddock. He detected between them a sense of the easy intimacy he occasionally saw in married couples. He knew Ruddock had a husband, though he had never met him, and he worried that his nephew might be embarking on an adulterous affair.

Should he talk to him about it? In his younger days, he would have felt it part of his priestly duties to do so, but now he hesitated. The world was changing, he had enough problems of his own and, most pertinently, he felt his nephew would tell him to mind his own business. And he had to admit, that they did look very relaxed in each other's company.

Bishop Mullins had announced his resignation as bishop the day after their last meeting. He said he wanted to do it as quickly and as quietly as possible, so he gave the story exclusively to Joey

Martin of the Brannocksbridge Observer. *Martin had an eye for a good story and persuaded Mullins to do an interview – just the one exclusive interview. In the interview, Mullins was frank, honest and respectful as he explained his frustrations as a bishop and his desire to get back to the essentials of his priestly vocation by becoming once again 'a simple priest of the people'.*

Martin kept his word and the story appeared exclusively in the Observer, *but he was a canny operator and had tipped off the national newspapers that he had a cracking good story coming up. As the man who had 'broken' the story, he would be available for interview.*

And Martin's instincts were right. It was a 'big one'. Bishops rarely resigned, except in rare cases of indefensible scandal, but this was different – a bishop resigning, giving up the perks and privileges to go back to the ranks. There had to be a story there and the journalists went about their job of finding it. Was he pushed? Had there been a scandal? Was there a woman involved? Was there money missing? The heavier papers carried articles speculating on the failure of the institutional Church to relate to the everyday problems of real people and took a few pot shots at the cardinal who was so clearly out of touch.

But as much as the journalists dug around in Kilderry and with their various clerical contacts, nothing emerged. The people of Kilderry liked and admired their late bishop. Nobody had a bad word to say about him. There was no 'story'.

Mullins had disappeared from view as the announcement was being made. He didn't expect much interest in his story and, after giving his only press interview to Martin, he felt it better to let things calm down. He had travelled down to Archie Bowe's holiday home in Kerry for a short break.

However, as the media interest continued, he was tracked down and eventually, on Martin's advice, he reluctantly agreed to do one more interview, as it happened on the Late Show, *which pre-viewed his appearance calling him 'the simple priest of the people'. The appellation stuck and, before long, people were talking about 'Father John, the people's priest'.*

Mullins was a natural storyteller, his sincerity was palpable and his openness in describing the work of Nurse Martha Keane and himself made an instant impression. Overnight 'the simple priest', as the newspapers had taken to calling him, became a national figure and, more significantly, donations began to pour in to Keane's charity. Mullins' simple life and plain talking were starkly contrasted with the gilded existence of the other bishops, most of whom wished to hell he would return to the obscurity he claimed to crave.

But he had no intention of so doing. He discovered he liked the media and the media liked him. He had never been short of an opinion and, before long, he was being consulted on all sorts of issues, social and political – even sporting at times. As far as the media was concerned, he was always available; always gave value, spoke clear, homely English; and was not worried about offending those in power.

And it was not just the media. He soon became a regular speaker at conferences, protest meetings and summer schools. Already one publisher had approached him about writing a book.

***

It was Morgan Dannaher who found out the inside story about Monsignor Nestor's quick appointment as Mullins' replacement. Normally a bishopric could lie idle for months but, within four weeks of Mullins' departure, his successor had been named and consecrated four weeks later. Dannaher was not the only one who saw this as unusual and set out to find out what happened.

Dannaher was a natural gossip, who now had a good story of his own to tell. Yes, of course he had been sworn to confidentiality by the other trustees and he would respect that confidence – but only up to a point. If by trading information he could get other valuable information from a person of utter discretion, then it was permissible. Or so he persuaded himself.

He was fortunate that Bishop Dominic Irwin was thinking along broadly similar lines. Irwin was indeed a holy man but he too had a great weakness for gossip. He had been intrigued by what was going on in Kilderry and by the sudden emergence of the well-funded Alsop Concannon Foundation. How had all that happened? Not even JJ Gilmartin could tell him. So he readily agreed to meet Dannaher in the Kildare Street University Club after Dannaher assured him the food was much better than it had been.

It was going to be a long evening and Dannaher told his side of the story over pre-dinner drinks – all in total confidence. Irwin was fascinated by the story of Concannon's adventures and his disagreement with de Valera, all of which was new to him, as was the source of the Bradley family fortunes. It was going to be hard to keep all this to himself, but he would be careful who he told.

When they had settled in to dinner – and the food was not great – Irwin told his side of things.

'John Mullins never realised the impression he made at our meetings in Maynooth and the impact he had. He had no guile and no diplomatic skills. He always asked the hard questions that the rest of us were afraid to ask and he always said what he thought – which was rarely what the archbishops wanted to hear. The truth is, they were scared of him. The cardinal patronised him as if he were a not-too-bright student and some of the others tried to bully him, but it never seemed to affect him. He was a loose cannon and one bishop told me it was only a matter of time before he broke ranks. He was at odds with them on at least a half-dozen issues.'

Dannaher wondered to himself how none of this had ever leaked out to the media. Mullins obviously was not a leaker and no other bishop saw it in his interest to do so.

'They expected a row, but the last thing they expected was his resignation. Bishops resign only in exceptional and utterly indefensible circumstance – a major scandal like poor Casey – but otherwise, I've seen bishops continue in to their dotage and not resign. But the resignation of a young bishop with no scandal and an unblemished record was something they had never experienced. A media sensation like that can open a can of worms and anything can crawl out. So when, out of the blue, Mullins resigned, it was red lights all round.'

Irwin paused to refresh their glasses.

'But there was a problem. Normally the nuncio would make contact with Rome, but with Valetti gone – and no one believes it was for health reasons and that's another story that could be damaging – with Valetti gone, the four archbishops had an emergency meeting and asked Rome to make a speedy appointment to Kilderry to try and close the story down as quickly as possible. Damage limitation they call it these days. Rome came back and told them to find a safe successor as quickly and with as little fuss as possible.'

'So that's how Jimmy Nestor got the job?'

'Exactly. Jimmy should have got the job last time round but was blackballed by one of my colleagues. But Jimmy is a good man, the priests in Kilderry like him and he is seen as a safe pair of hands. And most of all, Mullins likes and respects him and will not cause any trouble – at least for him. So with indecent haste, Jimmy was appointed and consecrated. Rome can move fast when it wants to.'

Dannaher was, in general, an admirer of things Roman ever since his days at the Vatican, but he had one more question.

'John Mullins? Will the appointment of Jimmy Nestor calm him down as far as the bishops are concerned?'

'Absolutely not. He's a bigger thorn in their side now than he ever was as a bishop. I was one of the few bishops he really talked to and he does have a weakness, as we all have. He is opinionated. He feels he has the answer to every problem and that was part of his difficulties with the bishops. He liked simple straight answers and was bored by complexity.

'All this new celebrity will go to his head. He now has endless platforms to sound off from. I spoke to him last week and it seems he's starting to believe all this "simple priest of the people" stuff. He told me he had invitations from all over the country and he's ready to take them on.

'And worse still, he's totally under the influence of that woman Martha Keane. I've had a few encounters with her. She's the brains of the outfit and, like a lot of holy women, she is utterly manipulative and a bit of a bitch – and she hates politicians as much as she hates bishops. But that's where he is, with her egging him on. I can assure you, neither the bishops nor the politicians will be happy.'

Dannaher, however, was very happy. He had his story. He just had to figure out how he could tell the others without revealing the price he had to pay.

He had no doubt he would find a way.

***

The trustees meeting had gone well. Heather Ruddock's work with the diocese was done and Archie Bowe would revert to working with the bishop – an arrangement that pleased them both. Heather would continue to chair the Foundation.

Peter O'Donnell did notice one big difference under the new bishop. There was decent wine and passable food, but otherwise normal life seemed to have returned to Kilderry.

There was only one major item of business. Ruddock announced a donation of £400,000 from the Joseph Bradley Foundation. It was accompanied by a warm letter from Jeremy Bradley saying how pleased his father would have been to see the great qualities of his close friend Thomas Concannon so suitably commemorated. And he finished with a promise of a further £400,000 in five years' time.

Morgan Dannaher felt he had done his work well with Bradley. He pointed out to his colleagues what he called the symmetry of the bequest – a five-year gap, just as there had been five years, 1940 and 1945, between the two occasions Bradley senior had robbed Concannon. Neat, thought Dannaher, but a pity about the interest.

As O'Donnell drove back to Dublin to the apartment on Pembroke Road that he now more or less shared with Heather, he turned on the radio. It was Five Seven Live *on RTÉ. 'The people's priest' was in full flight. He was sharply attacking the minister for health and politicians generally over the 'shameful underfunding' of the drugs treatment programme – and being egged on by the interviewer to say much more besides.*

O'Donnell switched off, inserted a Bruce Springsteen cassette. Darlington County *began to play and they drove in companionable silence, both Heather and himself looking forward to the evening ahead.*

70

....

Oct 16 2014

The young army officer had been having a long day. It wasn't the first time he had wondered how he, an army officer, was spending so much of his time poring over archive material dealing with the activities of the Irish Defence Forces during the Second World War.

'It's not as if we were doing any fighting; our only job was to survive,' he muttered to himself as he surveyed the seemingly endless stack of files in front of him.

But he didn't really wonder, nor did he complain. The army liked its officers to specialise. Some choose cyber security, others ordnance, others transport, but this officer had no difficulty in opting for a training course in archives. History was his passion. He already had a master's degree in History from the National University of Ireland Galway and it was the career he hoped to pursue in his post-army days.

He knew that the archives were as important to his superiors as they were to him. For them the army had a proud place in Irish life that was built on its traditions of loyalty, professionalism and, they would say, patriotism. They knew their archives were the bricks and mortar of history and were determined that the telling of their full story would not lack for the raw material.

Or at least as much of the story as it was politic to tell.

And so, late on this dark Thursday afternoon, the young captain was examining the wartime papers. His job was to decide which papers could move on to the National Archive to be exam-

ined by scholars and journalists and which records should remain
restricted. The rule was clear enough. Material that could defame
or damage the reputation of people still living or their families, or
material that might still be regarded as politically sensitive, was
to be marked 'restricted' and referred upstairs to be decided on by
a higher authority. He had been instructed that, if he had even
the slightest doubt, he was to 'refer upwards', but so far had very
little reason to do so.

That is until an hour ago when he opened a dusty box with
a number of files. The wording on the box simply said 'Military
College; Miscellaneous Matters 1955'. More boredom, he thought
until he saw the bulky file at the bottom of the pile. The title of the
file was unusual, strange even, The Kilderry Files; Matters relating to the Diocese of Kilderry and Bishop Concannon 1940-45.

What struck him was the official stamp, which said 'Highly
Restricted'. He checked further. The file had never been opened,
or at least it had no record of ever having been consulted, in the
59 years it had been lying in the archive since being deposited in
1955. That was unusual but not unique. Some files never needed
to be consulted simply because their contents were deemed to be
of no further relevance.

But what really excited the young officer was the author of the file
and the short note appended to the opening page. The person who had
compiled and deposited the papers was Colonel Dan Bryan. When he
saw the name, he felt that frisson of excitement only an archivist can
feel on the cusp of a major find.

And it was the name Dan Bryan that sparked it off.

Dan Bryan. Unknown outside a small circle of academics
but long a legend among generations of army officers. He had
been Ireland's main spy and spycatcher, head of G2 Irish Mili-
tary Intelligence during the difficult and dangerous years of the
'Emergency' as the government of de Valera liked to call the war.

He was the man credited with safeguarding Ireland's neutrality during that period, a man relied on by Michael Collins in the War of Independence, admired by WT Cosgrave in the difficult 1920s and eventually trusted by de Valera right through the war – though never rewarded by him.

But what was even more unusual was the handwritten note appended to the front page and signed by Dan Bryan.

> *This is a full record of events that have never been made public, and may never be, of major incidents, the first in 1940, the second in 1945, which had the potential to seriously damage the country's national interest. Both sets of incidents involved Dr Thomas Patrick Concannon, Bishop of Kilderry, and others mentioned in this report. The report also details possible illegal movements of large sums of money and the unexplained death, probably murder, of a diplomat, which has never been investigated to a conclusion.*
>
> *For cross-reference, see files in Garda Archive prepared by Superintendent John Gantly.*

Two hours later, the young officer had finished his reading. He thought he knew a great deal about the 1940s but all of this was new to him. He had never heard of Concannon but was vaguely aware of the other major protagonist mentioned. Of the two major incidents recounted by Bryan, he had not even heard the slightest rumour and none of the many recent historians who had written about these years had ever mentioned them.

Two thoughts immediately struck him. What was this sensitive wartime document doing in the Military College Archives in a box labelled miscellaneous? In that same box were files dealing with building repairs, the purchase of vehicles and some newspaper cuttings. How could such a sensitive file have been misfiled or misplaced?

The second odd feature was the date. 1955. A full decade after the events described. He quickly dismissed the possibility of human error. Dan Bryan did not do error. The most meticulous and secretive of men did not do things by accident. The only conclusion he could draw was that Dan Bryan, who had ended his career as Director of the Military College, had brought the files with him when he moved from Military Intelligence. Then shortly before he retired, he had hidden them away.

But why would he do that? The officer could only think of two reasons. Bryan may have feared the files would be destroyed if he left them in Military Intelligence. His fears may have been groundless, but Bryan knew the world he worked in and had taken his own precautions. That might explain why the files were moved, but why did Bryan leave them behind after he retired?

The officer thought hard about this. Maybe Bryan did so because he wanted the files to be found, the story to be told. Maybe not in his lifetime, but sometime. He knew that Bryan, like himself, was a keen historian – and historians do not destroy archives.

And now, 59 years later, the file had surfaced. The Kilderry Files.

Every historian's instinct in the officer wanted to publish the file. Every sense of justice in him told him the file should be opened up and let the pieces fall where they may.

But the realist in him said the case for opening the files would fall at the first hurdle. Its publication would not just defame but could shatter the reputation of one of the country's wealthiest families and might well open old political sores.

He wrote a short note, which he headed Urgent and Highly Confidential.

He explained to his superiors that the file was of prime historical importance, but its publication would run counter to the criteria he was obliged to apply. His recommendation was that the file remain restricted, but he would welcome the advice of his superiors.

The army officer did not have to wait long for a response.

Nothing was put in writing. Instead, three days later his immediate superior came to his office. He told him very firmly that the word from on high was that The Kilderry Files were to remain restricted and this restriction would be of indefinite duration.

He was told that the files were to be placed in a most secure place and then, hesitating for a moment, the superior suggested, though without enthusiasm, that some civil servants had indicated that, should the files disappear altogether, no questions would be asked.

'But I think I know you well enough Captain, to know how much respect you have for these records. If I were in your place, I hope I would give the same answer that I know you will.'

'Understood,' was the cryptic reply.

When his colleague had left, the army officer spent the rest of the day making notes from the files, notes which found their way in to his briefcase. Who knows he mused, in a few years this will be history, not politics and, if I am teaching history somewhere, and in a new climate of openness, Dan Bryan's story may yet be told.

And, who knows, I might yet be the man to write it.

And with that, he deposited The Kilderry Files *in a secure vault with a red tag saying 'Highly Restricted'.*

APPENDIX

Actual people were mentioned in the sections relating to the events of the Second World War. The most significant of these are listed below.

Archbishop Paschal Robinson (1870–1948), was papal nuncio to Ireland from 1929 to 1948. He was born in Dublin and moved to the US at an early age. He was a successful journalist before becoming a Franciscan priest and was a renowned medievalist and diplomat.

Eamon de Valera (1882–1975) was Taoiseach and later President of Ireland.

Colonel Dan Bryan (1900–1985) was Director of Military Intelligence in the Irish Army during the Second World War.

Professor James Hogan (1898–1963) was Professor of History at University College Cork from 1920 to 1963. He served as Director of Intelligence in the Free State Army during the Civil War, was a renowned medievalist and wrote widely on political issues. He strongly advocated Catholic Social teachings of the 1930s.

Bishop Michael Fogarty (1859–1955) was the Bishop of Killaloe from 1904 until 1955. He was a friend of Michael Collins and a bitter opponent of de Valera.

Superintendent John Gantly (1899–1948) operated from the Detective Branch at Dublin Castle. He was shot dead while arresting escaped prisoners.

Giuseppe Ramiro Marcone (1882–1952) was a Benedictine abbot, university professor and confidant of Pope Pius XII. He was nuncio to Croatia from 1941 to 1945 and was a supporter of the post-war Italian Christian Democratic movement.

Many other political and clerical figures of the period are mentioned, but all in incidental roles. They include politicians Seán Lemass, James Dillon, Frank Aiken and PJ Ruttledge; diplomats TJ Kiernan, Leo Macaulay and Leopold Kerney; clerics John Charles McQuaid and Pádraig de Brún; and academics Michael Tierney and Alfred O'Rahilly.

ACKNOWLEDGEMENTS

In the writing of this book I have been greatly helped by the encouragement, criticisms and suggestions of number of friends. In particular I would like to thank Eve Molony, Peter White, Nicky Kearns, Oliver Keenan, Conor Brady, John McMenamin, and Mike Burns. And as always, my wife Mary was patient and supportive.